South West Coast Path

Falmouth to Exmouth

Text and photography
by Roland Tarr

Aurum
Press

in association with

Walk
UNLIMITED

Brimming with creative inspiration, how-to projects and useful information to enrich your everyday life, Quarto Knows is a favourite destination for those pursuing their interests and passions. Visit our site and dig deeper with our books into your area of interest: Quarto Creates, Quarto Cooks, Quarto Homes, Quarto Lives, Quarto Drives, Quarto Explores, Quarto Gifts, or Quarto Kids.

Acknowledgements

My thanks to Malcolm Howell, Phil White and E. Reece NT Rangers South East Cornwall and South Devon, Richard and Judy Foss, Jonathan and Fran Ansell, the staff and volunteers at the wonderful Cookworthy Museum in Kingsbridge, Alison Talbot, Sarah Welton and Simon Conway Morris for their contributions and advice.

This revised and updated edition first published in 2018 by Aurum Press,
an imprint of The Quarto Group
The Old Brewery, 6 Blundell Street
London N7 9BH, United Kingdom
www.QuartoKnows.com
in association with Walk Unlimited
www.walk.co.uk • www.nationaltrail.co.uk

Design by Rosamund Bird

Printed in China

MIX
Paper from
responsible sources
FSC
www.fsc.org   FSC® C016973

Cover: *Portloe from the Flagstaff*
Half-title page: *Start Point at Dawn*
Title page: *Sharp Tor, the coast path approaching Salcombe*

Aurum Press want to ensure that these National Trail Guides are always as up to date as possible – but stiles collapse, pubs close and bus services change all the time. If, on walking this path, you discover any important changes that future walkers need to be aware of, do let us know. Either email us on **trailguides@quarto.com** with your comments, or, if you take the trouble to drop us a line to:

Trail Guides, Aurum Press, 74–77 White Lion Street, London N1 9PF,
we'll send you a free guide of your choice as thanks.

South West Coast Path

Falmouth to Exmouth

Roland Tarr, modern linguist and outdoor enthusiast, has served as Assistant Countryside Officer in Cheshire, Heritage Coast Officer in Dorset, and has worked as a consultant in informal countryside recreation for councils throughout the south-west, national government and the European Commission. He has always used photography to promote conservation and countryside recreation causes. Roland has been walking the cliffs of Devon, Somerset, and Cornwall for se...
anniv...

Contents

Part One: Introduction   13

Introduction · Planning your walk · What time of year is best?
Equipment · Camping · Youth Hostels, B and B and hotels
Safety precautions · Food and drink · Marine wildlife · Geology

Part Two:

Part Three: Useful Information   159

Websites · Smartphone apps for walkers · Transport · Accommodation
Tourist · Other useful addresses · Bibliography · Ordnance Survey maps

How to use this guide

The 630 mile (1008 km) South West Coast Path is covered by four National Trail guides. Each guide describes the section of the path between major estuaries. This book describes the path from Falmouth to Exmouth, 179 miles (288 km), and is in three parts:

• The introduction, including general information about the area and advice for walkers.

• The Coath Path itself, described in 14 chapters, with maps to accompany each section of the route description. This part of the guide also includes information on places of interest. Key sites in the text are marked by the same reference letters on the maps to make it easy to follow the route description.

• Useful information: the last chapter of this guide includes useful information such as local transport, luggage transfer services, organisations involved with the path, apps which may be useful on your smartphone, and further reading suggestions.

The maps used are those prepared by the Ordnance Survey using 1:25,000 Explorer® maps as a base. The line of the coast path is shown in yellow with the status of each section of the coast path - footpath or bridleway for example - shown in green underneath (see key on the inside front cover). In some cases the yellow line on these marks show a route which is different from that shown on the original surveys, and in such cases walkers are recommended to follow the guide which will normally be the route that is waymarked. Any parts of the path that may be difficult to follow on the ground are clearly highlighted. Important points to watch for are marked by bold numerals both in the text and on the maps.

Should there have been a need to alter the route for any reason walkers are advised to follow the way-marks or signs on site. Since this path passes through a military exercise area at Tregantle Fort, just before Freathy, walkers are advised to pay particular attention to any signs posted or flags flying around that area when firing is taking place.

KEY MAPS

South West Coast Path

Chapter start point

0 km   5

0 miles   5

KEY MAPS

South West Coast Path

Chapter start point

0 km   5

0 miles   5

Based on Ordanance Survey Road Map

PLYMOUTH to

Roscoff   6 - 12 hrs

Santander   20 hrs

(summer only)

Distance checklist

This list will assist you in calculating the distances between places on the Coast Path where you may be planning to stay overnight, or in checking your progress along the way.

	approx. distance from previous location	
	miles	km
Place (southside of Percuil River)	0	0
Portscatho	6.4	10.3
Portloe	7.2	11.6
Gorran Haven	8.4	13.5
Mevagissey	3.3	5.3
Charlestown	6.9	11.1
Polkerris	5.5	8.9
Fowey (Fowey Harbour - west)	4.6	7.4
Polruan (Fowey Harbour - east)	0	0
Polperro	6.9	11.1
Looe (bridge joining East and West Looe)	5	8.1
Portwrinkle	7.7	12.4
Kingsand/Cawsand	10	16.1
Cremyll (west side of ferry across Tamar)	3.3	5.3
Stonehouse (Plymouth)	0	0
Turnchapel (Plymouth)	7.3	11.7
Warren Point (Wembury) (Yealm Estuary - west)	7.8	12.6
Noss Mayo (Yealm Estuary - east)	0	0
Wonwell (Erme Estuary - east)	9.2	14.8
Cockleridge (Avon Estuary - west)	6.1	9.8
Bantham (Avon Estuary - east)	0	0
Salcombe (Salcombe Harbour - west)	12.3	19.8
East Portlemouth (Salcombe Harbour - east)	0	0
Torcross	13.5	21.7
Dartmouth (Dartmouth Harbour - west)	10.2	16.4
Kingswear (Dartmouth Harbour - east)	0	0
Brixham	11.2	18
Torquay Harbour	8.4	13.5
Shaldon (Teign Estuary - south)	11.3	18.2
Teignmouth (Teign Estuary - north)	0	0
Starcross (Exe Estuart - west)	7.6	12.2

Polrudden Cliffs and Black Head, between Pentewan Sands and Charlestown.

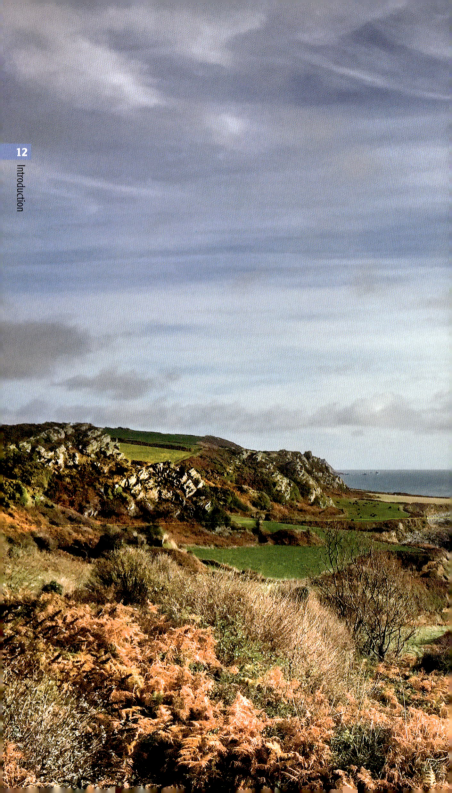

PART ONE
Introduction

The raised sea-cut platforms and old cliff-lines just east of Prawle Point.

Introduction

Sensational rocky outcrops, traditional fishing villages, natural harbours dazzling in the sunshine, not to mention the remarkable natural arches in the limestone and sandstone rocks of South Devon are the main features of this adventure. Those completing the section of the South West Coast Path described in this book will have climbed over 31,000 ft (9600m). Everest is 29,000 ft (8,850m). Most days will start from near zero height (sea level) and rise to several hundred feet multiple times. You will be much fitter and proud of your achievement by the end. During the year I have seen people of all ages tackling it, from octogenarians to toddlers and those carrying offspring in rucksacks. They looked, without exception, very happy.

The walk starts and finishes at wide wooded 'rias', the drowned valleys of the torrents which flooded across this area at the end of the ice age. This means the walk is served, in spring, summer and early autumn, by numerous ferries, each with their own character and method of signalling to the ferry you need to cross. The great headlands at Nare Head, Dodman Point, Rame Head and Start Point are magnificent. These impressive and chaotic masses of folded and faulted rock were formed at the same time as the Appalachians in eastern America.

The walking is not easy but always rewarding. The climbs and descents covered in a day, posted at the start of each chapter, are often the same as those which would be achieved during mountain walking in the Lakeland, Scottish Highlands or North Wales. Walkers need to take this into account when planning their daily route.

I have divided the text into 14 chapters averaging 12 miles (20km) per day. This may be too much for many people, though possibly too little for a fit young person travelling light. There are few settlements along the coast where you can stay, meaning that careful planning is needed to ensure the distances you travel each day are within your comfort zone.

The small Cornish fishing ports at Mevagissey, Fowey, Polperro and Looe still have lively fishing fleets with colourful traditional boats, coming and going at high tide every day.

The naval ports at Falmouth and Plymouth remain busy with the coming and going of large vessels, taking our forces to emergencies all around the world. Construction work takes place on both naval and merchant shipping, and the ports of Fowey and Teignmouth have busy commercial harbours importing and exporting massive quantities of clay and other goods worldwide virtually every day of the year. The ancient naval town of Dartmouth played a major role in WWII and is home to HMS Britannia, the British Royal Navy College, where a young Princess Elizabeth and the Duke of Edinburgh first met.

The Roseland and Rame peninsulas in Cornwall are particularly famous for their mild climate, sandy beaches, rugged cliffs and promontories, together with interesting village churches, congenial pubs and eating places, sheltered bays, sandy beaches at low tide and estuaries teaming with wildlife. They are also popular with people from the local towns and villages who often spend the weekend near the sea nearly all the year around. Even so, in summer this path never really gets overcrowded and it can still be enjoyed to the full by the visiting coastal walker.

The Devon coast has predominantly red sandstone cliffs interspersed with a number of Victorian seaside resorts. Each has a few fine buildings left from that era to remind us of their heyday. Today, there are amusement arcades and betting shops appealing to some, but search around a little further and you will find charming old fashioned English cafés serving cream teas, traditional shops and Old World service which is missing in many modern cities.

The National Trust owns substantial stretches of this coast. They manage it, amongst other things, with the aim of maximising the wildlife potential of the coastal slopes. This leads to superb displays of wild flowers, a better habitat for butterflies and small mammals, and the tuneful accompaniment of singing birds in the spring. The path is well marked through these areas, enabling us all to fully enjoy the delights on offer.

Dartmouth Castle.

The Salcombe 'ria', seen from East Portlemouth.

The marine wildlife of the area is also evident to the passing walker. In spring I saw seals and their pups cavorting in a rocky cove, with gannets circling above and fishing with their spectacular aerobatics and high speed dives. The less dramatic shags and cormorants also dived around the same spots. I saw the Lyme Bay dolphins performing once during my walk. Day outings from Paignton can be taken to increase your chances of seeing such species following the fish shoals here. See page 22 for more information about marine wildlife, and page 26 to discover the geology of the South Cornwall and South Devon coasts. There is also a centre at Wembury and the National Aquarium at Plymouth with excellent displays and further fascinating information.

There is a multitude of features to fascinate every walker of this route,

and I shall do my best to draw your attention to them as we go along. Many are hidden somewhere around a corner, behind a door or gate. All will be revealed in the text.

Planning your walk

Each of the chapters in this book describes one day of walking an average of 10 to 12 miles (16 to 19 km). This on the assumption that the walker will wish to spend time looking at some of the wildlife, the geology, the architecture of the small village churches or any of the other fascinating things that catch the eye along this coast. Allow a fortnight to three weeks to enjoy all that this section of the Path has to offer.

What time of year is best?

Autumn and winter are without doubt the most dramatic times to walk on this coast. In these seasons you will experience the southern Devon and Cornwall coasts at their wildest and most majestic. You may also see many unusual species of wintering birds which have migrated to escape the rigours of the Arctic regions.

Spring is good for flowers and for watching the cliff nesting birds and, taking care to avoid public holidays, the cliffs will be relatively uncrowded, particularly on weekdays. Early summer is also a good time for butterflies, though August can be too hot.

Although this is one of the milder and dryer parts of the United Kingdom, in winter, when the most beautiful views will be obtained, one should of course allow for the very occasional possibility of freezing weather, and be equipped accordingly.

Equipment

If you can afford it, a top grade hooded down jacket, which can be reduced to a minimal size when packed tightly into a purpose made bag, can guarantee warmth at all times of the year. On those days when it does rain, good quality waterproofs make an enormous difference to the enjoyment of your walking. Plastic waterproofs may be used for short excursions, but can be extremely sweaty and uncomfortable during a sudden downpour, or worse still, when it decides to rain all day. Some form of breathable waterproof gear is much better and in good camping shops the cost of jacket and leggings is about £200. It may seem a lot of money at first, but having bought it you will not have to worry about rainy days, and can even enjoy them.

In addition to bird and flower books or, better still, smartphone app equivalents, try to take some miniature binoculars which you can carry in your pocket. This will save weight, and also time if you need to get them out quickly before the bird has flown or the dolphin or seal has slipped away.

Essential on this mountainous, rocky, coast are walking shoes with mountain walking soles or actual mountain boots. These will save you slipping on steep slopes and sheer slate paths, making your walk easier as well as safer. Always run-in new footwear, even if it means wearing them around the house. This may save endless blisters and discomfort at the beginning of your walking holiday. As most of the directions in the book use east-west terminology you may find a compass or a compass app on your smart phone useful. There is a note about some of the apps I found useful on the walk in the useful information section at the back of the book (see page 159).

Camping

For camping a maximum of a 75 litre rucksack during the winter and a 50 litre rucksack in summer is recommended. The maximum weight including tent, sleeping bag, all spare clothing and cameras should not exceed 28 lbs (12.5 kg). It's amazing how little you need to exist for days on end without injuring your back. If you don't want to carry everything with you, there

Great Mew Stone from Lord Revelstoke's Drive. Rame Head and the Cornish coast in the background.

are luggage carrier companies who will take your luggage to your next location. There are quite a few campsites along the way, but, if it is not possible to reach one, farmers along the route are often happy to give permission to walkers to camp on their land. Always ask first.

Youth hostels, B and B and hotels

If you are you hostelling or staying in bed-and-breakfast accommodation, all you need is clothing for cold days, waterproofs, camera, and good bird and botanical apps for your smartphone.

Booking is absolutely essential during school holiday periods and spring and summer weekends, but during the rest of the year booking just ahead or taking pot luck can be much more relaxing. Late booking websites and Airbnb can often be used to find very good value accommodation at short notice, but there is always the risk that you may have to go inland if it's all booked up on the coast itself. The bus services at the time of writing were consistently reliable, and can be used to reach accommodation off route.

Camping rates varied in 2018 from £12 to £25 a night. Airbnb can of course be booked online, as can some of the excellent traditional B&Bs. Local B&Bs and hotels can also be contacted through Tourist Information Centres (TICs) listed on page 162. Typical 2018 prices are £30-£40 with separate bathroom, or £50+ for en-suite. Many will only do two nights at a time, so booking at least a day or two ahead, and use of the local bus services for exploration from a base may be

necessary to make the best of the situation. Roughing it some days and nights combined with occasional luxury treats can be a good way to enjoy the best of both worlds on this coast. A variety of opportunities abounds.

Safety precautions

Sensible, careful walkers have little to worry about on safety grounds but there are accidents each year. Many of the cliffs along this coast can be unstable at any time. Rockfalls can consist of many thousands of tons of rock. Always keep well away from the base of any cliffs. Avoid tripping on rough rocky paths or getting out of control on muddy slopes. There are many of both along this route.

An inadvertent slip on steep ground, or losing balance by not spotting a small protruding rock or hollow in the path, are often the cause of accidents. In this event a whistle may be useful to attract attention if you are alone, as well as some first aid kit. Mobile phone coverage is good on this section of the path but not 100%, so alternative ways of attracting attention may be needed.

Swimming is generally safe on incoming tide in coves. On exposed parts of the coast watch the water for currents and observe any warning signs. Walk along the beaches during falling tides only. Every year someone has been cut off by the tide or caught by an unexpected wave somewhere on the coast of Cornwall and Devon when attempting to do this without sufficient local knowledge.

Food and drink

When I first walked the path to write this series thirty years ago, good pubs were a rarity, good fresh locally sourced food was not even mentioned, and the beer was generally pretty boring. Wine? Don't sell that here! Coffee was two brands of instant. Tea could be from very old tea-bags.

The scene has changed completely. Many pubs do traditional or modern quality dishes at prices which are just about affordable. Local fish, meat and veg are often used. The day's fresh fish tastes totally different from anything you could buy in a city supermarket. Wines of most varieties are largely served at the right temperature. If you want to splash out at lunch time or at the end of the day you can really eat very well. If you are on a budget there are chip shops in the fishing villages, or you can buy good produce in the village shop and cook it at your camp site *en plein air*.

There is now a new phenomenon appearing on this coast; mainly outdoor places on or near the beach with a surprisingly varied menu. Often on National Trust property, and in simple huts or chalets, most eating happens on benches outside. Some aim at good value, some at the ultimate cuisine, others have menus catering for both. They are the first of many such small new open air enterprises aiming to supply tasty food at not too astronomical prices for the visitors to this area. They may supply fine wines, or you may be able to take your own. Just check ahead, they all have websites. You could make a point of visiting some of them as part of a gastronomic tour of South Cornwall and Devon. I shall try to mention them in the text as we go along. I hope they survive and prosper to the benefit of all coast path users. Please, whatever you do, buy locally in any case. I can assure you that the traditional pubs, cafés and restaurants can also be very good indeed.

Do your homework online, and avoid places that have no price list displayed outside. This applies as much to ice cream booths as to smart gastro pubs and restaurants along this coast.

The Victory Inn, one of the many watering places in St Mawes.

Stonechat. Along with the wren and the robin, this path-side bird will greet you along the way.

Marine wildlife along the South Devon and Cornwall coast

As you walk along the Coast Path, don't forget to look out to sea. If you are lucky, you might see bottle-nosed dolphins, seals or even a basking shark.

Headlands such as Pendennis Point are the best places to spot passing dolphins. Semi-resident pods move along the Channel, swimming in straight lines between headlands, or diverting for fish shoals.

Grey seals, one of the rarest seal species in the world, pull out on Looe Island and other rocky shores.

Basking sharks, the second largest fish globally, are the 'ultimate gentle giants' of the sea. They can be up to 11 metres long but their huge mouths filter plankton from the water – forget *Jaws*, basking sharks won't hurt you! This coast is one of the 'hot spots' for seeing this gentle species in the summer when the plankton blooms.

This coastline is especially important for its rocky reefs, which provide habitats for colourful invertebrates, such as soft and cup corals, gem anemones and tubeworms. The many wrecks in the area e.g. Plymouth Sound, provide

Introduction

22

A gannet flies over the sea.

Seal pups at play.

artificial reefs for marine animals to colonise.

Other important features are the maerl beds in Falmouth and St. Austell Bays. Maerl is a red seaweed but it is rock-hard, and when the knobbly, pink skeletons die they build up on the seabed, providing a hard substrate on an otherwise soft sediment. This 'reef' provides a habitat for seaweeds and plant-like animals.

If you wish that you could dive and see the secrets of what lies beneath the waves, seashores provide the perfect opportunity to explore the marine environment without getting your feet wet! Even better than that, there are several places along this coastline where you can take part in a guided 'Seashore Safari' or 'Rockpool Ramble' with an expert and see for yourself.

For details of events check out www. wemburymarinecentre.org and looemarineconservation.org/looe-marine-conservation-group/whats-on/

The coarse, artificial 'sand' of the shores of St Austell Bay – a by-product of the china clay mining industry – is highly mobile and supports less marine life than the natural sandy shores along this coastline. A walk along the strandline after a storm, however, can reveal some fascinating finds and clues to what lives below the waves: seagrasses, shells and cuttlefish bones.

Female Atlantic grey seal.

Bottle-nosed dolphin.

The Exe Estuary is of international importance for wintering waders and wildfowl, supporting thousands of birds. One of the best opportunities to view the wildlife of the estuary is at the RSPB's two nature reserves:

Exminster Marshes (SX 957874): an area of wet grassland drained by dykes and ditches, the Marshes are an important breeding ground for lapwings and redshanks. Ducks, including shovelers and teals, also breed here. In winter, the marshes provide roosting and feeding areas for waders such as curlews and black-tailed godwits, and brent geese graze the drier areas. The ditches have a good dragonfly fauna, including the rare hairy dragonfly.

Bowling Green Marsh (SX 973876): adjacent to the town of Topsham, this is the main high tide roost for the north of the estuary. Large numbers of waders and wildfowl gather here as the tide rises and covers the mudflats, especially in the winter. High numbers of black-tailed godwits can be seen and many widgeon graze on the Marsh.

During the winter the RSPB runs special cruises from Topsham, Starcross and Exmouth which provide an excellent opportunity to view the 20,000 birds to be found on the Exe Estuary, including hundreds of avocets. RSPB guides provide expert commentary. Booking is essential as cruises book up fast — please call 01392 432691 for details.

The Tamar Estuary is also important for estuarine habitats and species. The main features here are intertidal biogenic reefs, blue mussel beds and smelt. Smelt is a migratory fish species, which has suffered large declines throughout its range and is known to breed in the Tamar, which also provides a nursery for many other fish species. Biogenic reefs are made from the hard parts of animals, such as blue mussels, and are formed when the animals' shells are bound together with mud and sand by the sticky byssus thread, or 'beards', of the mussels. These living reefs are ecologically important as they provide a home or refuge for seaweeds and animals including barnacles, winkles and small crabs.

Marine Conservation has long been the 'poor relative' of conservation on land – 'out of sight, out of mind', perhaps. Now, areas of the sea are being designated as marine protected areas to protect habitats and species from human activities, with the aim of creating a coherent network of marine habitats.

Special Areas of Conservation along this coast include:

- Start Point to Plymouth Sound and Eddystone for its reefs, marine areas and inlets
- Fal and Helford Estuaries

Marine Conservation Zones - As a result of the Marine and Coastal Access Act 2009, a network of Marine Conservation Zones (MCZs) has been created that protect marine species and habitats. Sites were designated in Devon, Torbay and Tamar Estuary, along with Skerries Bank and surrounds – an area to the south and west of Start Point. In Cornwall, the second wave of MCZs includes the offshore Western Channel, 54 km off the Lizard Peninsula.

Other designations offer protection to the marine environment, although their primary purpose is to protect birds or other species or wreck sites:

- Exe Estuary Special Protection Area (SPA)
- Tamar Estuaries Complex SPA
- Falmouth Bay to St Austell Bay SPA

If you want to be amazed by our fascinating underwater world and how we all play a part in conserving it, the National Marine Aquarium at Plymouth is well worth a visit. www.national-aquarium.co.uk

Sarah Welton

Birds of the wild cliff – a shag, guillemot and three razorbills.

Geology of the Coast Path: St Mawes to Dawlish Warren

With its sea-girt cliffs, punctuated by labyrinthine estuaries (known as rias), occasional sandy bays and innumerable coves, the southern coast of the Cornubian peninsula exemplifies a monumental resistance to the surrounding ocean. This reflects its sturdy geological framework, principally ancient sedimentary rocks of Devonian age (about 400 million years old). This Devonian planet looked utterly unlike the familiar configuration of today's world. Not only was ancient Cornubia located somewhat south of the equator, but this wider geological story only makes sense if we consider how two ancient continents, Gondwana and Laurussia, ultimately collided, sweeping with them a flotilla of smaller pieces of the Earth's crust known as microplates. Though this story can only be fully told by looking at rocks as far apart as Texas and northern Africa, the cliffs of this coastline yield crucial information. They provide mute testimony to vanished worlds, albeit a history in deep time which even now has not been fully elucidated. The apparent continuity of outcrops, superbly exposed in long lines of cliffs, conceals a sequence of dramatic events. These are now telescoped into a complex series of deformed and folded rocks, but when unravelled reveal a now vanished seaway. Known as the Rheic ocean, its obliteration also involved immense tectonic events that were responsible for the construction of the Cornubian massif. Despite its attachment to the rest of the United Kingdom it has long been recognised that its geological aspect does not easily match equivalent-aged rocks elsewhere in the United Kingdom. We need to look to a wider setting to explain this distinctiveness. In essence it is the result of the Cornubian massif being once located hundreds of miles to the south of its present position. Transport along an enormous fault-line, analogous to the San Andreas fault of California, eventually parked it adjacent to the geologically incongruous South Wales.

Central to the interpretation of the geology is an episode of mountain building. This is referred to as the Variscan orogeny, a name derived from an ancient and long-vanished German tribe, the Varisci. This orogeny involved complex crustal movements that defined occasional episodes of volcanism, but more importantly the formation of a series of basins. These, it needs to be explained, are not structures equipped with hot and cold taps and plugs, but areas of crustal subsidence which allowed a vast thickness of sediment to accumulate. These ranged from muds to sandstones and accumulated in environments as different as lakes and the deep sea. In your peregrination and travelling westwards, the three principal basins that you will traverse are those referred to as the South Devon, the Looe and finally the Gramscatho Basins. Separating these and other basins are fault-bound regions of positive relief (horsts), often the site of limestone accumulation and even tropical reefs, such as around Brixham. This picture was far from static. Rather, on-going crustal compression resulted in a shifting pattern of basins, major faulting and complex episodes of deformation. The closure of the Rheic ocean also involved the violent scraping off of fragments of oceanic crust. The most spectacular manifestation is on the Lizard peninsula, but a near-equivalent is encountered at Start Point to Bolt Tail with highly deformed metamorphic schists.

As the Variscan orogeny drew to its close, melting of the crust produced a vast subterranean batholith, one that links outcrops of granite from the Scilly Isles to Dartmoor. Associated with this intrusion, a huge volume of hot fluids flowed through the Devonian sediments. This process would ensure later economic prosperity as these hydrothermal deposits yielded valuable minerals, notably tin and copper. The

termination of these igneous intrusions set the scene for the subsequent geological history of Britain. Adjacent to Dawlish Warren we encounter Permian sediments, especially desert sands and conglomerates, that accumulated deep in the newly constructed supercontinent known as Pangea. Time moved on, but if you wish to pursue that story then you must take the Coast Paths along the Dorset and north Somerset shorelines. These will reveal new worlds unfolding, first populated by giant reptiles and ammonites, and then a planet that moved inexorably to the present day. This brings us full circle to those distinctive rias. In part they owe their origin to slow subsidence of the crust combined with on-going sea-level rise.

Professor Simon Conway Morris

Bolberry Down, a wonderland for geologists.

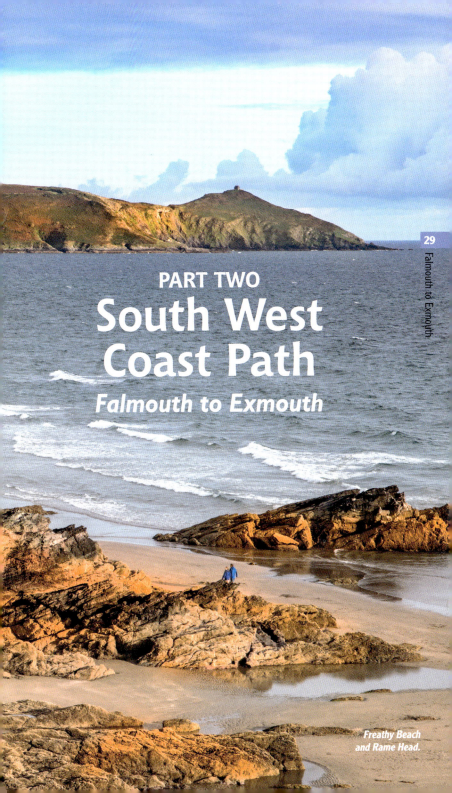

PART TWO
South West Coast Path

Falmouth to Exmouth

Freathy Beach and Rame Head.

St Mawes to Portloe

via Place, St Anthony, Portscatho and Nare Head
13.8 miles (22.28 km)

Ascent/descent 2,567 feet (782.5 metres)
Highest point 325 feet (100 metres)

Starting from St Mawes, take the little ferry to Place at one of the quays **A** near the Falmouth ferry terminus. The ticket office on the quay will direct you to the right ferry, and you will arrive near Place House. Turn right along the woodland path until you come to the ancient quay in front of Place House.

If you are travelling out of season and the ferry is no longer running, get the No. 50 bus towards Truro and get off at Gerrans Church, Highertown, where it turns round. Go down the narrow lane beside the Royal Standard pub and keep going past the village car park for 1½ miles (2 km). The lane becomes a bridleway and rejoins the road to St Anthony just before the Porth National Trust Car Parks. At Porth Farm turn right into the woods and follow a well defined path beside Porth Creek. The pond on your right is Froe tidal mill pond. The general idea was to fill the pond with water as the tide came in, and then release the water at low tide via an undershot water wheel. Many tidal mill ponds are recorded in the Domesday Book. They were certainly common throughout the middle ages

and until the Industrial Revolution provided cheap alternative sources of power in locations with perfect transport links. It seems likely that the Romans used them, including probable remains on the River Fleet in London, as in Fleet Street. Nowadays they are used to generate large quantities of electricity in many countries, and work in both directions, doubling the power output. More recent proposals to build them in Britain have been rejected on the grounds of marine wildlife conservation.

After another 1½ miles, with great glimpses of the calm, protected creeks, you will see the ferry landing stages and Place Quay **1**.

Go up the track to the left of the lawns and turn through a gate to follow the track to the church. Take the path above and left of the church and, when you reach the junction, possibly by some bee hives, turn right and follow the track northwest towards the sea, where you turn left again and continue through pine woods and out into the fields bordering the low rocky cliff top. Continue past the beaches and cross

Contours are given in metres
The vertical interval is 5m

the dam which holds back an area
of marshland. You soon come to the
entrance to the National Trust property
which has a gate and a style. Look
back here at the last views of St Mawes
Castle, with Pendennis Castle looking
down on you from its grand headland
to the west. The coast path continues
past the old lighthouse paraffin store on
your right, and then doubles back on
itself to the top of the hill by a range of
military buildings.

The granite St Anthony lighthouse was
constructed in 1835 as a navigational
aid and to warn passing ships of
the hazardous Manacles rocks. This
lighthouse has been automated since
1987 and is often open for visitors
during the summer months. Just near
the dam at the entrance to the National
Trust property is a shortcut which brings
you up to the National Trust car park
for St Anthony **B**. Either way, turn right
at the top of the hill parallel with the

Henry VIII's St Mawes Castle.

various military buildings and continue on the landward side of the coastal battery on St Anthony Head.

There is a birdwatching hide, a great spot for seeing cliff nesting birds, approached via the ditch which formed part of the fortifications, including a large bank, ditch and unclimbable fence. The battery is open to the public on selected dates advertised on the NT website and in the local Tourist Information Centres.

Place

The lawns in front of Place House were also once a tide mill pond, constructed and run for centuries in conjunction with the tiny church and monastery beside it. The grand, long house you see today is built on the site of an Elizabethan manor. It obscures the Victorian village church, which has an unusual steeple, echoed by a similar structure on the house, and a fine Norman doorway of Caen stone brought, by boat of course, from Plympton Priory. The other remarkable feature is the wonderfully ornate memorial to Admiral Thomas Spry.

Henry VIII comes into the story here. After the dissolution of the monasteries and his break with Europe he needed stone in large quantities to build fortifications to resist attacks from his former allies. Hence it seems almost certain that much of the stone from the small Augustinian monastery here, and the 12th century church on this site, was taken to build St Mawes Castle, leaving only the foundations of the church extant. So the Victorian church is almost certainly built on the original cruciform foundations. Samuel Thomas Spry, owner of Place and MP for Bodmin in the early 19th century, paid his cousin, the Reverend Clement Carlyon, to rebuild the church with new wooden roofs, glazed Victorian floor tiles and stained glass, and the genuine and beautiful Norman Caen stone doorway.

JUST OFF THE PATH

St Mawes

I can highly recommend pausing at least a day in St Mawes, perhaps staying near Portscatho (pronounced Portscatha), to get the best out of your visit to this area. Here I shall outline a few of the things that you can do to really get to know this beautiful corner of England properly before moving on to complete your next day on the official coast path.

There is a 2 mile (3km) walk along the coast from St Mawes to St Just in Roseland 13th century church. As a spur from the coast path this gives you good views across the Carrick Roads (Fal Estuary) as well as bringing you the idyllic sub-tropical surrounds of the waterside St Just Church. To start this walk go west along the St Mawes quayside and up the road until you reach the castle and then continue past the castle on the low clifftop.

At St Mawes itself King Henry VIII's gem of a castle is also worth inspecting. The English Heritage audio guide brings the place to life with its rumbustious humour and dramatic accompaniment. When you look back at the castle as you walk the first stretch of this section of the path it will add a completely new dimension to the experience. Many original carvings and decorations still survive within the castle walls, and it is considered to be one of the most perfect examples of Henry's forts. It was built between 1540 and 1542 when Henry VIII fell out with his European allies and decided that England should go it alone. On the coastal edge of the castle is a slightly earlier fortification. The round walls were built to resist heavy canon fire. Pendennis Castle at Falmouth, opposite, would be part of a dual defence of the Fal Estuary, known as the Carrick Roads. Falmouth Harbour would be well protected.

The sub-tropical gardens at Lamorran House, Upper Castle Road, are periodically open to the public. The views across St Mawes Harbour to the St Anthony Headland and lighthouse are beautifully framed by the palm-like leaves and other sub-tropical vegetation and they serve teas and cakes on the veranda.

As with several of the ports along this section of the path there are periodic festivals of sail, best seen from one of the vantage points I describe here, or from the Falmouth-St Mawes Ferry. The Tourist Information Centres should be able to let you know when these events take place.

The Fal ferries provide a very comprehensive travel service.

Keep on left round St Anthony Head across what was thick scrub and is now being managed to restore it to a flower rich meadow. Continue to Killigerran Head **2** and follow the clifftop all the way to Porth, where there is a car park, toilets and a seasonal cafe. The path is easy to follow along the low but jagged clifftop all the way to Portscatho. I've walked it in moonlight, the best, and during a gale, at high tide. Quite a dramatic scene.

There is no longer safe access to Porthbeor Beach. The former path to that beach really has completely collapsed and is totally unstable, but

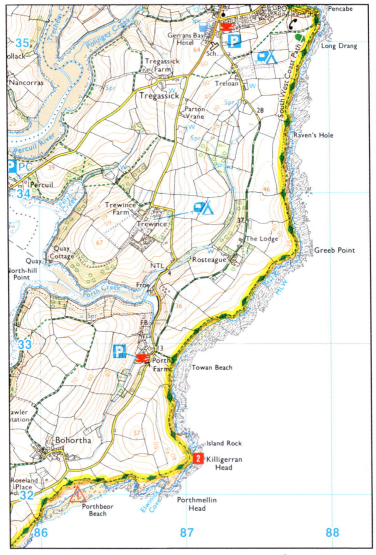

Contours are given in metres
The vertical interval is 5m

there are plenty of sandy (and rocky) beaches to descend to over the next few miles, so not to worry.

At Killigerran Head a short detour from the path seawards at Island Rock gives a strategic view of the rocky shore leading towards Towan Beach. There will often be oystercatchers flashing their black and white wings and making their familiar excited, distinctive, piercing calls as they feed on every living creature to be found on the rocks (not oysters, in spite of their name). Gannets may also circle overhead. Shags and cormorants may be fishing the seabed.

As ever on this walk, keep an eye open for the seals, which swim round from places like Tintagel for a winter break. See the information poster in the buildings at Porth (toilets and car park) about the sighting information relating to Cornwall's seals, each identifiable by their unique coat markings.

The path continues along the low cliffs to Portscatho, properly pronounced, and sometimes signed as, Portscatha, where the Wesleyan Chapel on your left as you round the headland at the western end of the village sometimes has coffee and tea for sale. Nearly every village on the coast here has or has had a Methodist Chapel, reflecting the discontent with the established church during the 19th century, and Wesley's preaching campaigns. Many of them are modest but attractive buildings.

Portscatho and Gerrans have a pub each, the Royal Standard up by the steepled church in Gerrans at the top of the street from the harbour and The Plume of Feathers near the harbour. Also near the church is a small museum about the area. Opening hours for

this museum are normally posted at the village shop which is also the Post Office.

Like many traditional village outlets you'll come across along the coast path over the next weeks, the shop is extremely well stocked with everything you need for your journey including a range of fresh food and a wide variety of drink. The shop is open from 7am to 7pm, the Post Office 9am-5.30pm except Sunday, with half day opening on Wednesday and Saturday. As there are few or no cash machines in many of the villages the path goes through on this coast, this may be your only source of cash, which can be issued by the Post Office for almost all bank customers nationwide, subject to proof of identity and a valid debit card. Some of the in-store Post Offices are now staying open for longer hours, (in Mevagissey for example) but that is the exception rather than the rule. The Co-op outlets in the larger villages have free cash machines.

Male Atlantic grey seal.

Starting from the square **C** by the shop and the Plume of Feathers, follow North Parade, which runs parallel with the beach until it becomes a path leading out onto the clifftop with rather fine Edwardian town houses on your left. As you come out of the village there is a car park on the clifftop. To your right is Porthcurnick Beach (NT). At low tide you can cross by the beach, at high tide continue east over the little valley beyond the Hidden Hut (food and drink on the clifftop, as mentioned in Part One). Cross the road, and continue along the clifftop towards the Pednvadan Coastwatch lookout station. The land around this lookout is National Trust owned and produces pretty magnificent wildflower displays throughout much of the year.

The National Coastwatch Institution (NCI) is a voluntary organisation and registered charity set up in 1994 to restore a visual watch along UK shores after many small coastguard stations closed. In 1994, when two fishermen lost their lives off the Cornish coast below a recently closed coastguard lookout, local people decided to open and restore the visual watch. When the first station was opened at Bass Point on the Lizard, NCI was born.

Contours are given in me
The vertical interval is

Pednvadan Coastwatch Lookout.

Today, 49 stations keep a visual watch around the coastline of England and work closely with the Maritime Coastguard Agency (MCA). Some of their stations have an information centre nearby. These cover all sorts of topics of interest and I found every one of them worth the time in getting to know that part of the coast better. The friendly local staff welcome questions, and will be pleased to give advice and information if it is requested.

Just up the lane here, at Rosevine and Trewithian, are several eating and accommodation facilities and a farmhouse B&B. If this is your first visit to the wonderful Roseland Peninsula and you have spent lots of time inspecting St Mawes, St Anthony Head, Gerrans and Portscatho, then this might be a good area to stay the night.

To continue eastwards keep on through the next fields on the landward side of the clifftop hedge. The path dips down through scrubland to Porthbean Beach, which is best not approached at maximum tide (check your tide tables), arriving by a wooden stairway and leaving up a pebble path. Keep right at the first fork and continue through the fields until you see a path coming down from Curgurrell Farm (farm and sea-food shop). Continue east for a short distance and the path brings you to the NT Treluggan Cliff property **3**, where spring grazing by Dartmoor ponies is beginning to produce one of the most remarkable wildlife displays of the Roseland Heritage Coast. These ponies keep invasive species like gorse and bracken under control, letting a whole variety of wild flowers flourish. The ponies go to Dodman Point in October each year. Early purple orchids and bluebells covered these fields in April and May. When I went through a few weeks later, a whole range of other species carpeted the ground. The habitat is perfect for voles, who are a great food source for birds of prey like kestrels, so keep an eye open for them as you admire the ground cover.

Contours are given in m
The vertical interval is

Eventually you will see a long white building ahead. The path curves inland up to the road just before this **D**. Follow the very quiet road past the white building and go through the car park. The road is a dead end for cars since the cliff gave way below. Keep on down into the valley, where some buildings are in a state of collapse. Cross the bridge and then follow the traces of the former road, or cross the beach to the low cliff opposite. Entering the fields you find more National Trust ground, which allows a wide margin for the path, since the cliffs here are eroding at a steady pace. When you come to the Nare Hotel, they have provided a path inland and round the back of the hotel buildings. Turn down the road to Carne Beach – in summer there is a mobile café serving snacks, drinks and ice creams in the car park just back from the beach.

A few yards along the road the clifftop path takes you through wild country to the top of the rocky Nare Head **4**, with close-up views of the jagged Gull Rock just offshore and panoramic views of the cliffs for miles all around.

I particularly enjoyed the views from the headland, which are well worth a few extra paces off the official coast path route. It is wild, rugged, lonely and a really good place to take photos. Much of the year round the flowers are pretty good too, and the headland is part of an SSSI (Site of Special Scientific Interest). Look the site up online for a complete list of rare plants if you are sufficiently interested in the detail.

Continuing along the path eastwards I like to follow the clifftop as far as possible for the best views of the island called, like many others, Gull Rock. This is home to several bird colonies, but a number of curious concrete structures, one covered by a large earth mound, also come into sight while you are still on the headland.

During WWII a secret department of the Air Ministry was asked to think up a strategy to deflect German bombs away from their intended targets – ports, airports and major cities – by creating the illusion of activity in a different place nearby in empty countryside. The first wave of night bombing would bring incendiary bombs to set the intended facility or city on fire. The fires would then be used as guides for the second wave, when the explosives would be dropped on that target.

The engineer, a retired Air Ministry officer, Colonel John Fisher Turner formed a team with an ex film studio staff, carpenters, engineers and others

to carry out the construction of an elaborate network of dummy airfields and other decoy sites.

The programme began in January 1940, by replicating the effects of a fire that a bomber aircrew would expect at their target. This cunning plan is deemed to have saved thousands of lives and hundreds of destructive air strikes. In these fields around the earth-covered bunker you can still see what would have been tanks of inflammable materials to be lit up to simulate Falmouth on fire, while the staff would take refuge in the bunker during the potential attack. There are interpretive signs illustrating the effect of this campaign.

The other, less conspicuous, structures mark a cold war bunker where the Royal Observer Corps were stationed to monitor radioactivity in the event of a nuclear attack. If you are interested in the history and use of these structures there are periodic guided tours which are advertised on the National Trust website for Nare Head, and in local Tourist Information Centres. There are also other websites and videos online covering the subject.

The view from Nare Head.

Contours are given in metres
The vertical interval is 5m

However, it is peace time at the time of writing, and most walkers may be ready to enjoy the superb vantage point which gives views to the west (which will soon disappear from view), as well as the floral displays resulting from the noble National Trust management efforts in recent years.

To continue to the fishing village of Portloe keep along the clifftop, around Kiberick Cove **5** (NT car park and beach), dip down to a stream and rather overgrown area, and rise through the undercliff to the top again, where the path becomes more open and well defined. At the right time of year the rocky outcrops on this cliff form a magnificent foreground to the approach to the tiny port and village of Portloe, with Dodman Point in the background.

There are two boats working from here, two pubs, and some other accommodation. The Lugger overlooks the harbour and advertises as a hotel, restaurant and spa. The Ship Inn, just up the road, left and up the hill, is definitely a traditional pub with traditional pub food as well as sea-food dishes, served in the garden if the weather is kind and you prefer that.

2 Portloe to Mevagissey

via Caerhays Castle, Dodman Point, Gorran Haven and Portmellon
11.87 miles (19 km)

Ascent/descent 2,695 feet (821 metres)
Highest point 374 feet (114 metres)

From the port of Portloe take the very quiet road past the phone box or one of the flights of steps. There is a rather wonderful epitaph to be discovered by one of the paths. In any event, you have to take to the road for a short distance. Soon you will see a ship's figurehead, where you turn right towards the former Methodist Chapel, right down the far side of the house with the slipway, and right at Anchor Cottage. Now follow the railings up to the NT sign at the Flagstaff for a good look back at the whole village and harbour.

From here to Portholland the path meanders along the clifftops and slopes until you come to a track leading right down to West Portholland **6**, which consists of the remains of a large limekiln and a few cottages. Turn right over the stream and along the road to East Portholland. The Post Office here is also a small café. To continue walk round in front of the Post Office and turn back up the slope behind it, taking a sharp right back onto the cliffop path, which comes to Porthlune Cove with views of Caerhays Castle (1807-1810). Take the quiet and narrow road past

the car park and the castle gateway, over the bridge and continue through the field. Turn round when you have climbed a little to assess the view of the castle.

Its architect John Nash is perhaps most famous for designing the extravagant oriental exterior of the Royal Pavilion at what had been the small fishing village of Brighton, where the Prince Regent had bought a farm by the sea on the advice of his doctor. This was after Nash had been engaged in London to set out the design of Regents Street, the Royal Opera Arcade, Regents Park, Regents Canal, St James's Park and its lake, Marble Arch and Buckingham Palace (not the facade you see now, the one behind it which you see if you visit the Queen). So the lake and castle in the Norman style you now see here is a significant part of British architectural history. Not only that, but the garden is famous for its oriental plant collection, and is open to the public in the spring, when these plants are at their best. Opening times are available online.

As you go away from the castle take the right hand path until level with the pine

Foxgloves near West Portholland.

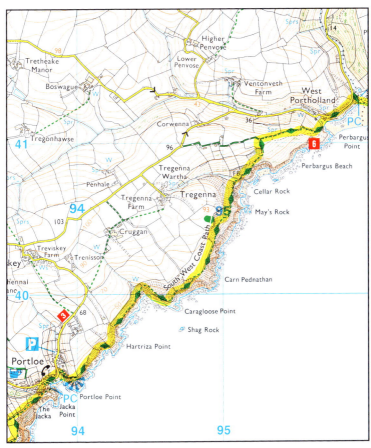

Contours are given in metres
The vertical interval is 5m

Contours are given in metres
The vertical interval is 5m

trees then turn right towards the cliff into the next field, following the cliff to the top of that field and through the woods above. At the top of the woods is a clearing beside the path, on the seaward side, giving one of the best late afternoon/evening views of the whole of this part of the South Cornwall path, with the jagged Greeb Point **7** forming a dramatic foreground to the view of the 325 foot high (114 metres) slate mass of Dodman Point jutting out of the sea. Time for a pause at least, or a photo, picnic and drink if you have time and the weather is kind.

The path from here clings to the slopes and eventually descends to the wild chaos of rocks around the sandy Hemmick Beach **8**. The (NT) parking for this beach is at Penare and a path separate from the lane links the two. The lane is definitely not suitable for vehicles unless you live along it, since there are no passing places and it is extremely narrow.

Your walk to Dodman Point (the highest point on the south Cornish coast) brings you to the plateau at the pre-historic 'Bulwark', a large bank and ditch, marking the inland boundary of this 'promontory fort'. The Bulwark is 600 metres long and 6 metres high in places, quite an impressive sight. If you have walked from Minehead you will have seen many such 'forts', with some sort of earthwork or rampart defending the neck of a high and prominent peninsula. We have no idea whether they were built to defend against human or animal threats, or whether they were constructed to appease the gods of their time, as grand temples with grand views. We can only speculate. If there was a threat, was it new arrivals defending themselves from hostile locals, or were they built to keep new populations from moving in and taking over? In any event there were very few humans here in those days. They were far outnumbered by the wildlife which kept them fed.

There were already Bronze Age burial mounds when the fort as we see it was built. Two still remain, as do the remains of a medieval strip field – an

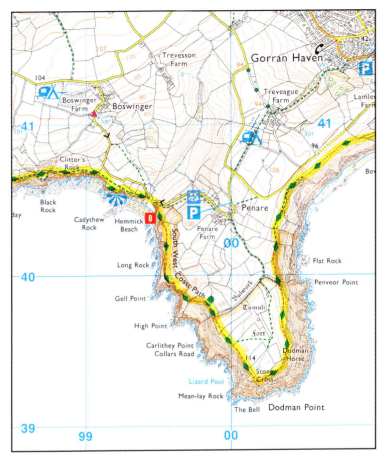

Contours are given in metres
  The vertical interval is 5m

archaeological treat. At the tip of the
headland is a massive granite cross,
inspired by the Victorian vicar of
Caerhays – 'In the firm hope of the
second coming of our Lord Jesus Christ,
and for the encouragement of those
who strive to serve Him, this cross is
erected AD 1896'. It serves also as a
navigational aid to seafarers. Here you
can take a minor diversion inland to
the watch house with its whitewashed
round tower (1795), one of a series of
Admiralty signal stations used by the

London HQ to communicate with the
Navy at Plymouth.

Grazing the area are Dartmoor ponies
and the tiny Dexter Cattle, native to
the west coast of Ireland, and thought
to be much like the cattle of Iron Age
England, forming a nice link with the
pre-history of this headland. These
cattle graze happily on the blackthorn
and gorse and trample on the bracken,
enabling a much wider diversity of
plants and creatures to establish and
thrive. This makes the area look more

beautiful, but more importantly helps to encourage a diverse environment rather than a monoculture, thus enriching our visit still further.

Peregrines may be seen swooping at high speed around Dodman Point catching small birds, while the kestrels hover, often from a fixed position, to detect and eat small ground creatures such as beetles and voles. Stonechat

and yellowhammer may be seen in the scrub. The white flashing wings of gannet may be detected out to sea, and watch for dolphin here, since the same shoal may have attracted them.

The view on the day I was there ('visibility excellent') from the headland extended from the eastern side of the Lizard Peninsula to Bolt Tail by Hope Cove, and included the twin islands of the Eddystone Rock lighthouse.

To continue the walk go to the north-east corner of the fort and keep going along the clifftop. Just after you come close to the lane from Gorran Haven to Penare the path follows the top of the undercliff scrub gently downwards to the eastern end of Vault Beach **9**. Ignore maps which show a lower path through the scrub. That path has long since tumbled into the sea. A path from the NT car park joins from the left, and the coast path goes past a simple bench and through a bridlegate into a wild area on Maenease Point. I took the path nearest to the low cliff here, but they all go round the headland and end up at the same point. You pass the access to Vault Beach, the distant part of which is listed by guides as a nudist area. Head along the clifftop path north-east now and you come down into the harbour of Gorran Haven. The old buildings clinging to the solid rocks close to the harbour are beautiful. Keep straight ahead through a boat parking area.

Gorran Haven has a general store, bakery and Post Office, eating and drinking facilities and a camping site at Treveaugue, as well as a chip shop. Some of these may be closed out of season, but you will not go hungry.

Continue to the top of the main street parallel with the sea, turn right into Cliff Road and go as far as the last house entrance gate. Turn left into a small enclosure and then into the fields uphill on the clifftop over one peak, down over a stream and back up to the hill where a tumulus is marked on the map. Sadly this piece of pre-historic England has been ploughed out since this map was made, but with a little imagination you may be able to place it. Slightly more of the earthwork **10** further along has survived. Looking on the bright side, the cliff has crumbled quite a bit, but the fence has been put well back and you are free to walk on open cliff all the way to the stream by the boat house by Chapel Point Peninsula. Daphne Du Maurier's novel *The House on the Strand* uses Chapel Point as a location.

Three cornered garlic at Portloe.

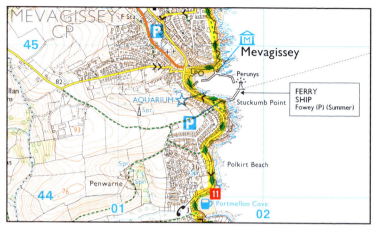

Contours are given in metres
The vertical interval is 5m

The three private houses here were designed in the 1930s by the Scottish arts and crafts architect John Campbell, and show that sensitive architecture can enable quite large structures to enhance the landscape rather than ruin it.

Go through an iron gate and cross the stream, walk behind the boat house and cross the private drive to Chapel Point at right angles. Curve left following the contours to the corner of the field. Here you cross a stone stepped stile and go through a gate to join the private drive. Turn right, pass all the houses on it and turn right again down the road to Portmellon Cove **11**. Here there is a pub, a very open harbour, and a boatyard still operating. You can see some of the old launching paraphernalia in the sea wall. Mevagissey has a perfectly protected harbour and built many boats, but had problems launching the larger ones because of the narrow harbour entrance, so they were often dragged over here for the launch, a formidable handling exercise. Hence

the easy answer was to build the boats here and launch straight in front of the yard, presumably taking them round to Mevagissey or their home harbour before the next storm.

And so we now walk up the road, turn right at the top, continue until we come into sight of the gardens, and a pretty good view of the coast ahead for many miles. Make for a steel staircase to the right, which takes us to the southern end of Mevagissey Outer Harbour. Walk right round the harbour to the museum at the far northern corner, and turn back up the zigzag cobbled street to the clifftop when you have made full use of all Mevagissey's wonderful walkers' facilities, including stores, the Post Office in the square, the old pubs and a very wide variety of accommodation. If you decide to make Mevagissey a base to cover walking the path round here, there are bus services to and from Gorran Haven and eastwards along the coast for returning, and you can walk to, or camp at, the Lost Gardens of Heligan.

Mevagissey fishing industry

Mevagissey was originally two villages, each with a dedication to a Celtic saint. St Meva was just inland, around what is now St Peters Church, and 'Ysy' the area around Cliff Street, a fishing village carved out of solid rock above the inner harbour. 'Ag' is the Cornish for 'and', hence the name Mevagissey, which has been in common use from the 15th century onwards.

Fishing used to involve every family – salting the pilchards and pressing them into barrels in the 'cellars' (fishermens' huts) or smoking them, pickling them in brine or canning them in oil. Coopers, boat-builders, net-makers, sail-makers, blacksmiths and fish merchants are just a few of the other occupations which depended on the annual reappearance of the pilchards. The village had ten pubs, two of which, the Ship and the Fountain, still remain, alongside a number of newer outlets, giving a wide choice for eating and drinking in the village.

There was a decline towards the end of the 19th century, although tourism was just beginning, sponsored by the new railways campaign 'Speed to the West'.

Mevagissey fishery declined even further at various times in the 20th century up until the 1960's, when the fishing industry started a revival. The mackerel boom that lasted into the mid-nineties brought boats back to this harbour. Pollack were landed in the winter months caught off the wrecks. Monkfish, turbot, sole, plaice, brill, cod, whiting, cuttlefish and squid began to be brought in in good quantities. These fish, together with crabs and lobsters, have a good market in France where the

Mevagissey harbour.

prices are higher. They are traded often via Plymouth Fish Market. The lorries take the ferries to France and Spain from Plymouth or Poole, and the fresh fish are served next day in French restaurants, as well as at the best Cornish outlets.

The pilchard is now marketed as the Cornish sardine and some of the Mevagissey fishermen have invested in ring nets and other efficient equipment. A website about the fishing industry is listed in 'Useful Information' on page 164 if you'd like to find out more.

In the meantime conservation measures have been introduced to protect the stocks for the long term health of the fishing industry and the environment – see page 22 for more information on the marine wildlife on this coast. An added bonus is that fishing is attracting younger people to work in the industry, which also helps to keep the fishing industry alive. New ice plants, cold stores, bait stores, lifting equipment, fork lifts and storage lofts have been built in support of the fishery, and Mevagissey in the 21st century remains a very lively fishing harbour, adding to its charm, much as it was in my youth in the 1940's and 50's.

The Mevagissey website states that in 1880 there were around sixty fishing-boats engaged in mackerel fishing and also mentions herring and pilchards. In 2018, sixty-three registered fishing vessels in the harbour worked by sixty-nine fishermen are recorded, hence the lively scene you will see around the harbour if you stay a while, which I recommend. I also recommend a visit to the Museum and the Aquarium.

The harbour offers fishing trips to visitors and there is a passenger ferry to Fowey.

Boats anchored in the harbour.

3 Mevagissey to Par

via Pentewan, Trenarren and Charlestown
10.64 miles (17 km)

Ascent/descent 1,909 feet (582 metres)
Highest point 300 feet (91.5 metres)

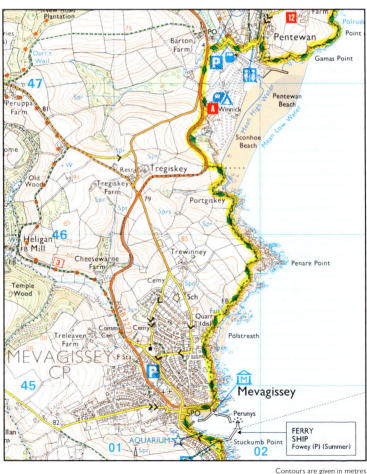

Contours are given in metres
The vertical interval is 5m

To start this section walk right round Mevagissey harbour to the museum at the far northern corner, and turn back up the zigzag cobbled street to the clifftop. As you near the top you get a good view of the rock strewn area below the cliffs, as well as a mile or so of very pleasant unspoilt coastline to come.

At the top you come out onto a recreation area. Keep roughly parallel with the clifftop, forking slightly inland as you ascend, and go to the right-hand side of the last white house facing you, at the end of the row and nearest the cliff (Beach Road). There is a hotel on the left open to the public which serves meals and drinks, including cream teas. A path also leaves on the right for Polstreath beach. Carry straight on into open country, down to a stream, and up to the heights of Penare Point. The path is wide and clear, and can be seen well ahead. Once on Penare Point it's downhill again to the stream at Portgiskey, once a tiny fishing settlement, and back up to the next hedge where we turn left towards the B3273 Mevagissey to London Apprentice road. Here there is an off-road path down to the entrance to the Pentewan Sands caravan park **A**, and from there we follow the pavement until the turning right for Pentewan Village **12**. (If you need a Post Office, it's at the Mill Garage just up the main road).

Pentewan too was a fishing village, with stone quarrying, farming and tin streaming supporting the population. In the early 19th century the local landowner, Sir Christopher Hawkins, built the harbour here, to help the pilchard fishing industry and to provide a sea outlet for china clay. It handled up to a third of all Cornwall's china

clay output for nearly a century, along with Par and Charlestown harbours. In 1829 a four mile horse-drawn tramway was built to connect Pentewan Port with St Austell. That tramway later became a steam railway.

On summer Sundays the wagons were used for Sunday school outings from the churches and chapels in the area, so that locals could go to the seaside at Pentewan. There are some old photos on display in the village showing the port and steam railway. The last train load of clay was delivered to the port of Pentewan in 1918. A further build up of sand in the entrance to the port meant that the last trading ship left in 1940. Now the harbour, still there, is no longer accessible from the sea at all, but the former railway forms part of National Cycleroute 3, and bikes can be hired in the village.

As well as the Post Office at the service station there is a pub, the Ship Inn, a café, public toilets, bicycle hire and a free car park in the village.

From the pub head up the road signposted for Trenarren, and take the first sharp rightx onto The Terrace. Pick up the coast path past the church at the end of The Terrace, turning left onto the footpath beside the gate to No.11.

The church is actually part of The Terrace, which is very unusual, possibly unique.

The clifftop path is quite narrow here, but great views suddenly open up just past Polrudden Cliffs, over Polrudden Cove to Drennick, the first headland facing us, and Black Head, yet another promontory hill fort.

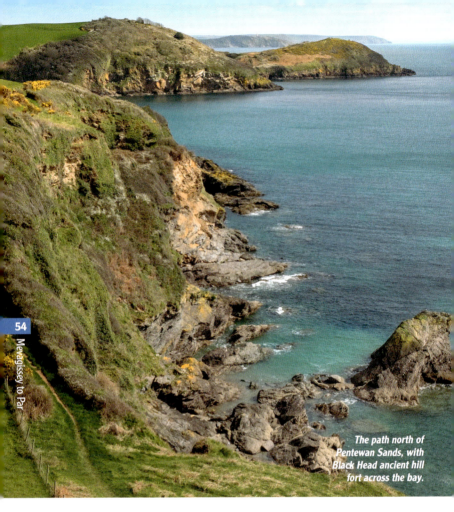

The path north of Pentewan Sands, with Black Head ancient hill fort across the bay.

It's rather less grand than the one at Dodman Point, but still has the same features, and its distinctive and attractive shape means you will be able to identify it on the skyline, starting with this view and the glimpses from Charlestown, and from quite a long way ahead if you look back. After Polrudden Cove the path widens out nicely. There is a substantial valley to negotiate, a further descent, crossing a small stream, and a moderately steep climb for even better views down the coast just before we descend again into the woods. Cross the rushing brook,

turn right over the bridge and follow the brook until we come to an old fisherman's house. The coast path keeps landward of this house and its garden, turns briefly left inland in a sunken way, and then right, turning back on itself to continue along the clifftop to Drennick and Black Head, where you can explore the promontory fort headland.

The 'rifle range' labelled on the map is a Victorian structure. There have been problems with the whole headland becoming overgrown, thus hiding its history, since it is difficult to graze such

Contours are given in metres
The vertical interval is 5m

an unfenced area. The rangers are attempting to resolve this problem.

Coming away from the fort and headland the path divides in two. The left hand track goes to Trenarren, so take the right hand path to continue along the coast. This path climbs gently to Gerrans Point and then comes along the top of the cliff, towards Ropehaven Cliffs Nature Reserve. Here you can look northwards to see the mounds made by the china clay industry over the last few centuries. In my youth these mounds were crystal white and were one of the great features of a holiday in Cornwall, called by us children 'The Cornish Alps'. Now they are sprayed and covered in vegetation, to stabilise the soil and stop the local streams being choked and polluted and running white with the china clay residues. I am told that the surplus content is now reused in the construction industry.

Where yet another path goes left to Trenarren, turn right into the woods for a few yards, and left by a rotting bench, keeping just inside the woods until a track leads out on to the road near Trenarren, and a parking area or roadside lay-by. At the far end of the lay-by return to the clifftop and stay on it past the dramatic cliff called Silvermine Point, past Phoebe's Point **13** and onwards towards Porthpean.

JUST OFF THE PATH
Castle Gotha

If you are especially interested in Cornwall's prehistoric past Castle Gotha, a circular earthwork just west of Castle Gotha Farm, is well worth a visit. It stands a few feet above the surrounding countryside, and is distinctly preserved on three sides by modern field boundaries. It is a miracle that it has survived for so many thousands of years, and I felt it worth a detour.

Although not impressive as an earthwork, the site was obviously chosen very carefully for its surprisingly far reaching and beautiful views. So, if you want to visit, leave the coast path by the lay-by at Trenarren and walk up the lane towards Lobb's Shop. Where the lane turns left, a footpath continues straight ahead around a marshy area towards the head of the valley and through a hedge in the right hand corner of that field. The path then forks. Take the left hand path north-west to a kissing gate which gives access to this 'castle'.

To return to the coast path after your visit, you can take the public right of way which runs landward of Castle Gotha Farm and rejoin the coast path at Flat Rock/Robin's Rock.

After Castle Gotha you come to Carlestown, specially built to export minerals in the nineteenth century, and now a historical film-making location.

Soon our path descends to Porth Pean Beach **14**, where there are public toilets and a café in the summer. Head toward and follow the concrete sea defence which backs the beach here, and take the flight of steps which zigzags back up to the clifftop behind Carrickowel Point. For access to Carrickowel Point turn off the coast path by a ruined multi-storey wartime lookout and circumnavigate the headland. The view is nothing special, and the cliffs there are crumbling and dangerous to the unwary, so the coast path carries straight on and I recommend sticking to it.

The cliff for the next few miles is crumbling, and you may have noticed the most recent falls earlier from the path around Ropehaven Cliffs.

The coast path has been closed for some time due to cliff falls. However, since 2018 it is now clear, after careful negotiation has restored a way through below a series of private gardens.

So wind along the cliff top, past the private area and a small beach (beware of cliff falls!). Just before arriving at Charlestown **15** there is one more curiosity to explore. In 1793 the Crinnis

Contours are given in me
The vertical interval is 5

Cliff Battery, or Charlestown Battery, was created by one Charles Rashleigh to defend the new harbour he had built at Charlestown.

Two hundred yards down the path we come to the exquisite harbour of Charlestown with its warehouses, working tall-ships and a fascinating two centuries of history, frequently reenacted on this spot for all manner of entertainment by the ever-successful British overseas-income-earning film industry. Visit the impressive museum, with its major collection, for stories of coastal life in the past.

Just up a cul-de-sac by the museum is a camping site with good views of the coast, and lots of accommodation, a choice of pubs, and a bus service for those wishing to base themselves in one place while doing the walk around this area.

Charlestown grew out of the small fishing village of West Polmear (or West Porthmear), which consisted of a few cottages and three cellars, in which the catch of pilchards were processed. The population amounted to nine fishermen and their families in 1790.

Charlestown – a minerals port now used for filming, and famous for its Poldark scenes.

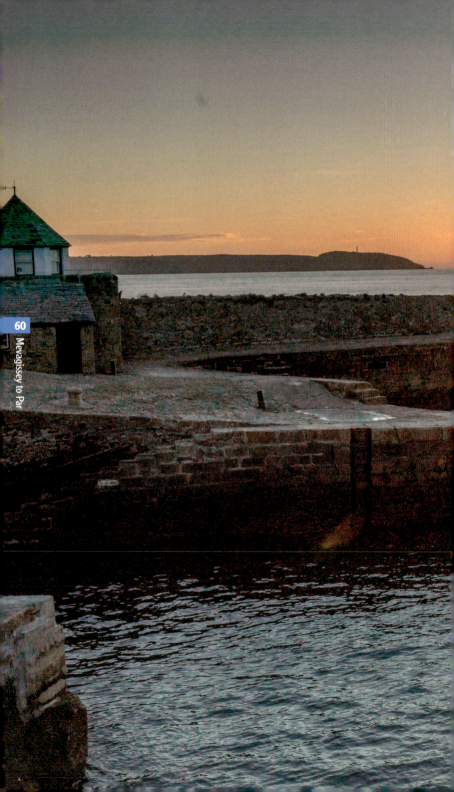

*Looking out to sea
from Charlestown.*

The port was originally built to export copper from local mines. Crinnis Hill Mine to the east of the village exported some 40,000 tons of copper ore between 1810 and 1813, and there were others just inland. By 1838 the port was employing around 800 individuals including child labour. As the mine output dropped the china clay trade started to replace it. Many of the structures around the harbour you can still see now were for the unloading of china clay into the ships below. The last full load of clay to leave Charlestown did so as recently as 2000.

There was of course competition from the ports at Pentewan and Par. Charlestown however was the first such port around here, did not get silted up like the other two, and was storm proof. The only disadvantage as time went on was that the harbour was originally designed for small sailing vessels, and an awkward turn was required involving complicated manoeuvres to get in and out. Following the widening of the entrance and the fitting of new gates in 1971, ships of up to 600 tons were able to enter the harbour, but could only do so at high tide, and a system of ropes still had to be used to manoeuvre vessels through the gates. By the 1990s, the size of vessels used for the transport of china clay had outgrown this port.

Very often the walkway above the sluice is open and you can cross to the northern side and straight on up the cliff edge. If not, walk right round the back of the port and back down the northern side to continue. The path rises through a couple of fields with good views, passes behind some houses, briefly joins a road opposite the traditional Porth Avallen Hotel, (bar and restaurant open to the public), and follows along the verge. It then arrives at the access to the National Coastwatch Institution Charlestown Station, which also welcomes visitors.

Continue past rather fine flowering garden escapes, with views of Gribbin Head and its distinctive and prominent red and white striped landmark tower.

You have now left the area of Heritage Coast and Area of Outstanding Natural Beauty which have protected the coastline you have walked since leaving Falmouth, and are entering, briefly, a mining area. Of this an 1824 travel guide said: 'The whole surface of the country in this vicinity has been completely disfigured, and presents a very gloomy aspect.'

On the whole, things have got better since then, but some of the development and urbanisation you will see, before returning to a protected area at the far side of Par Beach, will remind you how lucky we are to have the various designations to protect our coastal cliffs for future generations to enjoy. Economically that protection brings millions of visitors to the south-west to admire the scenery and that is a very important asset to protect.

So here, for a mile or two, you will pass some new clifftop buildings, lots of unnecessary signs, fencing, keep out signs, some derelict buildings and a degree of vandalism and lack of care for the environment. I would however say that this is very much the exception to the rule on this path. There are many great treats to come.

The path soon becomes narrower, bordered by high wooden fences and new flat-roofed developments, and then widens out onto open lawn.

We pass the Carlyon Bay Hotel, then a very large empty, sand covered area adjacent to a beach with private access. Next we enter a smart golf course **B** with a pleasant, well-defined path along its seaward edge.

At the eastern end of the golf course the path turns left and inland along the boundary fence of the china clay works, goes over a footbridge across part of the works, turns right alongside the London to Penzance mainline, and emerges onto the A3082 at the clay works' entrance. Go straight along the pavement beside this road, under the railway and turn right over the old-style level crossing by the colourful fruit and veg and freshly caught fish store. The road is signed A3082 Fowey.

Continue under the mainline railway bridge. Here there is a Post Office, a convenience store and traditional local pub, the Welcome Home, which has old photos of Par during the heyday of the china clay trade. Note that the phone box shown on maps is no longer there. This is Par **16**.

There is an hourly bus service which stops here for Par Station, Carlyon Bay, Charlestown and Duporth in one direction and Fowey in the other, should you be making use of the local bus services to return to base (First Kernow, No.25).

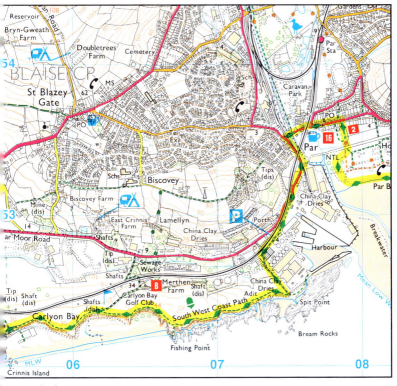

Par

In 1800 Par consisted of a few houses and a ferry, but a successful local businessman, Thomas Treffry, needed an outlet to the sea for copper and other minerals from his mines just inland. He wanted a route to Fowey and its deeper water natural harbour, but was unable to secure the land. So in 1824 he bought the ferry at Par and replaced it with a bridge, and went on to develop the port at Par instead, with a canal/tramway system to get the

copper to his new harbour. This later became a tramway and then a railway, and in 1859 the railway arrived from Plymouth, making Par accessible and leading to further development. His firm imported coal from Wales for pumping and power in the mines, and exported the copper to south Wales in return, but this involved the dangerous and problematic risk of ships rounding Land's End.

As at the other ports we have visited so far, the copper trade declined due to

The Lady Clarissa entering Fowey harbour on an incoming tide. Polruan in the background.

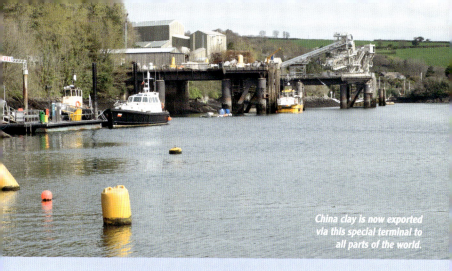

China clay is now exported via this special terminal to all parts of the world.

cheaper prices elsewhere in the world, but the china clay industry was on the way up. Thus the port was used increasingly for the china clay trade from the middle of the 19th century, and tens of thousands of tons of clay were being transported through Par every year in the second half of the 19th century. This became hundreds of thousands of tons in the course of the 20th century, a situation which just continued into the 21st century.

Now the port is closed to commercial shipping, all sea exports go via Fowey and you may see the boats coming and going there and the landing area by the car ferry. There is some industrial activity at Par Docks, but proposals are being considered to redevelop the area for residential use with a marina.

4 Par to Polperro

via Gribbin Head, Fowey and Polruan
14 miles (23 km)

Ascent/descent 2,829 feet (862 metres)
Highest point 350 feet (105 metres)

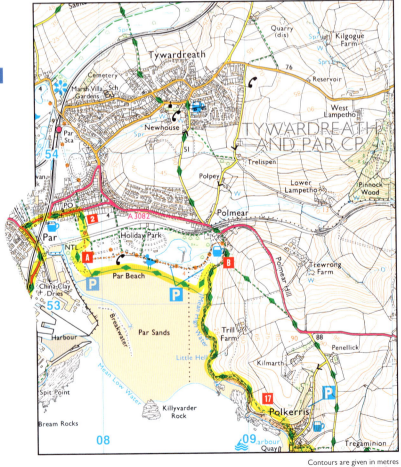

Contours are given in metres
The vertical interval is 5m

From Par, continue walking east past the Welcome Home pub until you see, on the opposite side of the road, a grass area with a concrete path down the right hand side, a litter bin and a park bench. Go down this path alongside a water course until you come to the former Par to Fowey railway track, converted to use as a private industrial road for lorries transporting china clay products around the area.

Cross this as directed and fork a few yards to the right in the woods before continuing more or less in the same direction as you have come from the village, and you will come out onto the beach. Follow the best surfaced path south to the small car park **A** next to the beach, which has an information sign about the life cycle of the sea trout.

Turn left and cross Par Sands according to the tide and as the mood takes you. You are aiming to get onto the low cliff facing you, but access is from the car park just inland, reached by turning landwards between the sand dunes. Go along the right hand side of the car park, and find the path just up above it **B**. Here we join the Pilgrims Way, of which more later. (The Ship Inn is on the main road here if you are thirsty or hungry at this point.)

Our path turns right and follows up through flower rich meadows above Par Sands when it is low tide, with good views looking back at Par and as far as Dodman Point. In the last field before Polkerris **17** you get glimpses of the little quay as the path rises up and you come towards woods into which the path has been diverted through a gate following cliff falls a few years ago. A set of steps takes you down into

Polkerris and past the cottages in this tiny fishing hamlet.

In season there is a range of activities on offer here including windsurfing, sail and paddle tuition and hire. There is a pub and eating places ranging from full meals to ice creams.

Make for the mock half-timbered building at the far side of the harbour, go to the left of it, then fork right up the path into the woods where the track goes straight on. At the top of the woods turn right into the fields. When you come to a very overgrown area ahead the path follows the field fences near the top of the slope, continuing to Little Gribbin. The cliff scenery becomes increasingly dramatic here and you round the southern end of the headland and start walking towards the Gribbin Tower.

The 84 feet (26 m) high, square Gribbin Tower was erected by Trinity House in 1832 to distinguish Gribbin Head from Dodman Point, making navigation into Fowey port safer.

This headland belongs to the National Trust and you can wander where you will and picnic. Since 1988 the National Trust has been removing the scrub, and re-introduced grazing by cows owned by a tenant farmer. In spring early purple orchid grows around the tower.

From the tower go towards the beach and lake at Polridmouth (pronounced 'Pridmouth') Cove by making for the north-east corner of the National Trust property and then following the low cliff to the cove where a track from Menabilly Barton meets the coast path. Follow the path along the back of the sandy beach and across the dam which

Great Pinnock

Trewrong Farm

Polmear Hill

53

53

Higher Lampetho

Polglaze

B 3269

102

Penventinue

Reservoir (disused)

Sewage Works

Saints' Way

Penventinue Lane

Kilmarth

Penellick

Reservoir

104

Penhale Farm

Newtown

A 3082

Lescrow Farm

Lescrow

Passage Lane

Resr

Reservoir

Polkerris

Harbour Quay

52

Tregaminion

Cross

Trenant

FOWEY CP

52

Saints' Way

Tristan Stone

B 3415

Polscoe

Lawhyre

FOWEY

FB

Sch

Menabilly Wood

Lawhyre

Hambland

62

Cross

Menabilly

Tregear's Wood

81

Coombe Farm

Readymoney

51

P

Menabilly Barton

Cross

Hooker's Grove

51

P

Allday's Fields

St Catherine's Castle (remains of)

Cross

St Catherine's Castle (rem

Coombe Cove

Penventinue Cove

South West Coast Path

73

10

68

Southground Cliffs

Coombe Haven

Lankelly Cliff

Poridmouth

Southground Point

50

Platt

Gribbin Tower

bbin Head

Sandy Cove

Brandis Rocks

10

Cannis

11

Contours are given in me
The vertical interval is

retains a very attractive lake. The low cliff here is eroding quite rapidly but at the time of writing there is a safe way through. At the far side of the lake another path joins from inland and the coast path goes south-east up through the woods, with a diversion up steps where the western tip of Lankelly Cliff has collapsed. Many features from this landscape were used by Daphne Du Maurier, who lived in various places around here.

Continue along the clifftop for a further mile past Coombe Haven where there is a path up to the National Trust car park at Coombe Farm. You will meet another permissive path coming from the left. Below the path you will see St Catherine's Point Lighthouse, a short red cast iron circular tower, operated by the Fowey (pronounced Foy) Port Authority. The tower is 20 feet high and the light is visible for 15 miles.

Soon you will find yourself on St Catherine's Point. Do not take the path to the right here which comes to an abrupt end. Take the left-hand path and then turn left through the woods, unless you want to visit the remains of St Catherine's Castle. I think they are worth it. A small sign points to the castle.

St Catherine's Castle augmented the medieval pair of forts further into the harbour and was built on Henry VIII's orders in the 1530's. It was also modified in the 19th century during the Crimean War, and again during the Second World War. Then, an anti-aircraft gun and an ammunition store were positioned there, latterly to defend the landing craft assembling ready for D-Day in the spring of 1944. It is open at all reasonable times. Above the fort is a bell shaped stone structure, apparently on the site of the ancient St Catherine's Chapel, a mausoleum constructed by the Rashleigh family. It has views across the estuary with St Catherine's Castle in the foreground.

Going back from the castle towards Fowey, go down through the woods, taking the wide track north-west and gradually descending to Readymoney Beach. Here there is a range of facilities, toilets and a sign explaining the history of the Saints Way, a 27 mile route signed with Celtic cross waymarks from Cornwall's north to south coast, Padstow to Fowey. It seeks to retrace the steps of early Christian travellers who might have been making pilgrimages from Ireland and Wales to holy sites in France and Spain.

From the far side of beach follow the road for half a mile to the quay, where the foot ferry service will take you to Polruan. Out of season you have to go a few yards further, where an all year round service operates back to the same quay in Polruan.

Like all the ports along this coast, Fowey and Polruan boat-builders have been active for centuries, but are now rare. C. Toms & Son is a family business based in Polruan, where they run a boatyard which builds and repairs fishing boats, commercial vessels and yachts. They also operate the Polruan foot passenger ferry, and the Bodinnick car ferry just upstream on the River Fowey. They deal with boat maintenance projects from major refits to basic hull cleaning. They build new vessels in steel or wood and can fit out fiberglass hulls. Associated services include marine electronics, chandlery, showers, laundry

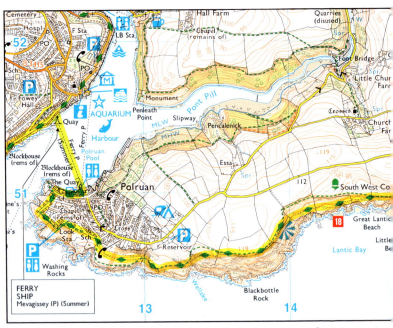

Contours are given in me
The vertical interval is

facilities and fuel supplies. They directly employ shipwrights, boat builders, welder fabricators, engineers, GRP specialists and marine painters. So, as a thriving business in an active port, and as a local employer, they help to bring life to the port and add to its interest for visitors.

Fowey has recently become a port of call for cruise liners, and has the advantage that it is a deep water port and can be accessed in all weather and at all states of the tide. There are also lots of interesting and beautiful places for cruise customers to visit nearby.

China clay is the the lifeblood of Fowey Docks. Around three quarters of a million tonnes are exported from Fowey annually. The product serves the paper industry in Norway, Sweden and Finland. It also supplies the ceramics

industry, that is tableware and sanitary ware, electrical insulation products and pharmaceuticals, in Britain and worldwide, including Egypt, Italy, Portugal and many other countries. Supplies of china clay to British buyers in the potteries and elsewhere often go directly by rail.

The ferry runs approximately every 15 minutes, and when I was there in March was operating from 7.30am until 9pm.

As you get off the ferry there is a small amenity area acquired on the initiative of Polruan people supported by public subscription, on the site of the old Coal Wharf. Just uphill is the Lugger Inn. Go up the narrow steps to the left of the Inn (Garrett Steps) and turn right up the very narrow road (West Street) until you come to Battery Lane. You can make a short detour to the nicely

Contours are given in metres
The vertical interval is 5m

restored Blockhouse which faced a
similar structure opposite which would
have closed the harbour with a chain
in times of stress. It has nice views
of the harbour. Having inspected the
Blockhouse retrace your steps and
turn right once again. At the top of
Battery Lane turn left, signed for
Polperro 6½ miles (11 km). The stone
track comes out onto a lawn with
another fortifcation below, worth
visiting for the view.

From here skirt around the seaward
side of the town and into a series of
fields where the coast path more or less
keeps to the level. When you get to the
next field boundary you have to cross
the stream. The lower path is for the
coast path. The upper path is trampled
by the cattle who graze these fields and
is therefore extremely muddy – you
have been warned! At Blackbottle Rock
the path is on top of the undercliff, in
the fields, and as you come into view of
Lantic Bay it takes to the undercliff with
superb views of Little Lantic Beach and
Pencarrow Head.

Follow the path out onto the headland.
I recommend going to the end of the
headland where there is a wild rocky
mass which I find quite spectacular.
Then continue along the clifftop around
the magnificent Lantic Bay **18**. A
path joins from the left from the car
park near Churchtown Farm and you
turn right, either along the top of the
undercliff, or down to the beach if you
wish. Either way, I highly recommend

Lantic Bay.

Par to Polperro

The Three Pilchards Pub, Polperro.

52

51

18
Landmark

19

Contours are given in metr
The vertical interval is 5m

ending up at Pencarrow Head. From Pencarrow Head to Polperro is 4 miles (6km) of superb scenic walking with wet slate rocks jutting in all directions, Especially dramatic if the sea is agitated.

At Lansallos Cutting there is a small stream, a waterfall, and an ancient path cut into the purple and green Devonian slate, cut out and then worn by centuries of passage by carts fetching seaweed and sand to spread onto the fields, and, quite possibly, kegs of brandy at the dead of night. The contorted rocks and complicated headlands here may confuse the walker. You loop inland briefly after

viewing the cutting, and the coast path is well signed with black and silver cast signs set in slate. If the path marked on some maps on the clifftop ever existed it has gone now, and the detour inland is the only safe way.

Once again we see ponies grazing the cliff here, and well-grazed vegetation improves the sward for a variety of plant and other dependent wildlife.

When you have climbed up above Lansallos Cove there is a superb view looking back at Pencarrow Head. Nearby Parson's Cove comes next, and a mile on, above Broad Cove, is a substantial Daymark with a pointed top

Contours are given in metres
The vertical interval is 5m

for the guidance of seafarers. Until the introduction of GPS technology lobster fishermen were still using them to place and find their pots just offshore. A kilometre further on, Nealand Point gives a good view of a small but dramatic slate promontory thrusting out into the waves at a steep 45 degree angle, the path just above it. Between here and Polperro look out for a nice rock archway best viewed from the east, i.e. looking back behind you.

The rock formations around Polperro **19** itself are particularly dramatic, and the path has some tricky slate sections which need special care. Just before you reach the inlet a path goes left, an alternative route, but the next one right is a cul-de-sac to a viewpoint.

The fishing village of Polperro has several pubs, excellent shops, cafés and enough facilities that are generally open all year. However, the bakery closes in the afternoon out of season, so if you just wanted a pasty or coffee you will have to ask in the pubs if you arrive later.

There are active fishermen working from Polperro, which has a floating harbour and quite a few facilities for boats both commercial and leisure. It always makes a pleasant scene, and there is a museum giving lots of information on the far side of the harbour.

Polperro.

5 Polperro to Portwrinkle

via Looe, Seaton and Downderry
13 miles (20.74 km)

Ascent/descent 2,430 feet (740 metres)
Highest point 500 feet (150 metres)

Leave Polperro by crossing the tiny pack-horse bridge and turning right towards the sea. Pass behind the museum and keep going up and down until you come out of the village. The coast path follows the slightly higher route of two which go east from this point, but it doesn't really matter which one you take. Below the path at Spy House Point is a small 10-foot high lighthouse built by Polperro Harbour Authority just over 100 years ago, which guides people into the harbour. The first significant place after Polperro is Talland Bay. The direct clifftop path which leads to it is deemed to be unsafe at the time of writing, so take the next left-hand branch off the path at the top of the hill before Downend Point War memorial, and then take the first right down a narrow track which brings you down to Talland Bay **20**. There is some holiday accommodation here, a café in season and car parking on the road, as well as public toilets and a telephone. Go up the road inland a short distance and turn right by the telephone box. The red slate rocks of Talland Bay are particularly striking, even when beneath the water on calm clear days.

On the corner is Smugglers' Cottage, a reminder of Talland Bay's chequered past. Probably not the original name, as that may have been something of a giveaway?

Not far along the road the coast path continues along the clifftop. As you reach the next headland you will see the Hore Stone just offshore, great to behold in stormy weather, and, rounding the corner, Looe Island comes into sight. Looe Island is a marine nature reserve and can be visited on certain dates.

This next day or two of walking are some of my favourites. Here the sight of Looe Bay and Whitsand Bay opens up, with the prominent landmark of Looe Islands at the western end and Rame Head at the eastern end. Both are very distinctive peaks, remaining in sight for the next 12 miles (20 km), although your view changes as the light shifts, and as you clamber on rocks and walk along cliff tops, exploring the coves around this magnificent continuum of rocky cliffs and sandy beaches. A good sunrise or sunset somewhere along the way may well make one of your most memorable experiences of this walk, with the island and the headland your companions, like book-ends, for the next one or two days.

In the last field before you reach the road at Hannafore, entered through wooden gates and over a small stream, up above the coast path, are

Contours are given in metres
The vertical interval is 5m

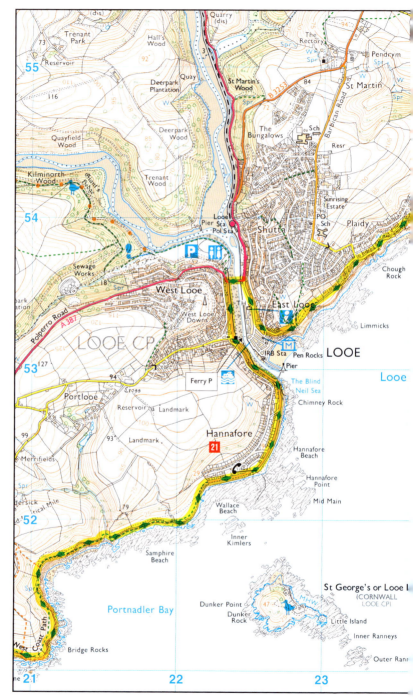

Contours are given in metre
The vertical interval is 5m

the remains of the medieval chapel of St Michael of Lammana. The chapel thereof and the monks' house were excavated in 1935 when these fields were threatened with development. The Priory was first recorded in 1144. The name Lammana means monk's church, and came into use as a chapel for the locals and then a dwelling since Henry VIII's Reformation. The priory chapel is high up in the field, and may have served as a sea mark, perhaps lit up by a flame maintained by the monks at certain times. There are accounts showing that monks did this as part of their duties, but the exact locations in Cornwall are not all known. The monks' house east gable end is incorporated in the garden boundary of the house adjacent to the gate onto the road.

After entering Hannafore **21** you can go down to and follow the sea defences to their end. Then you have to follow the road alongside the entrance to Looe Harbour. A strip of the road is marked for pedestrians.

As soon as you can, descend by the bronze seal to the quay of West Looe, which leads up to the main road bridge. The Atlantic grey seal was named Nelson and was a familiar sight in the harbour for a quarter of a century.

If you need bus services to return to base, the buses go from the Fire Station, just past St Martin's church. There is also a foot ferry across the harbour here. The current seven-arched bridge was built in 1853, and replaced the 15th century bridge which was just downstream of this. You can still work out where the medieval bridge was, by looking for the typical ultra-narrow road leading west up the hill, an indication that it was too narrow to

take even 19th century traffic, much like the rest of the streets in Looe. If anyone is coming to meet you in a car in any of the villages or towns along this route, tell them to turn off the satnav, park as soon as possible, and walk. The street network here was designed for pack-horses, and is often only really navigable on foot or by very experienced locals in tiny cars. You have been warned.

There is a fish handling facility opposite which services the fifty or so boats, trawlers, hand line mackerel boats and a variety of others. Leisure boats are also present, but not the sole use of the harbour, which gives the quaysides life all the year round and not just in the tourist season. The Cornwall Good Seafood Guide has a website www. cornwallgoodseafoodguide.org.uk which describes all the different fishing methods and gives advice on how to choose the best fish for your favourite seafood meals.

Turn right over the bridge and right into the town, leaving the car park to your right, and follow Fore Street, the main shopping area, straight ahead until you come to Castle Street by the Ship Inn, where you can turn left up Castle Street until you come to East Cliff, a tree-lined walk. Alternatively you can continue on Higher Market Street and turn left up by the Old Guildhall and Gaol onto Tower Hill. The third choice is to follow the quayside to the lifeboat station, follow along behind East Looe Beach and climb up the stepped path leading to the East Cliff.

Tradition has it that the local population went up to this area of public open space to watch the Spanish Armada come past. Look ahead at the cliffs

Flowers at Britain Point, just west of Portwrinkle.

contours are given in metres
the vertical interval is 5m

from this point and note the cliff falls on the other side of the bay. The old path there beyond Millendreath has disappeared completely, and I have given instructions on how to get round the problem. When you get there the National Trust has signed and waymarked the route, but I thought advance notice would be sensible here. The tree-lined path comes into Plaidy, a collection of 20th century bungalows fronting onto a rather crumbly cliff. When the road turns inland continue for a few yards and look for a footpath which goes right between the houses up to another residential street. Follow that straight ahead and go to the left hand side of the houses facing you at the end. The path between the houses then turns right and comes down to

Millendreath **22**, where there are more bungalows and a holiday village.

Go up the small lane next to the beach and climb up Bodigga Cliff on this old pack-horse route. At the top is Bay View farm camping site **A** and a National Trust picnic area. Do not attempt to follow the old route of the path which is currently inaccessible. Instead carry on along the road for a short distance, turn right and then left along a track in the woods **B**. When this comes to an end follow the road eastwards, straight on past the Monkey Sanctuary (6ft 6in width limit and Single Track Road sign) until you come to a trig point in the field on your left. Just past that is an entrance to the field on your right **C** (National Trust sign 'Struddicks'). The path crosses the field turning back briefly seawards, and then into the corner of a field before continuing slightly downhill and east and straight on through the next field, more steeply downhill on a well defined path which reaches the clifftop.

Looking back from this point you can see that the path still marked on most maps has completely disappeared into the sea. The replacement path now levels out, rising eventually into the woods on Looe Hill, at the far end of which it goes down wooden steps onto the lane into Seaton.

At Seaton **23** cross the river and make for the Smugglers Inn. Just round the

corner is a general store with a seaside theme, beach goods etc. Now, if the tide is in or advancing, you will have to take to the road for a mile. In the middle of the village, Downderry, is a well stocked village store, a pub and toilets. If the tide is on the way out and low, go onto the sea defence path, follow it east to the end and continue along the beach for just under a mile (1.4km).

Look up the cliff just after the stream running across the beach. Take the steps leading up to a wooden shelter, (and no 'private' sign). These steps lead to a path bordering the fenced school play area to which the wooden shelter belongs.

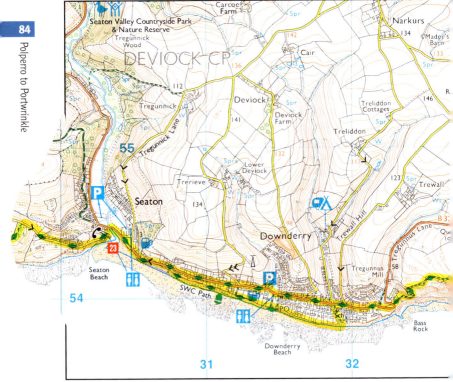

Contours are given in m
The vertical interval is

Turn right on to the road for a few hundred yards, round the hairpin bend, and take the path north-east to climb to the top of the undercliff. At the time of writing there is no other safe way of getting up the cliff, which has eroded considerably in recent years.

From this point the path is clearly defined along the top of the undercliff and brings you in behind the coastguard cottages at Portwrinkle **D**. Walk down to the tiny and quaint harbour, along the promenade, past the car park and Finnygook Café. Follow the road briefly east, and rejoin the coast path to Freathy and Rame Head.

Portwrinkle old port.

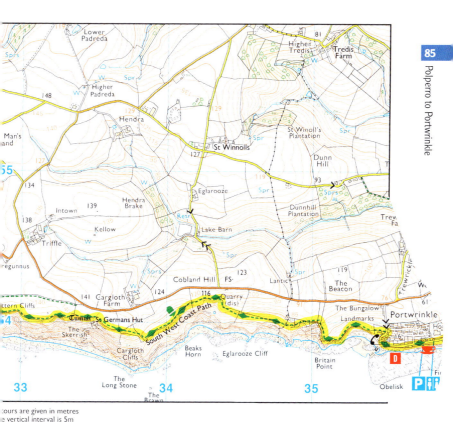

Contours are given in metres
The vertical interval is 5m

6 Portwrinkle to Cremyll

via Tregantle, Rame Head and Mount Edgcumbe
12.8 miles (20.6 km)

Ascent/descent 2,261 feet (690 metres)
Highest point 375 feet (112 metres)

Climbing out of Portwrinkle, after 500 yards the path borders on the Whitsand Bay Hotel golf course, where it is well defined with either a mowed grass or stone surface. Soon the path makes for a tall black and white striped post with a triangle on top of it. Straight ahead is a kissing gate and a flag post with lots of warnings not to stray from the path, not to enter when firing is taking place, and not to touch any ordnance. Below is Whitsand Bay with its magnificent sands.

If the range is in military use the signs will be quite clear and the gate will be locked, so turn left here and go inland, where a path adjacent to or on the road takes you round the outside of the firing area.

If the range is open to coast path users it is generally well signed. Keep approximately to the contours around the valley and on the landward side of the fence as it goes east towards the back of Tregantle fort. Where it comes through a gate to a rampart on the left with a small lookout on top, it carries straight on, curving very slightly inland down to a gap in the remnants of a

hedge and then follows the contours slightly seaward. The bare earth around the gap in the hedge is the place where the path goes through. I say that because the path ahead is briefly obscured by the lie of the land, and the signing was not entirely clear, but make initially for the landward side of the fort, the top of which is just visible at this point, and keep on the landward side of the aerial mast enclosure below. If it is blackberry time the blackberries are very good here, and toadflax adorns the path edges. Follow through another gate into a grazed field, keeping left of and close to the fence at the seaward side of the field, then turn right through another gate, along a path cleared through the scrub, where you come on to a military road.

Take the road around the seaward side of the fort. Turn right and then fork right at the eastern end of the fort though a six bar iron gate with a gap beside it, and then down a stone and grass track to an elaborate gate onto the road to Freathy. When the range is open a narrow stone off-road footpath continues, right, inside the range and comes out of it onto a National Trust path all the way to Freathy.

There is a branch on this path which takes people to the beach below the firing range during opening times. A notice here explains that public access to the beach is not restricted when the range is not in use. Local post offices, libraries and HM Coastguard are all informed of firing times, and a search online for Tregantle firing times will show the relevant information on the Gov.uk website.

Please note that these dates and times may be subject to change due to unforeseen circumstances or operational requirements, therefore the only absolute guarantee that there is no firing is the absence of the red flags on the range on the day. Changes are posted on the noticeboards next to the sentry posts on the coastal footpath. For up to date information on training activities, or for more detail call 01752 822516. Just remember that the red flags by day and the red lamp by night indicate that the range is active and live firing is taking place. The on- or near-road route is referred to as the 'Coast Path Permanent Route' and the one through the range the 'Coast Path Permissive Route'. As we leave the range a sign, 'Rame Head 4 miles' points the way for us to continue east off-road **A**.

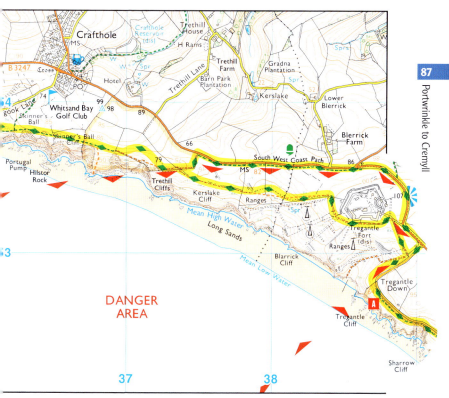

Contours are given in me
The vertical interval is

Now follow the path towards Freathy just away from the road or on the verge. This is the NT property of Sharrow Cliff. Just before Freathy is a car park, and signs warning that the path to the beach here has collapsed and no longer exists. If you want to access the magnificent beach here at low tide, fork right in the middle of this settlement and turn right down to the path to the beach, past the lookout. Because of rip currents it is not deemed safe to swim on this beach except when the lookout is attended, but at low tide you can explore amongst the rocks.

The path now follows the road for a mile at least. A second settlement of 1930's dwellings comes into view at Tregonhawke, where a sign explains the likelihood of cliff collapse and rock falls around here. Probably for this reason the path, shown on the maps as doing a dog-leg down the undercliff and back after Whitesand or Whitsand Bay Fort, is now signed along the road for a further 400 yards.

As a result of the 1859–1860 Royal Commission that reviewed our coastal defence arrangements in the wake of French rearmament, a chain of forts was built along the entire English Channel coast (and in South Wales) to protect both the land and sea approaches to naval dockyards. The budget for this large national initiative was huge and much disputed at the time, but the Prime Minister, Lord Palmerston, managed to steer the legislation through Parliament and the programme went forward. The jibe of those who opposed the expenditure was to call them the Palmerston Follies. Most of the facilities were never used in anger, having become obsolete in defence terms before any attacks happened. A major diplomatic effort with strategic alliances to prevent conflict had solved the problem of war with our neighbours in the later 19th century.

You have seen the major fort at Tregantle, built to prevent an enemy seizing the high ground overlooking the Plymouth dockyard. To prevent a landing in Whitsand Bay, Polhawn Battery had been built. However, within the two decades following the 1860 fort building programme, developments in marine artillery had made massive advances. It would have been feasible for ships to anchor offshore here and bombard the dockyard from the sea while being beyond the range of the existing forts. Accordingly two new installations were constructed to cover the bay – Tregantle High Angle Battery and Whitsand Bay Battery

Whitsand Battery has now been partly restored with the help of English Heritage, and is currently in use as a caravan park and leisure park, with pubs, cafés and a restaurant. A short detour coastwards by the main fort structure leads to the Cliff Top Café which offers a range of drinks and

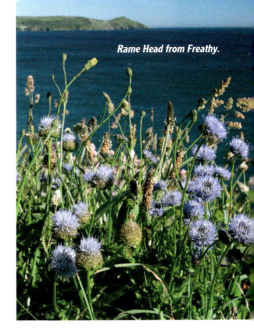

Rame Head from Freathy.

snacks in one of the chalets, with good sea views.

By Whitsand Bay Fort junction **B** there is a bus stop for the frequent 70A and 70B Plymouth Bus services. 70A starts at Cremyll and goes to Plymouth via Cawsand and Torpoint Ferry, while 70B goes from Plymouth to Portwrinkle via Torpoint. They may be useful if you are returning to a base anywhere along this road network.

I did walk the section east of Whitsand Bay Fort, marked with the diamond on the map, and it was passable at the time. It descends south-east past various huts, goes down into a small valley and onto a ridge near Ninney Rock. Steps then take it inland up the ridge above the last huts and right at the top back onto the road, about half a mile in all.

The route, now signed as the South West Coast Path with a black and white sticky on a round post, leaves the road again and travels south for a couple of hundred yards, then turns south-east, parallel with the road above, and gradually rises to meet the road once again via an access track. This is just before the junction with the road to Wiggle, where the road triangle is used for parking. Go briefly seaward and downhill along the grass-bordered path through the dense scrub, then swing left following the clifftop towards Polhawn Fort. A sign placed by Mount Edgcumbe Country Park explains why they now graze this area with Devon Ruby Red cattle, rather than Exmoor ponies, to improve the pasture for a species rich sward.

Take the higher path behind the old coastguard cottages and go up the steps and straight on across the access road to Polhawn Fort. The path curves right round the landward side of a tennis court and then runs parallel

to the sea and left round the last field to emerge on Rame Head with its 14th century chapel, Coastwatch lookout and extensive flowery, pony-grazed grassland. Rame is one of the promontory forts, and you can find the embankment where you cross the neck of the peninsula.

Having visited the ruined chapel and soaked in the views, retrace your steps and fork right, following the top of the low undercliff to Penlee Point (2 miles, 3 km). As you near the point you can fork right to go out on to the point, but the view is not special. The coast path goes straight on, and then turns left, becoming 'Earl's Drive', just above Queen Adelaide's Seat **24**, a gothic folly named after the visit of Queen Adelaide, Prince William IV's consort, after whom the city in Australia is named.

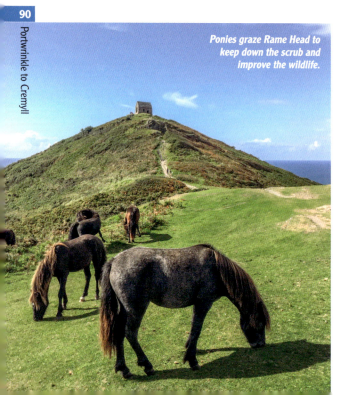

Ponies graze Rame Head to keep down the scrub and improve the wildlife.

50

Captain Blake's Point

Polhawn Cove

Crane Cove

Long Cove

49

...er Point

Western Gear

Chapel

...ort

Three Holes

Contours are given in me...
The vertical interval is 5...

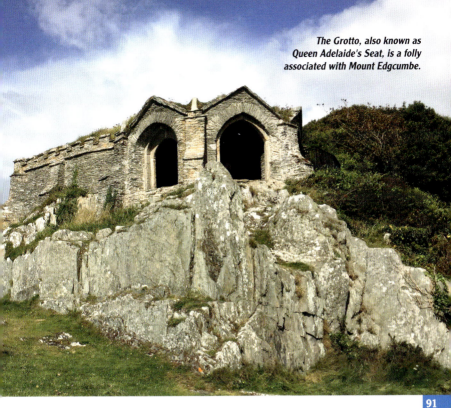

The Grotto, also known as Queen Adelaide's Seat, is a folly associated with Mount Edgcumbe.

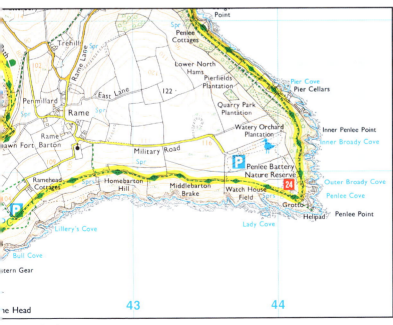

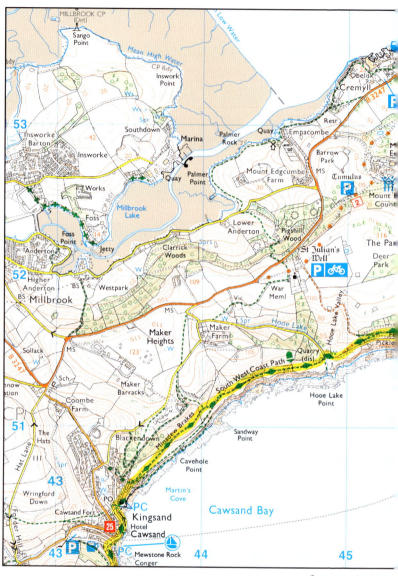

Contours are given in metr
The vertical interval is 5m

Continue along the path straight ahead and down through the woods until you arrive in Cawsand **25**. Look up above the beach and you will see the massive Cawsand Fort, one of the Palmerston forts, which has been converted into flats in one of the ingenious after-uses thought up for these imposing historic structures.

Down in the village there is a traditional square with a drinking fountain, pub and shop. Go to the north-east corner of

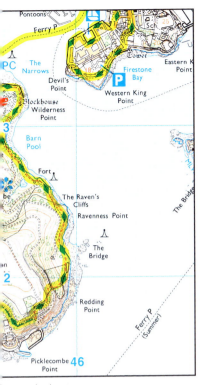

Pontoons
Ferry P
PC
The Narrows
Devil's Point
Blockhouse
Wilderness Point
Barn Pool
Fort
The Raven's Cliffs
Ravenness Point
The Bridge
Redding Point
Picklecombe Point
46

Sch
Tower
Eastern K Point
Firestone Bay
Western King Point
The Bridge
Ferry P (Summer)

ours are given in metres
e vertical interval is 5m

There are views ahead of the Plymouth breakwater and the Great Mew Stone at Wembury. You come to a white house, Hooe Lake Cottage, (lake often means stream in SW England) and a scout camp and there is a sign 'Mount Edgcumbe House 2¼ and Cremyll 2½'. Go to the kissing gate above the track and turn right along the narrower path. Watch out from here onwards for the fallow deer. Be quiet and stealthy and there is an outside chance that you will see them, especially in the very early morning.

This path gradually rises past another, recently restored, small folly with shelter and a bench, up above Fort Picklecombe (private, but there is a camp site in one of its fortifications), and higher still to by-pass recent landslips, via a wooden staircase and many steps, at Picklecombe Point. Here a public veranda makes a fine vantage point for the breakwater and Devon coast ahead.

As you make your way down to the Cremyll Ferry you will get glimpses of Drake Island, see a cottage designed by William Morris, possibly the deer, more follies and more forts, ending in the gardens where there is a café in the orangery, formal gardens, the stately home and a shop. There is also information about the many interesting conservation activities and entertainments which are organised here. This, like much of the Rame Peninsula, is the great playground of Plymouth.

The ferry goes on the hour and the half hour during the day, and buses leave for Portwrinkle and Plymouth on a regular schedule.

the square and follow the very narrow Garrett Street to Kingsand, with a fine view of the clock tower across the rocks on the way. At the Halfway House Inn turn right into Market Street and go towards the clock tower. Then turn inland up Heavitree Road until you see a pink house with a street either side of it, 'Mayflower House c. 1620'. You can go up either of these steep streets. The official path goes up the right hand lane and the left hand street goes past yet another pub, the Rising Sun. At the top is a sign pointing towards a wooden gate inscribed 'Welcome to Mount Edgcumbe, House and Country Park.' Just follow that well made-up path more or less on the contour into the woods beyond.

7 The Tamar to the Yealm

via Plymouth Barbican and by ferry to Mount Batten
10.5 miles (17 km)

Ascent/descent 1,435 feet (438 metres)
Highest point 320 feet (95 metres)

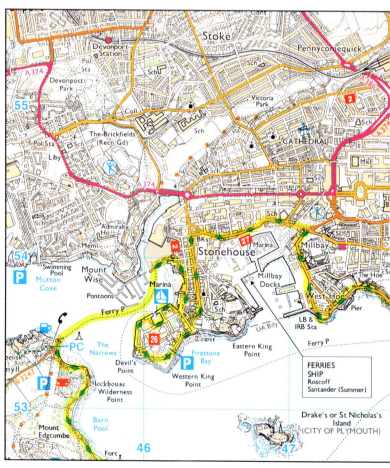

Contours are given in me
The vertical interval is

'Plymouth's Waterfront Walkway', a path which follows around Plymouth and its harbour and the estuaries of the Tamar and Plym, has been laid out over the years and has become defined as part of the South West Coast Path. I would say that the first part of this walk is a pleasant surprise for someone who does not much like cities. It includes several famous historic sites, some pretty good views of the island and cliff scenery we have been walking, and a trendy harbour scene with pubs and quayside eating places at various points. In particular it passes close to Plymouth Hoe, the site of Drake's first sighting of the Armada, and Smeaton's famously reconstructed, red banded, Eddystone Lighthouse. It also takes you past some spectacular listed buildings, some parkland and an early 20th century lido.

This first half will also bring you to the excellent National Aquarium, where you can polish up on your marine wildlife knowledge, on the far side of Sutton Harbour. Just before that is the historic Citadel and Barbican area of Plymouth where we can eat drink and be merry if we have the time and inclination.

The second half of the Walkway (east of the Aquarium) tours Plymouth's breakers' yards, sewage works, oil tank farms and gasometers, industrial estates and suburban streets. It is by its nature just away from, but within sight of, the water's edge for most of its length. The most dedicated and conscientious Coast Path walkers will want to walk it. Watching a whole luxury car being crushed in the breaker's yard was the highlight of my day there, and I could not help thinking that an extra day in the park at Mount Edgcumbe tracking the fallow deer, or more time in the National Aquarium would have been much more enjoyable and possibly enlightening. The alternative way of looking at it is that you get to know the part of Plymouth which you would not otherwise discover. You can see how Plymouth makes its living, get a general idea of the layout of the rest of the harbour, and experience the productive side of the city.

If you do decide to include it in your itinerary, may I recommend the excellent guide to the Plymouth Waterfront Walkway produced by the City Council, which you can obtain on payment at the Tourist Information Centre at the Barbican, or online for free from their website www.plymouth.gov.uk. The map shows each path and street to be followed by name, and has lots of relevant detail about the history and geology in addition to the route information.

The Royal William Yard **26**, from which all the naval ships used to be supplied, has become a centre with lots of restaurants, galleries, apartments and retail businesses and is circumnavigated by the coast path. A flight of new steps joins the Royal William Yard to the Devil's Point Park. From the steps you get a very good view of the harbour and at night it is lit up.

Next you come into Durnford Street. Carry on past the barracks and take the next turning right into Millbay Road. You come to Millbay Docks. These were formerly the Great Western Docks, in which Isambard Kingdom Brunel planned and constructed the world's first ocean-going screw steamer, the SS Great Britain, which set off from this quay on its maiden voyage in 1845.

This ship can of course now be seen near the centre of Bristol. The main use for this area is now by Brittany Ferries for their services to Spain and France.

Carry straight on down Millbay Road to the roundabouts and turn right down West Hoe Road on the western side of Millbay Park, forking right into great Western Road as you approach the West Hoe after which the walkway follows the shore all the way to the Barbican.

When you reach the Tinside Lido **27**, recently beautifully restored and still in use in the summer, I recommend a detour up the hill to Smeaton's Tower.

The Royal Citadel is open to the public by guided walk and notices are posted telling the times, or you can go online to find out details.

Just after the Royal Plymouth Corinthian Yacht Club you come round the corner to the Barbican **28**, with its theatre, information centre and range of eating places.

From this point you can take the ferry to the Mount Batten Pier **A** and continue the coast path walk in all its rural coastal beauty, having had a taste of the delights of the modern city of Plymouth.

Whether you take the ferry or continue to follow the Waterfront Walkway, I think a visit to the National Marine Aquarium **29** will give you a very good insight into life in the oceans. There you will see explanations of the conservation measures being taken, and how the fishing and fish and chip industry depend on them. You'll also see some excellent living evidence of life under the sea in the area in which you are walking.

To get to the National Marine Aquarium you have to cross a footway over the lock at the entrance to Sutton Harbour by the Barbican. At the time of writing this walkway has been closed for some time and when it will re-open is uncertain. This means you may have to take a detour around Sutton Harbour. This is not difficult. Merely follow the harbour around as close as to the quay edge as you can and you will come out behind the National Marine Aquarium. Make your way to the front entrance around the left hand (eastern) side of the building. The Sutton Harbour quayside is quite a lively scene, again with quite a few pubs, restaurants and other delights.

For those who wish to take the remainder of the walk I'm now going to describe its route from the Aquarium. Go over the bridge at the back of the Aquarium **29** and keep down Teat's Hill Road. The route is marked here and there with black acorns on the white background painted onto lamp posts. You come to a road called Breakwater Hill. Turn right into this. At the top of that road you'll see a missile like structure with South West Coast Path painted on it. Behind this is the pedestrian walkway, evidently an old road, which you follow over the hill and down through an industrial estate. As you come towards Cattedown Road there is a factory called Interfish. Carry straight on and then left past Neptune Park. Turn right into Maxwell Road and right again at the roundabout into Finnigan Road. Continue along this road parallel with the Cattewater and turn right over the busy road bridge. Having crossed the bridge look at the

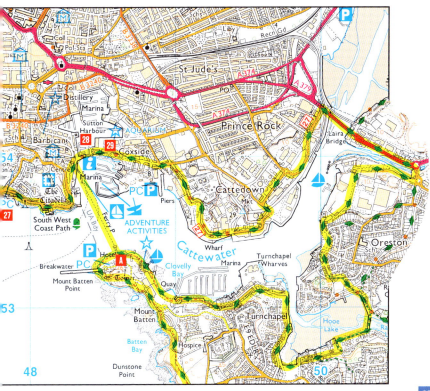

tours are given in metres
e vertical interval is 5m

wall on your right which has a poem on it, aptly known as the 'Poem Wall'.

Turn right at the next junction and right again into Breakwater Road, signed for the Post Office Sorting Depot, and pass various industrial concerns. At the end of this road turn left and continue straight on when you come to a range of industrial buildings on your right. Take the fenced path to the left of the waterside sheds and continue straight on until you come back on to the quay. Briefly follow the shoreline before turning left and then right into Park Lane.

At the top end of Park Lane there is a footpath going left after some stone steps marked by one of the red triangles which is an indicator of this route. Keep straight on right of the entrance to 'Windway' and left of 'Rose Bank' along a narrow path between two hedges, then the path skirts Hooe Lake to a dam at Radford Castle. Nearby was a residence of a gentleman who entertained, in Elizabethan times, Drake, Raleigh and other famous sea dogs of Plymouth. The uninhabited 'Castle' on the dam on the banks of Hooe Lake is an early 19th century folly which served as a house for the lake keeper.

Continue along the path parallel with the water and uphill on the southern

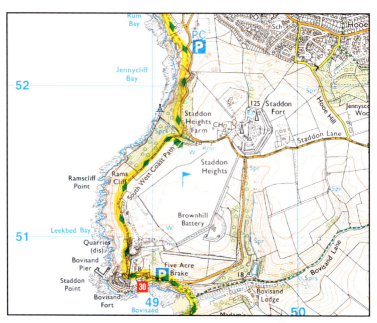

Contours are given in metres
The vertical interval is 5m

side of Hooe Lake, and then down along the road to the Royal Oak. Follow the water all the way past the new houses on your left and then turn left into Undercliff Road, Turnchapel. The walk comes back to the water's edge briefly, then back to St John's Road where we find the Clovelly Bay Inn.

Go up St Johns Road to the landward side of the Clovelly Bay Inn, away from the little fishing harbour, then follow the quayside to the Mount Batten Watersports Centre and the Barbican Ferry pier. Until 1992 this was the site of the RAF Mount Batten Station. A Colonel Thomas Edward Lawrence, also known as Lawrence of Arabia, was stationed here in the early 1930s. He helped to improve the performance of the RAF rescue launches.

Now the Mount Batten Pier is used as a popular public open space and by fireworks companies who come here each year in August for a national fireworks competition. The fact that it can be sealed off for safety is convenient, and the displays can be seen from miles around.

After passing Mount Batten Pier go east and round the southern side of the Mount Batten Tower, constructed at about the same time as the Citadel. The tower is named after Captain Batten, who defended it successfully during the English Civil War. The top of the hill is open to the public at all times and has good views. The tower is open to the public occasionally. Information signs explain its history.

The path going east now passes Jennycliff Café and goes briefly onto the road before turning left and down into the woods. Turn right over the bridge to continue past the golf course, leaving the radio station on your left. Descend and go to the landward side of Bovisand Fort **30**. You come down steps to the Cliff Edge Café. Go through a gate across the road and landward of the chalets of the Bovisand Estate. Continue on the clifftop all the way to Heybrook Bay **31**. Briefly go onto the road, and then back onto the clifftop before continuing around the headland. You now have 2 miles (3km) to go, easy walking between the field and the beach, all the way to Wembury.

At Wembury **32** there is a National Trust car park, a very comprehensive

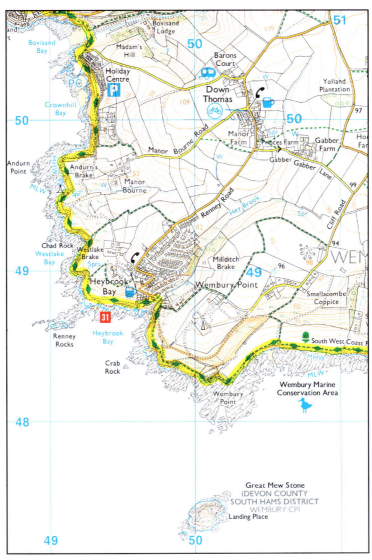

Contours are given in metres
The vertical interval is 5m

Battisborough. The view across the mouth of the drowned valley, or 'ria', of the River Erme shows Dartmouth slates on both sides of the ria mouth.

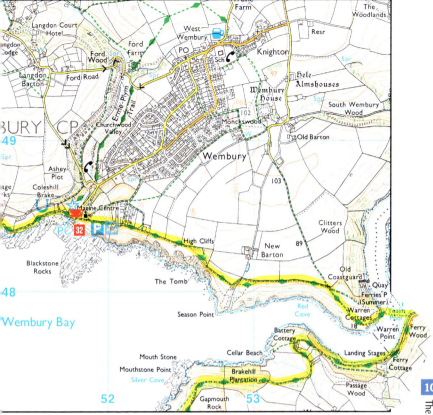

Contours are given in metres
The vertical interval is 5m

marine information centre, a café in the old mill and, just up the hill, a church which is worth visiting. From the car park make your way up towards the church and then turn east up through the scrub, keeping a lookout for some of the small birds which may come to greet you. Go briefly along the estate road with some houses on it and you soon come to a rather fine gate giving access to more open country. You come past the old small rocket house and gunpowder store for the Coastguard,

and down towards Warren Point. Follow the track past the Ferry Cottage. Further along you will see a small pier, on which there is a disc cut in half with a hinge in the middle. Fold open the disk to show that you want the ferry to come, and someone in the village will shout to the ferryman. Note the running times and season for this ferry in 'Useful information' at the end of the book.

8 The Yealm to the Avon

via Mothecombe, Wonwell and Bigbury
14.8 miles (23.8 km)

Ascent/descent 3,460 feet (1055 metres)
Highest point 340 feet (104 metres)

Arriving on the east side of the River Yealm, turn right along the track by the pier steps.

Should you be looking for an inn at this stage there is the Ship Inn in Noss Mayo on this side of Noss Creek and the Swan Inn on the far side, a short walk. To reach the village store and the Dolphin in Newton Ferrers you will have to go quite a lot further around the Newton Creek.

Soon after you start out along the road there is a quarry/lay-by on the left and a footpath branches off towards the Old Ferry House which has a very interesting ancient list of prices. Turn right off the road by the cattle grid to reach this Ferry House and keep walking along the waterside footpath until it rejoins the track. The track rises through the woods to Battery Cottage where there is a signed footpath down to Cellar Beach. 'Cellar', in this part of the country, means the shack where fishermen store their gear, not necessarily an underground hideaway for smuggled goods. The Revelstoke Drive curves around back towards the Coastguard Cottages, where you go

through the gate and gradually start going westwards along the Drive. After passing Millstone Point you reach Gara Point **A**, the most westerly part of this peninsula.

The Revelstoke Drive will take you along the first 6 miles of the 8 miles to Mothecombe. It remains on the clifftop and passes a number of small coves. It has superb views in both directions, especially to the west and the coast you have just walked. This includes the Great Mew Stone at Wembury, standing out spectacularly against the cliff scenery which can extend all the way to the Lizard Peninsula on a very clear day. As the path goes round to go eastwards again you come to Warren Cottage and a little later a turning for the Warren car park.

The Revelstoke Drive continues along the clifftop past the entrance of the Revelstoke (caravan) Park. At Stoke Point there is a small sign to the ancient church of St Peter the Poor Fisherman. This is a ruined former parish church which has been partially restored, although mostly roofless. It has a few fine features including an unusual tower and barrel roof. If you take this detour it is a pleasant walk down the undercliff until you enter the woods. Then follow through the caravan park until you come to the church. You can also visit the Stoke Beach here if you turn right after the church. Your route continues up the drive of the park to rejoin the Revelstoke Drive.

When the Revelstoke Drive comes to an end a well defined clifftop path dips up and down until you come to the mouth of the Erme. You come down a flight of steps beside an old lime kiln with a windowed building attached to it which was once a tea room. There is a permissive path here which goes left and inland up to Mothecombe and comes out by the Schoolhouse café/

restaurant. From here you can go down the road to the crossing point of the Erme.

The coast path however continues along a rather muddy clifftop path through woodland on Owen's Hill until it meets the road from Mothecombe. As is made clear in the information about river crossings in Devon, this river can only be crossed one hour before and after low tide. Tide tables are published on site and can of course be looked up online or in tide tables. If you have to wait for low tide the Schoolhouse Café is probably the place to divert to while you're waiting. There are clear maps when you arrive at the sandy beach. The water should not be more than knee deep. If you are crossing and the

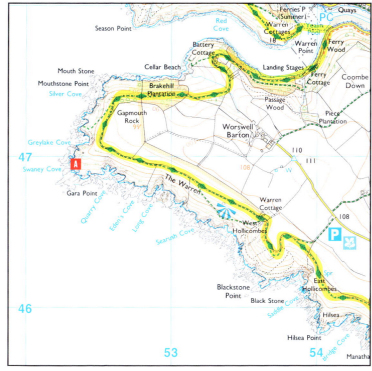

Contours are given in metres
The vertical interval is 5m

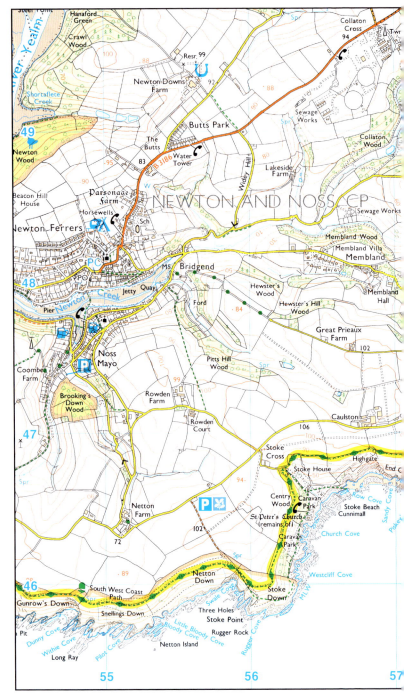

NEWTON AND NOSS CP

Steer Point

Hanaford
Green

Crawl
Wood

Resr. 99

Newton Downs
Farm

Shortaflete
Creek

Butts Park

Collaton
Cross
94

Twr

Sewage
Works

Collaton
Wood

49

Newton
Wood

The
Butts

B 3186

83

Water
Tower

Widey Hill

Lakeside
Farm

Beacon Hill
House

Parsonage
Farm

Horsewells

Sch

Newton Ferrers

Sewage Works

Membland Wood

Membland Villa

Membland

Ms

Bridgend

Hewster's
Wood

Hewster's Hill
Wood

Membland
Hall

48

Jetty

Quay

Pier

Newton Creek

Ford

84

Great Prieaux
Farm

102

Coombe
Farm

Noss
Mayo

P

Pitts Hill
Wood

Spr

Caulston

Brooking's
Down
Wood

Rowden
Farm

Rowden
Court

106

Stoke
Cross

Highgate

End

Stoke House

47

94

Centry
Wood

Caravan
Park

Stoke Beach
Cunnimall

Row Cove

Sandy Cove

Netton
Farm

P

St Peter's Church
(remains of)

Church Cove

Pokey

102

Caravan
Park

72

Spr

Netton
Down

Westcliff Cove

46

South West Coast
Path

Gunrow's Down

Snellings Down

Three Holes

Stoke Point

Stoke
Down

MLW

Swale Cove

Rugger Rock

Rugger Cove

Pit

Dunny Cove

Withie Cove

Pilot Cove

Little Bloody
Bloody Cove

Netton Island

Long Ray

55

56

57

Contours are given in me
The vertical interval is 5

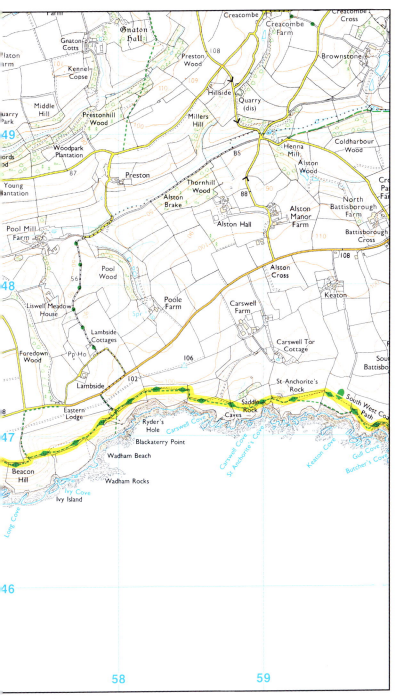

...ntours are given in metres
...e vertical interval is 5m

Contours are given in me
The vertical interval is 5

water becomes deeper than this you are probably crossing in the wrong place, or the tides have not worked out as predicted, and you should give up the attempt. There are local taxi services which will take you round by road to Wonwell Beach in the parish of Kingston.

At Wonwell Beach **33** you may well see egrets fishing in the river and there are several limekilns. These were for the production of mortar for building and for lime for spreading on the fields. The coal came from South Wales by ship and there are quarried limestone outcrops in Devon which

Contours are given in metres
The vertical interval is 5m

you will pass as you go along this coast. Developments in the methods of transport during the 19th century meant that the necessity to be near sea access was no longer so great. You'll see many limekilns in each port along the South West Coast Path. These fell into disuse with the coming of the railways, although some are still used as fishermen's stores.

Go south along the riverside path up to Malthouse Point, where you drop down to Wonwell Beach again. This too can only be crossed when the tide is not fully in, but as you had to wait for low tide to cross the river there should not

Gutterslide Beach and Meddrick Rocks from the Beacon.

be a problem. Continue south-east to Fernycombe Point where the National Trust has a permissive path going to Scobbiscombe Farm and Kingston. After Beacon Point, by Meddrick Rocks, the foreground view east towards Bolt Tail becomes quite dramatic. Rock strewn coves and high cliffs lie ahead, with good views of Burgh Island. There is a steep dip at Freshwater and a substantial rise to nearly 100m at Hoist Point. As well as Burgh Island you are looking at Bigbury on Sea, Thurlestone at South Milton, Hope Cove, and, on the extreme right, Bolt Tail with its prehistoric promontory fort.

At Westcombe Beach there is a permissive path which goes back up to Kingston again, but the coast path continues along the clifftop to Ayrmer Cove, where the path eastwards has eroded away and been brought back towards a new fence-line to Toby's Point, another relatively steep climb, the last one before the end of this section at the Avon.

From Toby's Point the path descends to Challaborough **34**, which has a large beach, and an even bigger holiday park. Continue along the low clifftop and you come into Bigbury. Walk down the road and into the car park. There is a café and shop in the top car park and an eating place popular with surfers which open from 10am. Now it's time to visit Burgh (pronounced Burr) Island, which I recommend. On the island is an Art Deco hotel much visited by high society in the first half of the 20th century, and more recently renovated and revived in the original style but with 21st century luxury facilities. There is also a pub, the Pilchard Inn, and a number of footpaths on which you can follow the island cliffs, with good views looking eastwards above the rocky inlets of the island. The island is only accessible on foot at low tide or by tractor at high tide.

To continue eastwards leave the beach east of the car park by a small track which joins the road, and turn right out onto Sharpland point. The path then goes to the landward side of a number of houses and crosses the road into a field where you turn right up through a summer car park overflow (and camp site), running parallel to the road up Folly Hill to Folly Hill farmhouse across the road. Go into the farmyard and to the left of the farmhouse then continue across the field south-east to Cockleridge Point. At the bottom of this field the path is quite narrow and near the cliff edge. Should that cliff collapse before you get there you may have to follow an alternative route. Please look out for appropriate signs.

When you get to the bottom of the narrow path there is a sunken way which you follow south-east across an area which is inhabited by many rabbits. As you come out of the sunken way you'll see the ferry point where it says to shout and/or wave to attract attention. There is no phone signal here following objections to having a mast in the hinterland.

This ferry is only available early morning and late afternoon during defined dates in season, so take a taxi or, better still by far, take the easy and well signed Avon Estuary Walk to Aveton Gifford, (pronounced as in Jill), where there is accommodation and a shop. Come back to Bantham along the same Walk on the eastern side of the Avon.

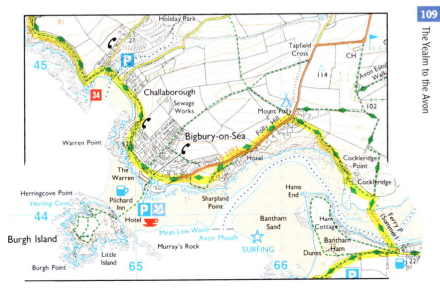

Contours are given in metres
The vertical interval is 5m

9 Bantham to Salcombe

via Hope Cove, Bolt Tail and Bolt Head
11.8 miles (19 km)

Ascent/descent 2,133 feet (650 metres)
Highest point 380 feet (130 metres)

From the ferry come up the hill from the Bantham Sailing Club to the road and turn right, keeping to the main track through the car parks going seawards. Make your way to the left of the rescue establishment. Then follow the clifftop around the perimeter of the big field and up the hill until you come to the corner of the golf club greens. Go to the seaward side of the last tee on Warren Point, turn left to the small sandy beach, still by the golf course, and join a track which leads to some houses and follows the cliff up to a triangular car park. In season there is often a mobile café here.

There are good views of Thurlestone itself and all the watersports activities which continue right through the year (for the very brave).

Continue along the clifftop side of the car park and keep on down the road until it ends. Take to the path, cross the stream by the bridge and rejoin the road again. There are toilets and a café called the 'Beachhouse' here, a wooden shack which is one of the food outlets/ informal restaurants I mentioned at the beginning of the book.

You are now at the National Trust South Milton Sands property. The Trust lease the wetland to the Devon Birdwatching & Preservation Society (DBWPS) who manage it as a wetland bird reserve. In 2017, I saw cattle egrets there for the first time. They are slightly smaller than the little egret and have been a rare sight, although they are now visiting the UK. This might be your first chance to see them. The egrets here like being close to livestock and eat the insects, worms, reptiles, frogs and mice, all of which the hooves of cattle and horses disturb. Cattle egrets have yellow or greyish legs and a yellow beak, compared to the black legs, black beak and yellow feet of the little egret. They also have some ochre feathers.

Follow the track behind the long beach until you get to the new-ish flats. Go up the road from here to the left of these flats and then turn down the first track right, which takes you back to the clifftop. Follow the clifftop all the way to Hope Cove. The path is very clear and there are some very nice views looking back at Thurlestone.

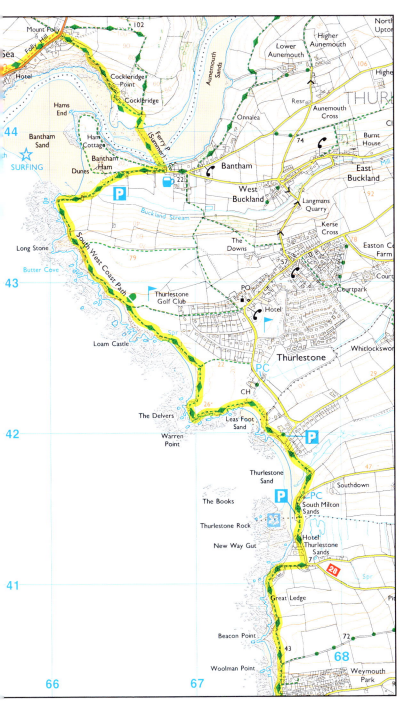

Contours are given in metres
The vertical interval is 5m

Contours are given in metr
The vertical interval is 5m

At Hope Cove **35** you descend to the Hope and Anchor pub and a range of eating and drinking establishments can be found in the village.

Take the road which runs in front of the Hope and Anchor and follow it down to the Watchhouse. The coast path now goes to the landward side of some houses which border on the beach/slipway/sea defences, and then sticks to the clifftop all the way to St Clements church. Now follow the road down to the old lifeboat house at the far side of the beach. Here a set of steps will lead you up into the woods. Just keep following this path until you come out onto open grassland. This is the Bolt Tail, where there is yet another promontory fort. This is a National Trust property where you can explore anywhere,

but the path goes through the centre of the massive embankment which demarkates the fort.

To protect this ancient monument visitors are asked to keep to the marked path to Bolt Tail. Then retrace your steps and continue south-eastwards on the well defined clifftop path to Bolberry Down **36**, until you come to the NT car park there. This is a 1km level access for people with limited mobility. From here the path goes along the highest point of the ridge of the Down and continues fairly close to the field boundaries until you come to the rocks at the end.

It skirts round the landward side of the rocks and descends to wild and beautiful Soar Mill Cove **37**, still keeping to the ridgeback until a zigzag

Contours are given in metres
The vertical interval is 5m

Contours are given in metres
The vertical interval is 5m

path goes down left and then right into the valley and the beach. Here there is a bridge over the stream and the path forks right to continue along the clifftop.

Unless you want to take a shortcut make sure that you keep along the more rugged clifftop path and do not go straight ahead up the hill on the much more distinctly marked track ahead. That would take you to the top of a plateau which makes slightly boring walking all the way to Bolt Head **38**. So keep on the undercliff path until you face the next rocky ridge and then go to the left of it.

Bolt Head has very distinctively shaped craggy rocks all over it and is fun to explore. Go around the end of the headland and then descend the undercliff round the back of the much indented and wild Starehole Bay.

Keep parallel with the water's edge along the rocky path which rounds Sharp Tor (see image on page 2) under the pierced crags. After you round the corner a more gentle path takes you northwards through the woods after which I recommend a visit to the National Trust house called Overbecks.

There is an NT café which does a range of meals and drinks, with superb views of Salcombe from the outside terrace of the lush sub-tropical gardens.

There is also a museum which was kept by the owner, Otto Overbeck, a research chemist and collector, at the beginning of the 20th century. The house was built in 1913 for a younger son of the 5th Viscount Gort whose widow sold the house to Otto Overbeck, who lived here until his death in 1937. I found the

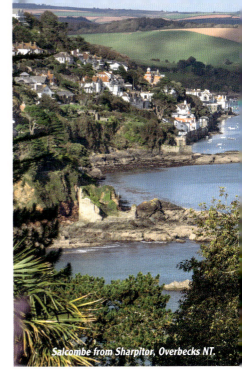

Salcombe from Sharpitor, Overbecks NT.

collection interesting and if you are a National Trust member you can view it free of charge. The 6-acre garden has many palms, olives, mimosa, pines, cypresses as well as magnolia, planted when the gardens were laid out around an earlier house.

From Overbecks the coast path follows the road down to the South Sands Hotel. Turn right here and walk along the road behind the beach and up the hill past the toilets. Keep on along this road until you come to North Sands. Continue to follow Cliff Road parallel with the shore all the way through Salcombe and past the harbour until Fore Street, where a narrow passageway leads through to the ferry to East Portlemouth. Out of season take the ferry at the harbour a little further down the road.

Bantham to Salcombe

10 Salcombe to Start Point

via Gara Rock Beach and Prawle Point
9.27 miles (14.9 km)

Ascent/descent 1,908 feet (582 metres)
Highest point 225 feet (72 metres)

The ferry from Salcombe brings you to the road along which you turn right to Mill Bay. There is a café by the ferry pier. If you have time for a small diversion as you come away from the ferry, go straight on up the narrow track, a bridleway, above the café. This goes up the hill to the phone box and car park at East Portlemouth. From this car park is a view of the Kingsbridge ria, which is one of the best panoramas along this route, especially at high tide in summer, when hundreds of boats are moored upstream. The view of the Devon countryside looking inland is magnificent on a fine clear day. If you take this diversion there is another path back forking right which leads back to the lane.

The whole of this route to Start Point is easy to follow, runs parallel with the clifftop all the way, and gives good views of wild rocky scenery, some of the best in Devon. However, I will describe the way so that you have some idea of what to expect on the day. The road

continues to a National Trust car park after crossing the sandy end of Mill Bay. Go past the entrance to the car park, taking the path to the right of the entrance and continuing parallel

Contours are given in metre
The vertical interval is 5m

Salcombe to Start Point

to the sea. The path gradually rises through the woods. As you round the end of Limebury Point you leave the woods behind, and after Leek Cove the path continues about halfway down the undercliff, following the contours to Gara Rock where you will see a white painted thatched lookout on the skyline. This belongs to Gara Rock Hotel, where the café welcomes walkers. Below is Gara Rock Beach, a good stretch of sand and rocky shore. The path climbs up to Deckler's Cliff through the undercliff, gradually rising but generally following the contours. At Hamstone Cove the path starts to rise to the top of the undercliff and on your right you can see the distictive Gammon Head, with

Start Point from the Coast Path.

a small sandy cove below. Go round the back of Elender Cove and Black Cove and then climb to the top of the undercliff where you'll see a distinctive stile ahead.

On Prawle Point is the white Coastwatch station which is visible for many miles and is often mistaken for the lighthouse at Start Point when seen in the distance.

Prawle Point is the most southerly place in Devon. Prawle comes from an old English word for 'lookout'. A small chapel dedicated to St Brendan is believed to have stood on the site of the Coastwatch station in the middle ages, and would have served as a seamark. These were often manned by a small group of monks who would keep a flame or fire going at appropriate times.

Contours are given in met
The vertical interval is 5

Gammon Head
from Deckler's cliff.

Contours are given in met...
The vertical interval is 5...

An Admiralty Signal Station was on the point, and this would have been able to communicate with the similar station on Stoke Point which you may have passed a couple of days ago on the Revelstoke Drive out of Noss Mayo. Relay signals could be passed along the whole coast in this way, but only when it was clear.

Continuing along the coast path you will pass Ivy Cove, where there is a terrace of former Coastguard cottages which the path circumnavigates on the cliff slopes above. This cove is no longer easily accessible to the public due to cliff falls, but in the first half of the twentieth century a number of fishing boats operated from this cove, and the south-easterly facing coves to the west of it. Often protected from strong south-westerly gales and dangerous

Contours are given in metres
The vertical interval is 5m

waves, the coves would be used by returning longhaul Hallsands fishermen as a safe haven from which they could walk home along the Coastguard Path.

Lannacombe Beach had a busy limekiln, now converted to a cottage. Note the front entrance arch, a mill driven by a leat from the stream, and the old millstones embedded by the path.

The coast path now follows the cliff edge to Peartree Cove, where, by a rather grand rocky outcrop above, it turns southeast to rise up towards the lighthouse at Start Point **39**. There is a B&B at nearby Down Farm, west of the giant aerial array.

Lighthouse at Start Point.

11 Start Point to Dartmouth

via Torcross Strete and Stoke Fleming
13.5 miles (22km)

Ascent/descent 2,584 feet (787 metres)
Highest point 400 feet (120 metres)

From the lighthouse at Start Point retrace your steps for 500 yards up the road through the gate, then fork right out of the car park. Here the path follows the top of the undercliff, starting off on the level and gradually descending to the clifftop at Hallsands.

Note there is a viewing platform at the top of the old village road with a series of signs explaining the history of the destruction of the village. Geologists still argue as to whether the removal of the gravel for the Royal Navy contributed towards the disaster, or whether this is a naturally occurring process taking place during the current millennium of rising sea levels and global warming.

After the information boards the path continues parallel with the cliffs past a number of clifftop houses. You come to North Hallsands, where the car park is already being washed away. You can cross the beach, where the path has been diverted slightly inland to allow it to continue along the clifftop. At Beesands **40** there is a pub and a new gastronomic outlet which was in tented accommodation on my recent visit, but had submitted a planning application for a more permanent restaurant at the time of writing.

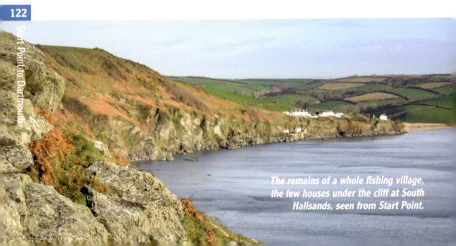

The remains of a whole fishing village, the few houses under the cliff at South Hallsands, seen from Start Point.

Beeson

Beesands

P

40

PC

81

67

109

110

40

Higher Middlecombe
Farm

84

South West Coast Path

Tinsey Head

Hall Sands MLW

39

Bickerton

P

Hallsands

Greenstraight

Lamacraft
Farm

Wilson's Rock

LOST
VILLAGE

P

Hollowcombe
Head

Long Rock

119

124

38

Hare Stone

Long Cove

wn Farm

Lobster Rock

Great Broad Cove

Little Broad Cove

129

Shoelodge Reef

Shoelodge Cove

99

Start
Farm

Spr

P

Freshwater Bay

Nestley Point

122

Yellow Rock

Frowder Point

The Halftide

Black
Hole

The Warren

Start Point

King's Head
Rock

Copper Stone

The
Benches

Chap
& Crater

Sea Rock

37

Fowhole
Cove

Blackstone Lake

Limpet
Cove

Two
Stones

Great Mattiscombe
Sand

Peartree
Cove

Bullock Cove

Gull Island

Black Stone

Frenchman's Rock

Ravens Cove

Barler Rock

Great Sleaden Rock

Little Sleaden Rock

Peartree Point

Sleaden Halftide

81

82

83

The destruction of South Hallsands

The best view of what has happened here is from the Lighthouse Road through binoculars or a telescopic lens. From this vantage point you'll see a few ruins at the bottom of the cliff and a couple of houses which remain in use. Until 1917 it was a fishing community, first mentioned in the 16th century, before which the coast was deemed too dangerous for permanent settlement. A similar village underneath the cliff at Strete, just ahead, was also lost in the 18th century. The fishing community which perched on the ledge above the pebbles at South Hallsands was more or less destroyed in 1917, although quite a few of the ruins were clearly visible and identifiable on the ledges even 40 years ago when I first visited the site, when the village street could still be traced along the undercliff.

Hallsands probably came into existence when threats from pirates and sea raiders were brought under control at the beginning of the 17th century. The first mention of the village is in 1611. The original houses were built on solid rocks which projected some 10 to 15 feet (3-5m) above high water level and about 30 yards from the waters edge.

In 1891 the population of the village was about 160, there was a public

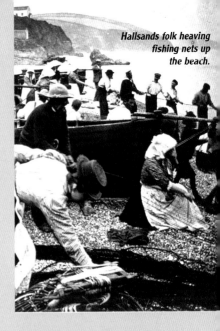

Hallsands folk heaving fishing nets up the beach.

house called the London Inn, and during the summer paddle steamers were beginning to come from Torquay for outings for the day to the beach.

In the 1890's the Devonport Naval dockyard construction was in need of sand and gravel. Thousands of tons of material began to be moved from the Skerries Bank just offshore. By the end of the 19th century the beach had begun to recede and villagers began to protest, leading to a cessation of extraction at one point. On 26 January 1917, high tides reached the walls beneath the houses and it is reported that by the end of the storm most of the houses on the main street had become uninhabitable.

At the end of Beesands continue along the track northwards and turn left at the houses beyond the lake. Go to the left hand side of the garage and round the back where the path climbs up. Turn left round the landward side of the large quarry and then right, out into the open fields. Here you will descend to the far corner of the field. Join the track and follow it right and then left past a few houses, then right out to the small promontory called Torcross Point **A**.

contours are given in metres
the vertical interval is 5m

D-Day landings

What you see before you at Torcross Point is the site of a series of practice landings during the period leading up to D-Day towards the end of WWII. About six weeks before D-Day, on 28 April 1944, an exercise codenamed Tiger involved the landing of numerous craft and amphibious tanks in one last practice for the landing at Utah Beach in Normandy. The Supreme Allied Commander General Eisenhower was on a naval vessel offshore here, ready to watch and assess the exercise. A naval bombardment preceded the landing, and the experiences of previous exercises were used to try and perfect the action for the real thing. The troops were to land on the beach and secure various installations just inland and then start to invade, just as they would in Normandy.

The naval bombardment took place, but as the landing time approached it became apparent that the boats which were meant to come in were not all present and that something had gone seriously wrong. The idea had been that the vessels would come out of all the ports in this area and assemble before proceeding across Lyme Bay to simulate the crossing of the English Channel on the day.

Unfortunately, during the previous night, German torpedo boats were on a patrol and intercepted the convoy. Two of the boats sank and one was very seriously damaged during this incident, and hundreds of the occupants had to jump overboard or sink with the boats. The incident happened 25 miles off Bridport in Dorset and approximately the same distance from

Portland Bill. For a matter of seconds in the confusion following the fire which broke out in the engine room of one of the boats, another American craft fired and several people were injured, but not killed, which has led to a series of misunderstandings about the nature of a 'friendly fire' incident during the exercise.

The main problem was that no rescue procedure had been prepared. The life jackets issued were of a new type and many of the men had not been trained how to use them. The message which ordered the torpedo boats out, sent out by the Germans the previous afternoon, had been intercepted by our intelligence services, but had remained in the queue for decoding for 24 hours. Thus it was not known to the commanders of Exercise Tiger until it was too late. The last major factor was that the two participating forces, the Americans and British, were operating on different radio frequencies and were unable to communicate, leading to deadly delays to the rescue effort. By the time this rescue operation took place late the

Sworn to secrecy: Years later the publican at the Cove House Inn Portland was able to tell the story of the disaster which befell Operation Tiger in Lyme Bay in April 1945.

following morning many of the men had been in the cold water of the English Channel for several hours. Many died, though many were rescued and brought ashore at Chesil Cove, Portland. This was related by the publican at the Cove House Inn there in later years and was also carefully recorded in the official documents relating to burials, as well as accounts by medics at the hospitals the survivors were taken to. The new medical facilities had been installed in the previous months all over the south west of England ready for D-Day. Accounts of the arrival of the survivors have been given by the staff who were at the Coldharbour Hospital in Sherborne. Other survivors were taken to Taunton and other facilities which were at this date ready and staffed for the D-Day casualties, but came into use six weeks earlier than expected. Immediately afterwards the whole exercise was necessarily shrouded in secrecy, and participants who had seen any part of it sworn to silence. In the following half century many strange stories of bodies being buried behind the Chesil Bank in Dorset and the lagoon at Slapton Ley developed, based on recycled gossip rather than any concrete facts.

The stories have been extremely upsetting for the survivors and their families in the United States and a number of books have been written, based on documentary evidence and the accounts of the survivors. All these books, each the result of very careful research, recount the story outlined above and not the fictions which thrived during the last 70 years. The fact that the Chesil Bank in Dorset resembles very closely the beach at Slapton Ley led a lot of the survivors to believe that they had seen bodies floating in this bay. The recorded deaths at this site for that day total only one. The American authorities were extremely conscientious in following up all injuries and deaths at this time. One hopes that a film will not be made based on the myths rather than the carefully researched accounts of the massive tragedy, for which there is a memorial at the far end of the village. For books on the subject, see the 'Useful Information' section at the back of this book.

As a result of the decision to evacuate this area in 1943-4, the local villagers had just six weeks to leave their homes, find alternative accommodation for their families and livestock, lift any crops and take valuable ancient furniture form their churches. The Cookworthy Museum in Kingsbridge has records of this event.

Slapton Ley is now a reserve, particularly remarkable for its population of cetti's warbler and the resident bittern.

After Torcross the next village just up the road is Slapton, which has two pubs and an unusual medieval tower which is the remains of a medieval collegiate chantry.

The coast path follows the landward side of the road east until the Slapton junction and then crosses briefly to the seaward side before reverting to the landward side all the way to Strete Gate **B**, where the road turns inland. Here the coast path keeps parallel with the beach and rises for about a mile before joining the main road into Strete.

Strete **41** has a store, Post Office and public telephone (the pub shown on

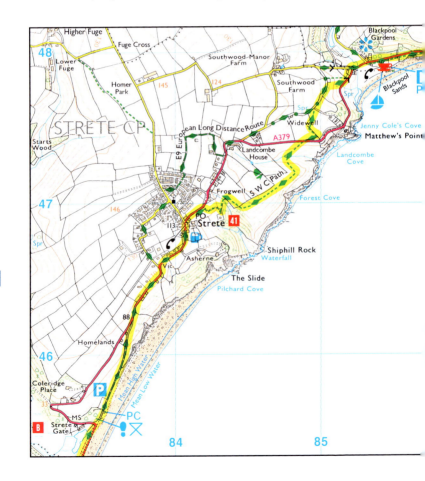

the map below has sadly closed). Go through the village along the main road until you come to a footpath going seaward, just after you come out of the village. This path turns back on itself, down to a stream, then towards the coast and finally follows the contours outside the field boundaries. It then crosses the main road once again and continues through the fields until reaching a narrow lane.

Follow this lane north for a short distance and then take the path right back to the main road, which has to be followed again briefly up to the

Slapton Ley.

Kingfisher.

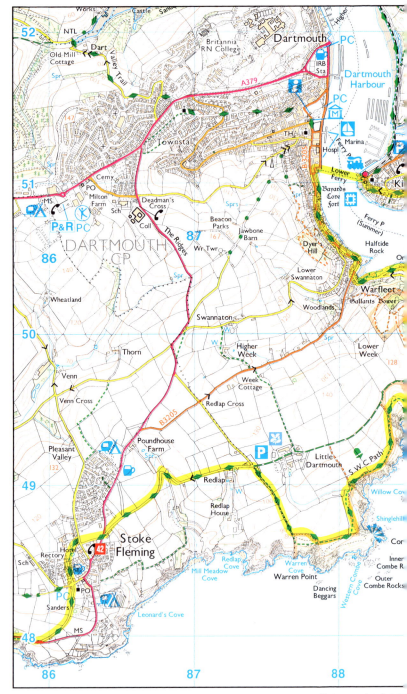

Contours are given in met
The vertical interval is 5m

Dartmouth Castle.

next junction left where the coast path leaves the road and follows it closely on the right hand, seaward, side. Leave the main road as soon as you can, turning inland along the lane which runs up towards Stoke Fleming **42**. Go straight across the crossroads by the church and carry straight on until the footpath forks right across to another road. Turn right again and then left back to the main road which you cross, going into a very narrow lane which leads you to Little Dartmouth. When you get to the National Trust car park at Little Dartmouth turn right towards the sea and then left along the clifftop all the way to Dartmouth Castle **43** (2 miles, 3km). This piece of path has excellent displays of flowers and their associated butterflies in spring and summer.

Dartmouth Castle is 600 years old and has stunning views of the mouth of the Dart. The defence works were begun in 1388 by John Hawley who was a privateer and mayor of Dartmouth and who features in Chaucer's hilarious *Shipmans Tale*. Chaucer's day job was as a customs official and he had to visit John Hawley as part of his official duties, after some unfortunate incidents relating to the treatment of some important overseas visitors to our monarch. Read Chaucer's poem to see how these people worked and made their money, as seen by a customs official of the time.

There is a tea room at Dartmouth Castle which is of course open to the public (English Heritage members free). I recommend a visit to explore the fascinating history of this place. Turner's much romanticised picture of the castle has probably been a major factor in encouraging tourism in recent centuries. Here you can take a ferry into town which runs regularly during the summer months. The coast path continues along little used roads and paths into the town centre where you can take the Lower Ferry to Kingswear, preferably after exploring the town, beautiful medieval church and museum, which gives an account of the commercial history of the town as well as some information about Exercise Tiger.

Start Point to Dartmouth

12 Dartmouth to Brixham

via Coleton Fishacre
11.5 miles (18.5 km)

Ascent/descent 3,825 feet (1,165 metres)
Highest point 420 feet (125 metres)

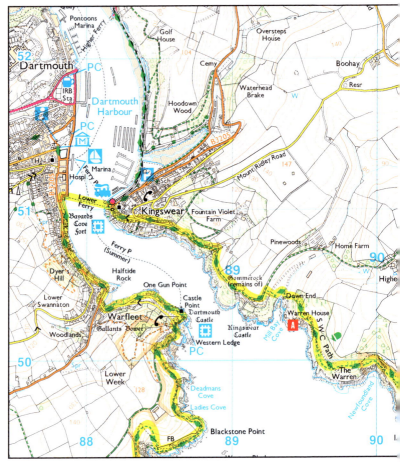

Contours are given in me
The vertical interval is 5

After you have tasted the delights of Dartmouth, its historic forts, churches and museum, and possibly a boat trip or two on the River Dart, take the Lower Ferry to Kingswear. As you come off the ferry go through the archway next to the Post Office and left up the steps. At the top of the steps turn left, not right as shown on some of the older maps, and then right up the steep road past the church entrance. Keep straight on at the first junction along the road which now follows the contours. The older route which is closer to the sea has fallen away at the far end. You can still follow the old route as far as a very long flight of steps back up to the new route described, and turn right at the top. Continue along the road which you're now on for a little less than a mile past various houses and through the woods until you come to Warren House **A**, a large house immediately adjoining the road. Go to the landward side of this house and after a short distance you come to a granite inscription commemorating

Dartmouth Castle and St Petrox Church.

Dartmouth to Brixham

Froward.

Colonel Jones and his heroic role in the Falklands War. Eventually you come towards Lower Froward Point where the Coastwatch lookout has a very informative display/museum about the immediate surroundings. I recommend going into it if it is open. It describes the events at Froward Point during WWII. Even if this period of our recent history isn't of personal interest, you can follow a multiplicity of paths and steps down the steep sloping cliffs, passing many of the military installations, from which there are good views, especially of the Mew Stone. Continue westwards to Outer Froward Point, taking the upper path across this headland. Advance round Old Mill Bay and Kelly's Cove through the undercliff until you come to the back gate of the garden of Coleton Fishacre **44**.

Coleton Fishacre was built as a country home for the D'Oyly Carte family and they chose the architect Oswald Milne, onetime assistant to Edwin Lutyens, to build it in the arts and crafts style with an Art Deco interior. They lived there from 1923 until 1949. The lush 24-acre garden runs down the valley towards the sea at Pudcombe Cove and is planted with subtropical exotic plant species which survive here because of the warming influence of the Gulf Stream. The garden is Grade 2 listed in the national register of historic parks and gardens. Since 1982 it has been owned by the National Trust, bought with funds from Project Neptune, enabling the coast path to pass through the area. Now the house and gardens are open to the public. The house has been kitted out with furniture of the period, and is well worth a visit. You can play the piano in the drawing room and admire the wind indicator, with its amusing paintings of birds-eye views of the peninsula. Allow at least a couple of hours to visit the house and gardens.

There is of course a restaurant, toilets and a National Trust shop.

Pudcombe Cove was sadly no longer accessible when I visited because of coastal erosion. To continue along the

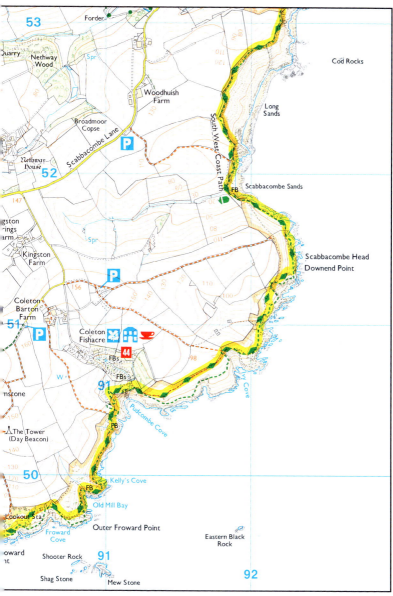

tours are given in metres
e vertical interval is 5m

coast path go north-eastwards along the top cliff path and choose the upper path wherever there is a choice. You'll come to Scabbacombe Head and then Scabbacombe Sands where you drop into a valley with a stream. Cross the stream and walk up towards the top of the undercliff around Long Sands. There is a permissive path to the car park in Scabbacombe Lane. Continue round the back of Long Sands on the clifftop where the path rises to a plateau and then descends into another valley with a stream, to rise again to the top of Southdown Cliff. You have crossed the stream at Man Sands. The adjacent Mansands Lane will lead you inland to Brixham if you need to take a shortcut. The coast path continues along the top of Southdown Cliff until Sharkham Point. Continue around the back of St Mary's Bay where you begin to see the urban parts of Brixham, and continue to Durl Head and Berry Head **45**, which is a country park.

The path comes to the top of the slope and turns left and then joins the road for a short distance around Shoalstone Point. Turn right towards the sea as soon as you can and the path continues along the clifftop on the landward side of some gardens. It rejoins the road again until it is level with the breakwater, where you can descend to the harbour, which has some excellent information displays. Continue around the quayside until you get to the trawler harbour. Here there is a fish outlet where you can eat fresh fish of the day; as elsewhere in fishing ports along this walk, this is a rare and delightful experience. There is also a viewing

platform where you can see the trawlers being loaded and unloaded and preparing for their sea voyages, as well as explanations of the various types of trawler design. Also in the harbour are some restored ancient sailing vessels. If you look at the online information about these vessels you'll see that they welcome visitors when volunteers are working on them, and this should be quite interesting.

Brixham town has a range of shops where you can buy food as well as seaside goods, and there is a museum which is currently being upgraded along with other accredited museums in the bay.

The bus services from the town are very good with frequent services to Paignton, Torquay, Teignmouth, Dawlish and Exeter, should you be choosing to base yourself at some point ahead and walking the path from that base.

Brixham harbour is home to one of the largest fishing fleets in the UK and has a thriving fish market. Over 100 fishing boats land and sell their catch at the fish market on the quayside. Brixham claims to have invented the trawler in the days of sail. Many of the modern boats are large beam trawlers, along with smaller boats which you may see working just out to sea as you walk the coast path. The Brixham Heritage fleet of six sailing trawlers is also resident in Brixham Harbour, built during the 19th and very early 20th century.

You will see them berthed at the town pontoon and may find local craftsmen and -women working on them. They will be pleased to show you around.

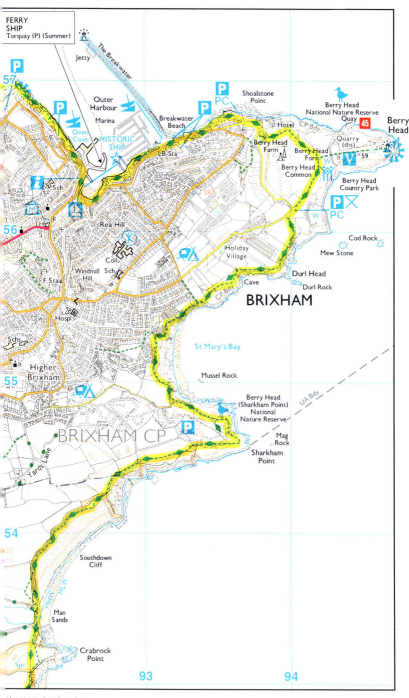

The Breakwater

Jetty

P

57

P

Outer
Harbour

Marina

Oxen
Cove

HISTORIC
SHIP

Breakwater
Beach

LB Sta

P
PC

Shoalstone
Point

Hotel

CP Bdy

Berry Head
National Nature Reserve
Quay   45

Berry
Head

Berry Head
Farm

Berry Head
Fort

Berry Head
Common

Quarry
(dis)

V 59

Berry Head
Country Park

P

W   PC

Sch

Rea Hill

Coll.

Windmill
Hill   Sch

F Sta

Hospl

Schs

Higher
Brixham

56

55

59

Holiday
Village

BRIXHAM

Durl Head

Cave

Durl Rock

Cod Rock

Mew Stone

Mag
Rock

Sharkham
Point

St Mary's Bay

Mussel Rock

Berry Head
(Sharkham Point)
National
Nature Reserve

UA Bdy

CP Bdy

BRIXHAM CP

P

Yards Lane

54

Southdown
Cliff

Man
Sands

Crabrock
Point

Spr

MHW   MLW

93   94

ntours are given in metres
he vertical interval is 5m

Inner Froward Point and the Mew Stone, between Dartmouth and Coleton Fishacre.

JUST OFF THE PATH
Berry Head

I recommend going out to Berry Head, past the Napoleonic fort, to the lighthouse. Berry Head Lighthouse is unusually short and the revolving reflector was originally turned by a weighted cable which descended 45m down the shaft below. It was also fired by gas and controlled by a bimetallic strip which cut off the gas when the sun shone on it and turned it on when it became dark. The lighthouse still emits a nice bright light – with a range of 20 miles (30km) it can be seen from more distant locations on a clear night across Lyme Bay. Before 1875 there was also a Lloyds signal station, which communicated with shipping and passed messages onto London through the Post Office Telegraph system. The Guardhouse café is located in the Napoleonic guardhouse on the headland, open every day of the year except Christmas Day, and from 9am to 4pm in winter months. There is also a very large colony of guillemots at Berry Head. An information centre in the Country Park gives details of the fascinating and varied aerial, marine and plant life.

Berry Head is remarkable for the fact that it is constituted of limestone, not slate, and the headland has been extensively quarried for this valuable building material. It was much used during the Napoleonic era for the construction of the many fortifications around these parts.

To return from the lighthouse, retrace your steps along the crest of the headland to the southern side of the quarry and turn right, signed for Brixham, across Berry Head common.

13 Brixham to Babbacombe

via Paignton and Torquay Harbours
12.95 miles (21 km)

Ascent/descent 2,550 feet (777 metres)
Highest point 325 feet (98 metres)

Contours are given in met
The vertical interval is 5

Perhaps having looked at some of the historic ships in the harbour and the modern trawlers in the commercial port (from the viewing platform), go to the left of the Fish Market and down an alleyway towards Oxen Cove. Continue along the water's edge into an area called Battery Gardens (WWII), until you come to Churston Cove. If you want to take a detour here, you can go down some steps and through a romantic mock-gothic doorway to the cove.

Once you are back on the coast path follow it back inland a few yards, before turning right and right again back towards Fishcombe Point. Continue along the low undercliff. After Elbury Cove and Churston Point you will come to Broadsands **46**. Here you have to go inland, under the railway, and turn right and keep parallel with – and immediately inland of – the railway, for about 1½ miles (2 km).

ntours are given in metres
he vertical interval is 5m

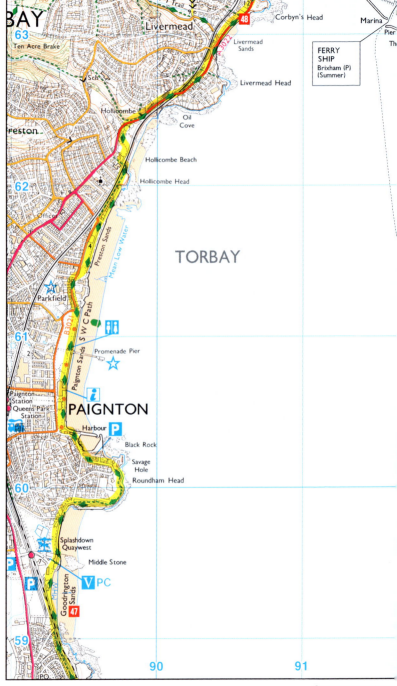

Contours are given in met
The vertical interval is 5

Go under the railway once again to come out behind Goodrington Sands **47**. Goodrington Sands Station is on the heritage railway which goes from Paignton to Kingswear. I can recommend a trip from Paignton with a day return and perhaps a stop off at Greenway to visit Greenway House (NT), the home of Agatha Christie.

The path follows behind Goodrington Sands and around the headland going just to the landward side of some flats by Savage Hole. Here you come to Paignton Harbour. This harbour was established after the Paignton Quay and Harbour Act of 1837 and was open for trade by 1839. You can see some of the old buildings still intact including one of the many fish houses, now the Harbour Light Restaurant. In the early days agricultural produce and fish were exported, and coal and building materials imported, at this quay. Imagine it like one of the small fishing villages you have gone through. The Great Western Railway's 'Speed to the West' advertising campaign changed that quite quickly and from the arrival of the railway in 1859 until its closure in 1972, tourism was the greatest source of income for this town. Continue along the seafront at Paignton Sands. Admire the renovated promenade pier, first opened in 1879.

Continue parallel to the beach for another few hundred yards to Preston Sands. Towards the end of Preston Sands follow a good path up to the seaward side of the railway line before going over another railway bridge. Turn right and keep parallel with the railway line to start with, gradually curving round towards the main road again in a park. Here the path goes onto the road and follows the pavement to Livermead Sands **48**. The road is quite busy and this is not typical coast path stuff, but you realise when you are there that there is little alternative for the route as the road, railway and pleasure path all compete for the tiny space available. The next major features are a massive Victorian hotel on your left and Torquay Station.

A modern Brixham trawler in its home port.

Beyond come the ruins of Torre Abbey **49**. Torre Abbey was founded in 1196 when the abbott and six canons came from Welbeck in Nottinghamshire. This abbey led to the naming of the town of Torquay and the Bay of Torbay. There was rich fertile land in this valley, and in the past you would have come to a huge outcrop of limestone, from which much of the abbey was built. The various headlands which we will now walk round are formed of this limestone. You may notice that a completely different plant life from that on the ubiquitous slate and sandstone which you have been following exists here. Torre Abbey is worth a visit and you can learn about the history of the building as an Abbey and then as a home for a wealthy family after the dissolution. This family invited Nelson for a dinner party and this event is recreated in the dining room for visitors to enjoy. The art collections displayed in the abbey are also highly rated.

Continue your walk around to Torquay Harbour. Here there are wildlife and other boat trips advertised, so you may want to try your luck with viewing the secretive dolphins or other wildlife. There is always a chance that you may come across some extraordinary sightings. If the dolphins do present themselves and decide to show off while you are in the boat, it will be an unforgettable experience. If they don't you will still get some lovely views of the cliffs you have been walking and a dramatic alternative view of some of the geological curiosities of this coast.

Keep to the quayside and take the bridge across the harbour. Note that the concrete ramps still visible to your right were laid at great speed ready for the embarkation of troops for D-Day, and would have been used for the preceding exercises including the ill-fated Exercise Tiger. Continue past the cafés and round to the 'Living Coasts'

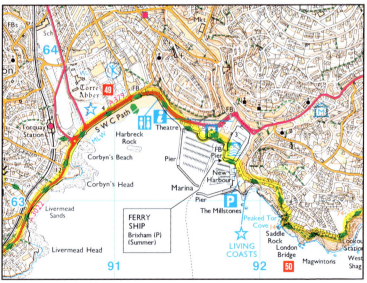

Contours are given in metres
The vertical interval is 5m

entrance. A range of captive Antarctic penguins and other species are on show to the public there, and you will catch sight of some of them inside the netting as you continue along the coast path. Turn right up the road which we follow very briefly before the coast path goes onto an old drive towards London Bridge. Go to the landward side of the large modern building and keep straight on until you are running level on the old driveway.

Follow the old clifftop drive parallel to the clifftop, past the bollards, until the path quite suddenly ends with a stone wall overlooking the famous and remarkable 'London Bridge' **50**, a natural stone archway in the limestone. Having viewed the 'Bridge', retrace your steps for a short distance and go up into the woods above, on the path which takes you through a man-made archway to the Coastwatch lookout station overlooking Daddyhole Cove.

('Daddy' comes from 'devil', and 'hole' meaning 'cove' they do say round these parts...)

There is an interesting and informative display by the lookout station which I recommend viewing. Now cross the lawns at the clifftop and rejoin the path at the far end until you reach another road. This is also evidently part of an old coastal 'ride' but is open to cars, although it is a quite quiet and pleasant walk. Now follow the road, with one footpath link at the halfway mark, for about ¾ of a mile (1 km). Then take the path that rounds Thatcher's Point and Thatcher's Rock, another limestone promontory and island. This path brings you back to the road which you follow briefly to the entrance gate giving access to Hope's Nose.

Some maps mark the coast path as going to Hope's Nose and you might like to explore the headland in any case. For geologists this is a fascinating series of formations which are famous, not least for the discovery of gold in the early 20th century.

If you do go out onto Hope's Nose and explore, return to the road and cross it going diagonally across to the footpath which goes to the landward side of the coast road, and above it, for the next 500 yards or so. Cross the road before you come to the next road junction. Go down the lane to the seaward side of the road travelling east, and then north by turning left off that track to go through woodland to Black Head. After this a pleasant woodland path brings you to Anstey's Cove. Again if you're interested in geology you may want to descend to Anstey's Cove, but the coast

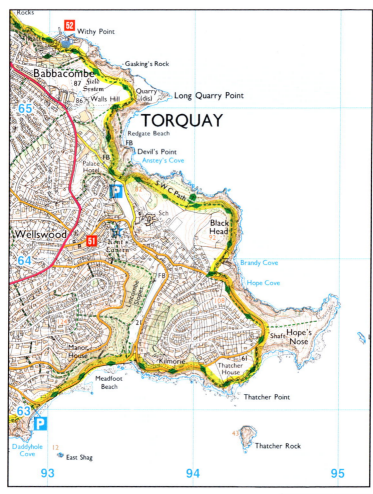

Contours are given in metres
The vertical interval is 5m

Brixham to Babbacombe

path continues along the road north west for a very short distance past the car park.

From this car park there is a green and grassy piece of parkland leading inland and almost due south to a residential road. Turn right along this road for a matter of yards and you will come to the entrance of Kent's Cavern **51**, Britain's oldest ancient monument. The millions of years of geological and human prehistory represented in these caves are well presented in displays. Take some time to absorb them at leisure while waiting for your timed ticket entry. Photography is allowed, and the finds and formations are quite remarkable by any standards. Local residents Agatha Christie and her father come into the story, as does Beatrix Potter.

North-east of the Anstey's Cove Car Park, turn right where an old iron sign points into the woods, seawards. This woodland path continues along the clifftop and comes out on to grassland at Walls Hill. Keep on across the lawns following the clifftop here. Beneath you is the much quarried Long Quarry Point which is clearly the source of stone for much of the building in this area over the last millennium. Just keep to the clifftop now across very open country, keep right along the clifftop where a path leaves to go inland. Keep curving round to the left on the path down through the woods and the path emerges by the tiny quay and hotel at Babbacombe **52**. This beautiful, quiet, rural spot gives an illusion of remoteness when in fact Torbay, the second largest conurbation in Devon (after Plymouth), is just up at the top of the cliff. Apart from the relatively small and even genteel seaside resorts of Teignmouth, Dawlish and Dawlish Warren you will be walking in rural surroundings for the rest of this walk.

Long Quarry Point, with Devonian limestone, which was the former source for many of the buildings, bridges, railway platforms and older sea defences along the path.

14 Babbacombe to Torcross

via Paignton and Torquay Harbours
14.29 miles (23 km)

Ascent/descent 3,203 feet (976 metres)
Highest point 420 feet (130 metres)

From the Cary Arms at Babbacombe go east through the woods and keep parallel with the sea until just before the cliff railway, where the access road/track to Oddicombe Beach meets the coast path. Follow that track uphill to the next hairpin bend, and then keep straight on and bear left to follow the cliff railway up to a bridge/underpass. Once on the other side of the railway turn right towards the coast once again and then turn left. Keep parallel at the top of the steep slopes for about 300-400 yards. Then you will turn left and inland again until you come to the main A379 road. Walk along this for about 150 yards and take the next turning right which takes you back to the cliffs and the woods. Turn left and continue along the top of the undercliff for about 400 yards where you choose the path forking right. This zigzags down to Shag Cliff and then runs parallel to the sea once again past Smugglers' Hole, where it turns inland towards Watcombe. Cross the access path to Watcombe Beach and continue north across the Valley of Rocks. The path turns seawards again and then keeps to the clifftop due north to Maidencombe. Here there is the Thatched Tavern pub, car parking and access to a frequent bus service along the main road between Teignmouth and Torquay.

After crossing the access path to Maidencombe Beach **A** turn right along a residential driveway, keep straight on at the next junction, and left at the end, just before a house and garden where the path goes left, and landwards of, the garden and buildings.

The path continues along the clifftop for two miles where it rises to the Teignmouth Road, which it follows on a separate pavement very briefly, before returning into the clifftop fields all the way to Shaldon. There are numerous permissive paths along this section which link to the coast path. Pathside maps show where they lead, and the whole area is managed for wildlife, particularly the rare cirl bunting. The life cycle of this colouful little bird is well explained on the display boards. In Britain it is almost exclusively found on this coast between the Tamar and the Exe.

The glimpses of views of the high red sandstone cliffs around Labrador Bay

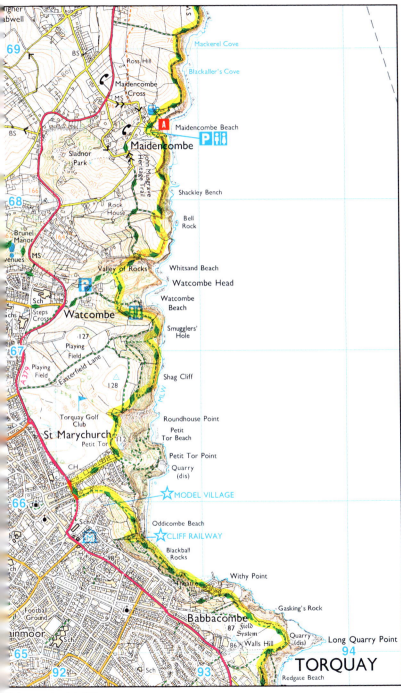

69

Mackerel Cove

Blackaller's Cove

Higher
abwell

BS

Ross Hill

Maidencombe
Cross

MS

A Maidencombe Beach

P 🚻

Maidencombe

Sladnor
Park

166

Shackley Bench

68

Rock
House

John Musgrave Heritage Trail

Bell
Rock

Brunel
Manor

164

venues

MS

P

Valley of Rocks

Whitsand Beach

Watcombe Head

Watcombe
Beach

Sch

Watcombe

Steps
Cross

Smugglers'
Hole

chs

67

·127

Playing
Field

Playing
Field

A 379

Easterfield Lane

Shag Cliff

MLW

128

Torquay Golf
Club

Roundhouse Point

Petit
Tor Beach

St Marychurch

·112

Petit Tor

Petit Tor Point

CH

Quarry
(dis)

66

☆ MODEL VILLAGE

Sch

Oddicombe Beach

☆ CLIFF RAILWAY

Blackball
Rocks

Withy Point

Theatre

Gasking's Rock

Football
Ground

ainmoor

Sch

Babbacombe

87 field
System

86 Walls Hill

Quarry
(dis)

Long Quarry Point

94

65

92

93

TORQUAY

Redgate Beach

Contours are given in metres
The vertical interval is 5m

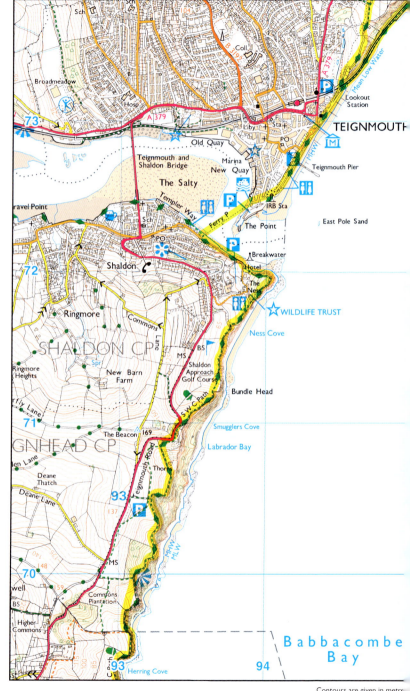

Contours are given in metre
The vertical interval is 5m

and Ness Cove are dramatic, even more so viewed from one of the boat trips you can take across the bay in summer. Just for the record, Labrador is an anglicisation of the French *La Baie d'or*, the Golden Bay, to which local lads from this coast went to fish every summer for generations. So two reasons for the name. One trade related, one a reminder that what is now part of Canada was first settled by our neighbours across what we call the English Channel.

Coming down into Shaldon the view opens up to the whole of the remaining stretch to the Exe, with the Jurassic Coast beyond. A Unesco World Heritage Site, the most beautiful coast in the south west of England is the final climax to walking England's longest long-distance path.

At Shaldon, towards the end of the golf course, the path is in an old lane which starts going inland and joins a similar path coming up the hill from the Ness. Double back down this path (right, and north-east) and follow round the Ness until the coast path joins the road at the mouth of the Teign. Take the foot passenger ferry across to Teignmouth. It runs pretty much all the year round during the day, check online before you get there if that is practical. In the event of no ferry being available, continue the very short distance to the road bridge into Teignmouth and make your way back to the sea front, a small detour, but not so much fun as taking the ferry.

Teignmouth is a resort with a pleasant sea promenade, a station a few hundred yards from the beach, a museum and a good variety of retail and eating establishments.

At the far end of the seafront the coast path follows a stone paved promenade

The Coastguard cottages at Dawlish, built of Torbay limestone. The Catholic church to the right is built from a local red sandstone, which makes a nice contrast on the red cliff top.

Contours are given in metres
The vertical interval is 5m

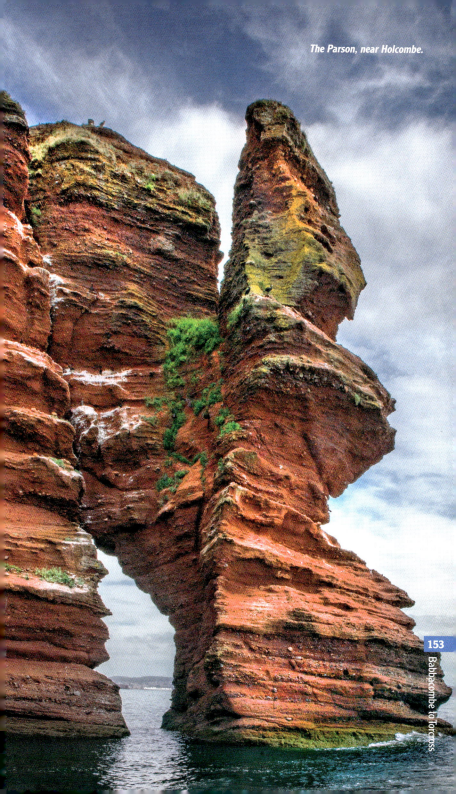

The Parson, near Holcombe.

Langstone Cliff, Dawlish Warren

on the seaward side of the railway for about a mile, to Holcombe. This is the only rail link to Cornwall, so there should be a few high speed trains as well as local ones going past while you are doing this bit. The drivers often love to wave to passers-by as they did years ago. Just before the line goes into a tunnel, the path crosses under the line and goes inland to the main road by a stream. Follow the main road north for a couple of hundred yards on a pavement on the inland side, and then cross back over at the second turning right. You'll immediately go onto a fenced path across the fields coastwards up to the clifftop, then left for 400 yards before returning to the road at the southern end of Dawlish, turning off the new main road down the peaceful old toll road. Rejoin the main road on a pavement again for a very short distance before entering a park and following the clifftop down to Dawlish beach.

Do not attempt to use the railside paths out of Teignmouth or Dawlish described at high tide or in stormy weather. Always check that the tide is low enough, and the sea calm enough, to avoid waves breaking anywhere near the top of the beach or over the walkway. If in any doubt at all, take the alternative routes which leave each town at the northern ends of their promenades. These are signed and waymarked, but not so beautiful as the seaside walk. They both share main roads for some of the length, and I would advise waiting for low tide and safe passage if you have the choice.

So, a mile after Dawlish Station you come to the caves of Langstone Rock **53** where the railway, and the coast path, turn north. Unless you have arranged with the Exmouth water taxi to be picked up from the Warren, cross the railway on the footbridge. Take the first path right and north until it hits the road. Follow the path/cycleway Route 2 along the main road to Eastdon, Cockwood (port) and Starcross Station **A**. In season take the ferry to Exmouth, in winter the train, or take up one of my suggestions overleaf.

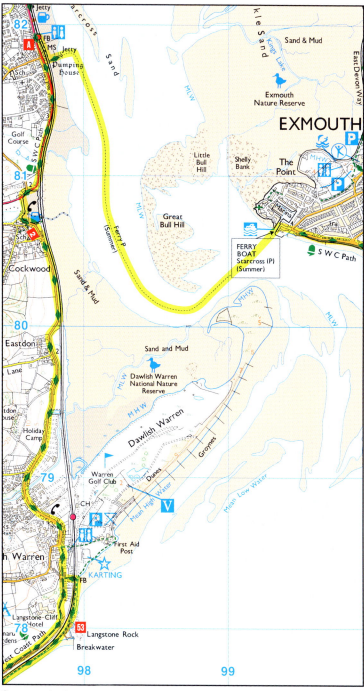

Jetty

82

FB

MS Jetty

A

Pumping
House

Golf
Course

S W C Path

Sch

81

Sch

Cockwood

Sand & Mud

Sand

Ferry P
(Summer)

kle Sand

Kings Lake

Sand & Mud

Exmouth
Nature Reserve

EXMOUTH

Little
Bull
Hill

Shelly
Bank

The
Point

Great
Bull
Hill

MLW

MLW

MHW

Marina

P

P

East Devon Way

MHW

MLW

FERRY
BOAT
Starcross (P)
(Summer)

S W C Path

80

Eastdon

Lane

tdon
ouse

Holiday
Camp

79

h Warren

Langstone Cliff
Hotel

78

naru
dens

East Coast Path

Sand & Mud

Sand and Mud

Dawlish Warren
National Nature
Reserve

MLW

MHW

Dawlish Warren

Dunes

Groynes

Mean High Water

Mean Low Water

Warren
Golf Club

CH

P

V

First Aid
Post

KARTING

FB

53 Langstone Rock
Breakwater

98

99

Contours are given in metres
The vertical interval is 5m

Crossing the Exe

It is possible at any time of the year to walk or cycle around the Exe Estuary. It is part of Route Two of the National Cycleway Network and is clearly signed as such all the way to Exmouth. From Dawlish Warren to Exmouth station is 16 miles (26 km) and the whole route is more or less flat. In winter there are large numbers of migrating birds on the route around the RSPB reserves. There are excellent pubs and cafés along the route. There is also cycle hire at either end and I was informed by the cycle hire by the railway bridge in Dawlish Warren that they would be quite prepared to allow you to cycle the bike to Exmouth and hand it to an associated cycle hire enterprise at the other end. A nice variation on walking, exercise for the muscles that walking does not reach.

So if you allow a couple of hours for cycling and a couple of hours for a pub meal and tea this would be an excellent way of reaching Exmouth under your own steam at any time of the year.

The route is nearly all off road and takes you around the small harbour of Cockwood. Then you pass the pumping station at Starcross, and continue along the Exe through the Powderham Castle Estate. Here there is a large herd of deer, which you will almost certainly see on your walk.

You then join the tow path of the Exeter Canal, built after a disagreement between the City Council and a Countess, who built a weir across the River Exe and prevented boats from reaching the City of Exeter. This canal was built in retaliation, as an alternative route into the city, and is one of the earliest ship canals in the country. After 6½ miles you come to Topsham, where the ferry can take bikes across at Easter and from 2 April until the start of October. See the further details section at the back of this book for operating times. If the ferry is not running you can continue for a further 2 miles on the cycleway, cross the Exe on the cycleway, and return on the north side of the river. In that event, after the bridge river crossing, there is a short urban distance to cover into Topsham, though Topsham itself is extremely pleasant. A new path crossing the river Clyst with the railway bridge then takes you through to Exton, where the cycleway goes through the village just away from the coast, but returns to the riverside within a few hundred yards. Then the path follows the Exe all the way to Exmouth via Lympstone Commando Camp and Lympstone.

Sailing boats at The Turf Inn on the Exeter Canal.

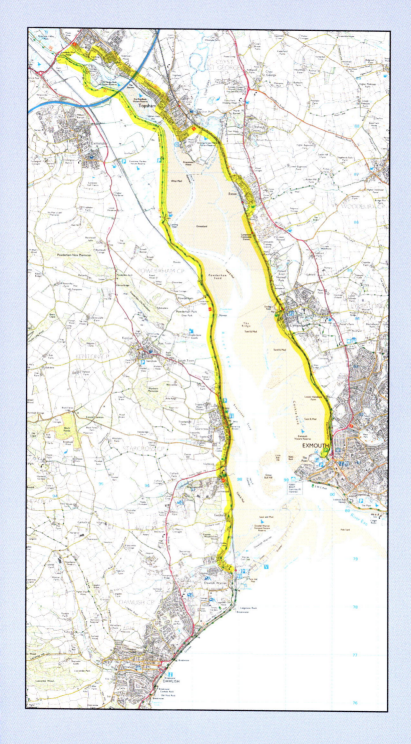

PART THREE

Useful Information

Websites

National Trails Official Site
(i) www.nationaltrail.co.uk/south-west-coast-path
For countryside-related government organisations go to
(i) www.naturalengland.org.uk

Tidetables can be found at
(i) www.bbc.co.uk/weather/coast_and_sea/tide_tables/

English Heritage forts, castles, and other historic monuments
(i) www.english-heritage.org.uk/

National Trust properties you may visit along the route (i) www.nationaltrust.org.uk

The **South West Coast Path Association** is an independent voluntary organisation representing the users of the trail. It campaigns to improve the path and raises money to help this happen. You can find out more about its work at
(i) www.southwestcoastpath.org.uk

Smartphone apps for walkers

There are quite a few smartphone apps which will help you on your way. Some cost a nominal sum or are free. I quote iPhone apps, but a similar range is no doubt available for other operating systems.

Tide Times – finds when it's safe to walk on the beach before you get there. It can be particularly dangerous to swim on outgoing tides on this coast.

Go Skywatch and Sky Guide – find out which planets and stars you can see by pointing at them with your smartphone.

SunSeeker – tells you which direction the sun will be coming from, and how high it will be plus sunrise and sunset – vital for the best photo angles!

Moon – tells when the moon will rise, what direction it will be shining from, which phase it is in. Ideal for moonlit walks by the bay or harbour, and/or photos of the same.

BBC Weather – a website, and an app, but if you press the right buttons you can put it on your start screen for regular use.

Tomtom – *Which?* magazine recommended satnav for getting there in a car (but trains are greener).

Outdoors GPS – 1:50,000 OS maps and 1:25,000, often bought one for each county. Map will accurately locate your current position, record average speed and progress. Will need additional charging for full day use on a smartphone, but lasts all day on an iPad. GPS capability needed, but not G3.

Ordnance Survey maps now often include downloadable maps when you buy a paper version, which can be read while out and about through a smartphone app.

Transport

Detailed information about all public transport journeys in the UK is available from the Traveline (i) www.traveline.info/

Also useful:
(i) https://www.cornwall.gov.uk/media/28932744/public-transport-guide-2017-51-113-bus.pdf
(i) https://www.cornwall.gov.uk/media/28933622/countymap.pdf
(i) https://www.cornwall.gov.uk/media/28932740/public-transport-guide-2017-22-50-maps.pdf

Air

The nearest airports are at Newquay (on the north coast of Cornwall) and at Exeter
ⓘ https://www.cornwallairportnewquay.com/flying-to-cornwall
ⓘ https://www.exeter-airport.co.uk/

Rail

ⓘ www.gwr.co.uk
ⓘ https://www.crosscountrytrains.co.uk/
For timetable and fare enquiries contact the Traveline (details on page 159).

There is also a privately operated steam railway – from Paignton to Kingswear and Heritage lines to Falmouth and Looe
ⓘ greatscenicrailways.co.uk/lines/looe-valley-line/
ⓘ greatscenicrailways.co.uk/lines/maritime-line/
ⓘ www.dartmouthrailriver.co.uk/

Buses

ⓘ www.traveline.org.uk. You can use the Traveline service for details of local buses along the route. Printed summaries and timetable booklets for local services may also be available from main bus stations, or from local Tourist Information Centres.

Timetables for all the services for towns and villages along the coast path can be downloaded, and maps show all routes in the area. Search for 'Devon Bus' and 'Cornwall Bus' ⓘ www.nationalexpress.com

There are normally daily express services by coach from all parts of the country. Tickets for these services should be bought in advance online, from travel agents, or from offices of the company concerned.

Ferries and river crossings

Falmouth to St Mawes and the following ferries:

An all the year round ferry, as at Fowey, Plymouth, Salcombe and Dartmouth. So you can cross those at any time of the year, just check the hours they start and finish each day on the websites given.

St Mawes to Place, then at Wembury, and Starcross to Exmouth have seasonal services outlined below.

Instructions for bus routes for St Mawes to Place (Portscatho Church) are in the text.

The next estuary has no ferry, but the stream, the Erme, is so small that one hour either side of low tide you can take your boots off, paddle though it and walk to the other side across the sandy beach, a great feeling. Just make sure you have a tide table or a tide app on your smartphone, and read the signs which the council displays each year, which give low tide times along the coast path crossings for different dates. If you get it wrong or conditions are unusually wild, ring for a taxi.

Wembury usually runs from spring to the end of September, Starcross from April to October. When there is no service at Wembury a taxi is the best option, at Starcross take the short train journey into Exeter for Exmouth. (That's the last ferry on the path until you get to Poole, which is also virtually all the year round.)

Wembury

ⓘ www.yealmharbourauthority.co.uk
ⓘ www.nationaltrust.org.uk/wembury/features/wembury-ferry

Operating hours

The ferry usually operates from **Easter to mid September**, subject to weather conditions.

Busy days, including school holidays: 10am–4pm

Quiet times including bad weather: 10am–12pm and 3–4pm

When the ferry isn't running, we advise taking a bus or taxi. Walking around the estuary is not recommended and swimming across should not be attempted.

Water taxi/Ferry service

A local boatman offers an independent and limited water taxi service between 1 April and 30 September. Water taxi hours are as ferry hours plus evenings by prior arrangement. Contact on mobile: ☎ 07817 132757

Ferry operating hours are usually Easter to mid September: Daily 10am–12pm and 3pm–4pm, then 10am–4pm during the summer school holidays.

Salcombe to East Portlemouth

ⓘ www.southsandsferry.co.uk/
☎ 01548 561035 All year round daily service 8am–7pm, reduced hours from September to June and weekends plus Bank Holidays. For Portlemouth ferry: ☎ 01548 842061

River Dart Ferry - Dartmouth to Kingswear

ⓘ www.dartmouthrailriver.co.uk
Passenger ferry daily all year round 7:30am–11:10pm with 9am start on Sundays. To check times: ☎ 01548 561035
ⓘ www.teignmouthshaldonferry.co.uk/

Teign Ferry charges

Dogs Go Free, Bicycles taken.

Teign Ferry timetable

Check online as above but normally the last ferry loads 15 minutes before finishing time, which is 6pm or, in winter, in daylight hours, starting at 8am weekdays and at weekends 10am in summer, and 9am in winter. Service operates between Teignmouth back beach, near the Lifeboat House and Shaldon Beach running daily, with restricted service in winter. Does not run on Christmas Day or New Year's Day.

The Exe

ⓘ www.exe2sea.co.uk takes you to their Facebook page
ⓘ https://www.facebook.com/StarcrossExmouthFerry

Operates April to October. Please note due to limited space they cannot take return bicycles on weekends/bank holidays and in the high season.

Accommodation

Finding last minute accommodation in the peak holiday period is not easy, especially for single nights, so at these times booking in advance is recommended.

Airbnb is the online solution for advance reservation and payment. You can choose your price, select your location and read reviews before booking. ⓘ https://www.airbnb.co.uk

Others prefer to make use of the personal service in our Tourist Information Centres, who have local contacts with all types of accommodation. See contact details below.

A comprehensive listing of walker-friendly accommodation is maintained by Luggage Transfers Ltd in conjunction with the South West Coast Path Association. This can be found on the website ⓘ www.luggagetransfers.co.uk. The guidebook is available from many bookshops, and is free with membership to the Association.

Youth Hostels and campsites are noted on the Ordnance Survey maps in this guide. Many additional campsites spring up during the summer. The solitary backpacker may be able to camp in a farmer's field, but permission should always be obtained first. For details of all Youth Hostels visit ⓘ www.yha.org.uk. A centralised telephone booking service is also available on ☎ 0870 241 2314. There are also a number of independent hostels – an annual guide is published by the Backpackers Press, ☎ 01629 580427, or visit ⓘ www.independenthostelguide.co.uk/ for details or to email hostels directly.

A list of Tourist Information Centres (TICs) is given on pages 162-3; they will answer enquiries about accommodation, including camping. It is best to approach the TIC nearest to the place you wish to stay. Note that not all TICs are open throughout the year. Most operate a 'book a bed ahead' service for personal callers for the same or the next night. A fee is charged but will be deducted from your bill by the accommodation provider.

Tourist

Cornwall Tourist Information Centres

Visit Cornwall Information Service, Municipal Buildings, Boscawen Street, Truro TR1 2NE
☎ 01872 261735
✎ visitcornwall@truro.gov.uk
ⓘ www.visitcornwall.com

Bodmin, Shire Hall, Mount Folly, Bodmin, PL31 2DQ
☎ 01208 76616
✎ bodmintic@visit.org.uk
ⓘ www.bodminlive.com

Falmouth - Fal River Visitor Information Centre, 11 Market Strand, Prince of Wales Pier, Falmouth TR11 3DF
☎ 01326 741194 (Press 4)
calls cost 31p per minute + network charges if applicable
✎ vic@falriver.co.uk
ⓘ www.falmouth.co.uk

Fowey, 5 South Street, Fowey, PL23 1AR
☎ 01726 833616
Fax: 01726 834939
✎ info@fowey.co.uk
ⓘ www.fowey.co.uk

Liskeard, Foresters Hall, Pike Street, Liskeard, PL14 3JE
☎ 01579 349148
✎ tourism@liskeard.gov.uk
ⓘ www.visitliskeard.co.uk

Looe, The Guildhall, Fore Street, East Looe, PL13 1AA
☎ 01503 262072
✎ looetic@btconnect.com
ⓘ www.looeguide.co.uk

Mevagissey - Visitor Information Point (seasonal service), Hurley Book Shop, 3 Jetty Street, Mevagissey, PL26 6UH
☎ 01726 842200
✎ hello@visitmevagissey.co.uk
ⓘ www.visitmevagissey.co.uk

St Austell, By Pass Service Station, Southbourne Road, St Austell, PL25 4RS
☎ 01726 879500
Fax: 01726 874168
✎ staustelltic@gmail.com
ⓘ www.staustellbay.co.uk
Kiosk at the rail/bus station, High Cross St, St Austell, PL25 4LA

St Mawes & The Roseland, The Roseland Visitor Centre, The Millennium Rooms, The Square, St Mawes, TR2 5AG
☎ 01326 270440
✎ enquiries@roselandinfo.com
ⓘ www.stmawesandtheroseland.co.uk

Truro, Municipal Buildings, Boscawen Street, Truro, TR1 2NE
☎ 01872 274555
✎ tic@truro.gov.uk
ⓘ www.visittruro.org.uk

Devon Tourist Information Centres

Visit Devon, Tourist Board, Devon, England
ⓘ www.visitdevon.co.uk

Brixham Tourist Information Centre, Hobb Nobs Gift Shop, The Quay, Brixham, Devon, England, TQ5 8AW
☎ 01803 211 211
ⓘ www.englishriviera.co.uk/brixham

Dartmouth Tourist Information Centre, The Engine House, Mayor's Avenue Dartmouth, Devon, England, TQ6 9YY
☎ 01803 834224
ⓘ www.discoverdartmouth.com/

Dawlish Tourist Information Centre, The Lawn, Dawlish, Devon, England, EX7 9PW
☎ 01626 215 665
ⓘ www.visitsouthdevon.co.uk/

Exeter Visitor Information & Tickets, Civic Centre, Dix's Field, Exeter, Devon,

England, EX1 1GF
☎ 01392 665 700
ⓘ www.visitexeter.com

Exmouth, Tourist Information Service,
42 The Strand, Exmouth, Devon, England,
EX8 1AL
☎ Tel: 01395 830 550
ⓘ Web: www.exmouth-guide.co.uk

**Kingsbridge Tourist Information
Centre,** The Quay, Kingsbridge, Devon,
England, TQ7 1HS
☎ 01548 853195
ⓘ www.welcomesouthdevon.co.uk/

Modbury Tourist Information Centre,
5 Modbury Court, Church Street, Modbury,
Devon, England, PL21 0QR
☎ 01548 830 159
Fax: 01548 831 371
ⓘ www.visitsouthdevon.co.uk/

**Plymouth (Plymouth Mayflower)
Tourist Information Centre,** Plymouth
Mayflower Centre, 3–5 The Barbican,
Plymouth, Devon, England, PL1 2LR
☎ 01752 306 330
✉ barbicantic@plymouth.gov.uk
ⓘ https://www.plymouth.gov.uk/
visitorsandtourism

Salcombe Tourist Information Centre,
Market Street, Salcombe, Devon, England,
TQ8 8DE
☎ 01548 843 927
Fax: 01548 842 736
✉ info@salcombeinformation.co.uk
ⓘ www.salcombeinformation.co.uk/

Shaldon Tourist Information, Blue Cabin,
Ness Car Park, Shaldon, Ness Drive, Devon,
England, TQ14 0HP
☎ 01626 873 723
✉ info@shaldon-village.co.uk
ⓘ www.shaldon-village.co.uk/

Seasonal opening

**Teignmouth Tourist Information
Point,** Pavilions Teignmouth, Den Crescent,
Teignmouth, Devon, England, TQ14 8BG
☎ 01626 215665
✉ dawtic@teignbridge.gov.uk
ⓘ www.visitsouthdevon.co.uk

Torquay Tourist Information Centre,
5 Vaughan Parade, Torquay, Devon,
England, TQ2 5JG
☎ 01803 211 211
ⓘ www.englishriviera.co.uk/torquay

Packaged walking holidays

Several firms operate guided or unguided
holidays along sections of the South West
Coast Path and a list of operators can be
found on the official South West Coast Path
website ⓘ https://www.nationaltrail.co.uk/
south-west-coast-path

Luggage transfer

While some B&Bs and hotels will deliver
your luggage to your next overnight stop
for a small fee, the easiest (and normally
cheapest) option is to book through Luggage
Transfers, ⓘ www.luggagetransfers.
co.uk ☎ 0800 043 7927, who move
bags between accommodation along the
entire path.

Other useful addresses

**English Reviera Unesco Global
Geopark**
ⓘ www.englishrivierageopark.org.uk/
A host of fascinating information about the
geology of Torbay, the UNESCO recognition of
the work being done on 32 geosites covering
three geological periods, and the facilities
for education, and the opportunities for
enjoyment of the area which it affords.

The Cornwall Wildlife Trust, Five Acres, Allet, Truro, Cornwall, TR4 9DJ
☎ 01872 273939
ⓘ www.cornwallwildlifetrust.org.uk

Devon Wildlife Trust, 35 St Davids Hill, Exeter, Devon, EX4 4DA
☎ 01932 279244
ⓘ www.devonwildlifetrust.org

National Trust, Cornwall Office,
Lanhydrock, Bodmin, P120 4DE
☎ (01208) 74281. Publishes leaflets about its properties along the coast.

National Trust, Devon Office, Killerton, House, Broadclyst, Exeter, EX5 3LE
☎ (01392) 881691. Publishes leaflets about its properties along the coast.

The Ranger's Office, South Down Farm, Malborough, Devon TQ7 3DU
☎ 01548 562344
✎ southdevon@nationaltrust.org.uk

Natural England ⓘ https://www.gov.uk/government/collections/england-coast-path-improving-public-access-to-the-coast

The Cornwall Good Seafood Guide
ⓘ www.cornwallgoodseafoodguide.org.uk
Describes different fishing methods and gives advice on how to choose the best fish for your favourite seafood meals.

Contact the coastal access team

Contact Natural England with any comments, suggestions or queries you have about improving coastal access.

Coastal access delivery team (South west), Natural England, Ground Floor, Sterling House Dix's Field, Exeter, Devon, EX1 1QA
✎ southwestcoastalaccess@naturalengland.org.uk
☎ 0208 026 7602

South Devon AONB, Follaton House, Plymouth Road, Totnes, TQ9 5NE,
☎ 01803 861384
✎ enquiries@southdevonaonb.org.uk
ⓘ www.southdevonaonb.org.uk/our-work/active-projects/

The Ramblers, 2nd Floor, Camelford House, 87-90 Albert Embankment, London SEI 7TW,
☎ 020 7339 8500.
Handbook with many B&B addresses: available free to members; available to non-members from bookshops and newsagents.
ⓘ www.ramblers.org.uk

Bibliography

Barrett, Roger, *Salcombe, Schooner Port...* (Salcombe Museum, 2018)

Haughton, John, *Follow The Acorn: A Very Unofficial Guide to the South West Coast Path.* (Kindle)

Freeman, Ray, *Dartmouth, A new history of the Port and its People* (Harbour Books)

Hall, Jean, *Railway Landmarks in Devon* (David & Charles, 1982)

*Hoyt, Edwin P., *The Invasion before Normandy* (Hale)

*Lewis, Nigel, *Channel Firing* (Harbour Books)

*Murch, Muriel and David, and Fairweather, Len, *The American Forces at Salcombe and Slapton during WWII*

Pevsner, *Devon* (Penguin Buildings of England Series)

Pevsner, *Cornwall* (Penguin Buildings of England Series)

Rose-Price, Robin, *Torcross and Slapton Ley* (Orchard)

*Small, Ken, *The Forgotten Dead* (Bloomsbury)

Stanier, Peter, *Cornwall's Geological Heritage* (Twelveheads Press, Truro, 1998)

Stanier, Peter, *Cornwall's Mining* (Twelveheads Press, Truro, 2002)

Wallington, Mark, *500 Mile Walkies* (Hutchinson/Arrow, 1986)

There is also a thorough and engaging account of the events leading up to this wreck of the East India Company's megaship, the Halsewell, on the south coast of England on a cold and tempestuous January night 130 years ago. The title is *The Unfortunate Captain Peirce and the Wreck of the Halsewell, East Indiaman, 1786*, by Philip Browne.

It describes graphically why this English Channel trading route was so important to our economy in the 18th and 19th centuries, tracing real people who ran the trade and all it meant to Britain at that time in our history.

* books relating to Exercise Tiger, 1944

Ordnance Survey maps covering the South West Coast Path (Minehead to Padstow)

Landranger Maps: 204, 200, 201, 202, 192

Explorer Maps:
103, 105, 107, 108, OL20, 110, 115.

The more recent versions of these maps indicate all coastal access land
ⓘ www.ordnancesurvey.co.uk

The Official Guides to all

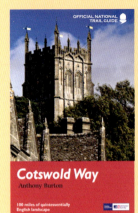

Cotswold Way
Anthony Burton

100 miles of quintessentially
English landscape

ISBN 978-1-84513-570-5

Cleveland Way
Ian Sampson

Over 100 miles of magnificent
walking on the North York Moors

ISBN 978-1-84513-781-6

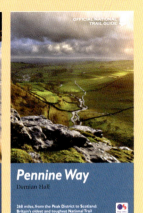

Pennine Way
Damian Hall

268 miles, from the Peak District to Scotland:
Britain's oldest and toughest National Trail

ISBN 978-1-78131-565-1

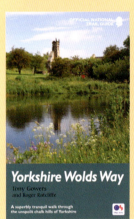

Yorkshire Wolds Way
Tony Gowers
and Roger Ratcliffe

A superbly tranquil walk through
the unspoilt chalk hills of Yorkshire

ISBN 978-1-78131-568-2

Pembrokeshire Coast Path
Wales Coast Path: St Dogmaels to Amroth
Brian John

ISBN 978-1-84513-572-9

South Downs Way
Paul Millmore

100 miles of glorious chalk downland
for the walker, cyclist and horse rider

ISBN 978-1-78131-563-7

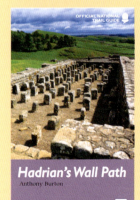

Hadrian's Wall Path
Anthony Burton

Follow the Roman Wall
from coast to coast

ISBN 978-1-78131-571-2

The Ridgeway
Anthony Burton

87 miles of downland walking
from Wiltshire to the Chilterns

ISBN 978-1-78131-573-6

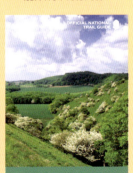

North Downs Way
Colin Saunders

Follow the chalk ridge across South-East
England all the way to the sea

ISBN 978-1-78131-500-2

# of Britain's National Trails

Thames Path
in the Country
David Sharp and Tony Gowers
From the source to Hampton Court

ISBN 978-1-78131-575-0

Thames Path
in London
Phoebe Clapham
From Hampton Court to Crayford Ness:
50 miles of historic riverside walk

ISBN 978-1-78131-754-9

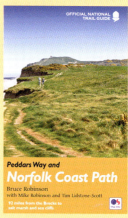

Peddars Way and
Norfolk Coast Path
Bruce Robinson
with Mike Robinson and Tim Lidstone-Scott
92 miles from the Brecks to
salt marsh and sea cliffs

ISBN 978-1-78131-566-8

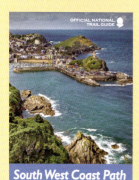

South West Coast Path
Minehead to Padstow
Roland Tarr
160 miles of coastal walking from
Exmoor to North Cornwall

ISBN 978-1-78131-564-4

South West Coast Path
Padstow to Falmouth
John Macadam
From golden beaches to rugged coves
around Britain's southernmost tip

ISBN 978-1-78131-580-4

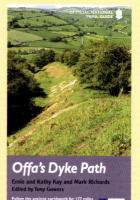

Offa's Dyke Path
Ernie and Kathy Kay and Mark Richards
Edited by Tony Gowers
Follow the ancient earthwork for 177 miles
from the Severn Estuary to the Irish Sea

ISBN 978-1-78131-066-3

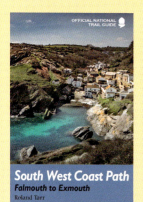

South West Coast Path
Falmouth to Exmouth
Roland Tarr
From St Mawes Castle to the Exe Estuary –
179 miles of dramatic and historic coastline

ISBN 978-1-78131-579-8

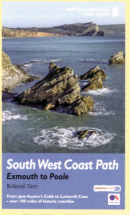

South West Coast Path
Exmouth to Poole
Roland Tarr
From Jane Austen's Cobb to Lulworth Cove
– over 100 miles of historic coastline

ISBN 978-1-78131-567-5

Other guide books from

The Capital Ring
Colin Saunders

76 miles of green corridor encircling inner London

ISBN 978-1-78131-569-9

The London Loop
Colin Saunders

150 miles of secret countryside to walk in a green corridor around London

ISBN 978-1-78131-561-3

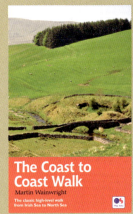

West Highland Way
Anthony Burton

94 miles of Scottish moor and mountain in Britain's most spectacular long-distance walk

ISBN 978-1-78131-576-7

The Coast to Coast Walk
Martin Wainwright

The classic high-level walk from Irish Sea to North Sea

ISBN 978-1-84513-560-6

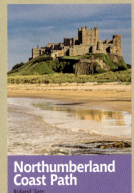

Northumberland Coast Path
Roland Tarr

From the centre of Newcastle to the Scottish border

ISBN 978-1-78131-562-0

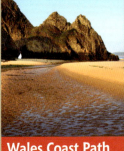

Wales Coast Path
Tenby to Swansea
Chris Moss

Endless sandy beaches and the beautiful Gower Peninsula

ISBN 978-1-78131-067-0

Somerset Coast Path
Damian Hall

121 miles of beautiful scenery, history and surprises

ISBN 978-1-78131-185-1

Camino de Santiago
Sergi Ramis

The ancient Way of Saint James pilgrimage route from the French Pyrenees to Santiago de Compostela

ISBN 978-1-78131-223-0

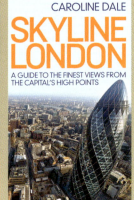

CAROLINE DALE

SKYLINE LONDON
A GUIDE TO THE FINEST VIEWS FROM THE CAPITAL'S HIGH POINTS

ISBN 978-1-84513-762-5

Acknowledgements

Thanks to all those who have made this book possible.

To all those fine people at Quercus especially my editor, Jon Butler, for his tireless enthusiasm for the project and his insightful suggestions for which I am most grateful.

To my brilliant team at Glassbox, for all their support, Luke, Davey, Raymond and Lucinea.

To all those wonderful people who have helped to look after our animals, to Will and Marina, Roman, Joe and Teddy.

To my mother and father who instilled in me a love of nature and the outdoors.

To all those with whom I have shared adventures and amazing animal encounters, especially Dax.

And to my wife Kris, who's unfailing support and encouragement has kept me on track.

To all of you, my heartfelt thanks.

BILL BAILEY is a comedian, musician, actor and presenter. He is perhaps most well-known for his live shows, including *Larks in Transit*, *Qualmpeddler*, *Limboland* and *The Remarkable Guide to the Orchestra*. His work on television includes programmes such as *Never Mind the Buzzcocks*, *Black Books* and *QI*. He is also the author of *Bill Bailey's Remarkable Guide to British Birds* and *Bill Bailey's Remarkable Guide to Happiness*. He lives in west London with a small menagerie of animals and humans.

PRAISE FOR BILL BAILEY

'Bill Bailey knows how to make you happy'
Mirror

'Gently amusing and frequently informative . . . Just a chapter with my morning tea lifted my mood, and helped me approach the day with a dose of Bailey-esque curiosity, tolerance and humour'
Daily Telegraph

'You can tell a true naturalist from a hobbyist by the fact that they can get madly smitten even by animals they can't cuddle – so, hello bats, cockroaches, a tasselled wobbegong . . . Bailey can find affection almost anywhere'
Guardian

Also by Bill Bailey

Bill Bailey's Remarkable Guide to British Birds

Bill Bailey's Remarkable Guide to Happiness

BILL BAILEY

My Animals
and
Other Animals

A memoir of sorts

Written and illustrated by Bill Bailey

QUERCUS

First published in Great Britain in 2024 by Quercus Editions Limited
This paperback edition published in 2025 by

QUERCUS

Quercus Editions Limited
Carmelite House
50 Victoria Embankment
London EC4Y 0DZ

An Hachette UK company

The authorised representative in the EEA is Hachette Ireland,
8 Castlecourt Centre, Dublin 15, D15 XTP3, Ireland (email: info@hbgi.ie)

A CIP catalogue record for this book is available from the British Library.

PB ISBN 978 1 52943 618 1
EBOOK ISBN 978 1 52943 616 7

1

Designed and typeset by EM&EN
Printed and bound in Great Britain by Clays Ltd, Elcograf S.p.A.

Papers used by Quercus Editions Ltd are from well-managed forests
and other responsible sources.

To Kris

Contents

Contents

~~~~~~~~~~~~~~~~~~~~~~~~~~~~~~

Contents

Preface

This is a memoir of sorts.

It's a stroll through my life so far, pausing at those moments where creatures of one sort or another have appeared in a series of incidents, excursions and mishaps . . . The pets that I've shared my life with and my wild animal encounters act as waymarkers, points of interest that blink and buzz and glow in my recollection like a festoon of lightbulbs strung out on the thread of memory.

An errant hound, a kung-fu chicken, a laughing parrot: I've lived with all kinds of critters for most of my life. The fun and companionship they bring is undeniable, but animals give us something more. They teach us lessons about loyalty and responsibility, and even loss. They reflect the arc of our own human experience. Apart from a couple of special, long-lived parrots that you'll meet a bit later on in this book, our pets — pets in general — tend to have short lifespans compared to ours. The times we spend with them are often marked as milestones in our own lives.

And I think animals gain something from us, in return. From the modest beginnings of a few rescue guinea pigs, the menagerie in the Bailey household has grown over the years to include all manner of unexpected guests. They obviously benefit from the care and attention we give them, but they also clearly enjoy our company: I think back to the hens that loved to sit on my head, the ducks that didn't mind a cuddle, the armadillo that liked a scritch behind the ear . . . I loved having them around. Animals give us perspective on our own lives. They cheer us up, they shake us out of gloomy introspection and, sometimes, they remind us of a fundamental truth. Who are we anyway? We're just the lucky winners in the evolutionary lottery. We are their cousins, after all . . .

Part One

FAMILY

For most of us, our first sight of an exotic animal, up close, might well be at the zoo. You can't help but smile as penguins fling themselves into a pool, or when you're being eyeballed by an inquisitive ape, or at the sight of a gentle giraffe's tongue snaking out to implausible lengths. These moments leave a powerful impression on you as a child. The debate about the very existence of zoos might still be contentious, but at least since 1981 the Zoological Act has enshrined in law that zoos should no longer capture animals and should strive instead to educate, and focus on conservation and research. I think that, on balance, they have earned a place in our society. They allow us to see, hear and smell animals, to get a tangible sense of these creatures that we will never get from watching a documentary. For that, they have a potent role to play in illuminating our lives, offering us a glimpse of the marvels of our planet, maybe even encouraging an inquiring mind to take more steps to acquire a greater knowledge of the natural world.

As a child, our family outings were often to a bird reserve or wildlife park and these excursions always seemed more fun as a result. My mother particularly loved these trips and her enthusiasm was infectious. I remember her repeating her mantra to me: 'I just want you to love Nature!' I have fond memories of days out with my parents, my maternal grandparents and me crammed into my Dad's Austin, watching the Somerset countryside roll by on our way to Rode Bird Gardens or the wetland centre at Slimbridge.

As the youngest on these road trips by some distance, I was lost in my own world and devoted myself to the 'acquiring knowledge' bit of the excursion. A lifelong love of our distant animal cousins was the result.

Chapter 1

The Beast of Woolacombe Bay

My first memorable encounter with a dog was characterised by sand in my eyes and ears, and a degree of public
humiliation.

It happened in the summer of 1970 and involved a
boisterous red setter pup on a Devon beach. It galumphed
towards me and, in what I now imagine was just a gesture
of affection, knocked me flat on my back. I was banjaxed
and body-slammed by this massive red-haired beast,
who skittled me over with a double-pawed lunge to my
shoulders.

Came out of nowhere. One minute I was pottering
about with a bucket and spade and then, WHAM, I was
staring up at the blue, cloud-studded sky, suddenly forced
to consider the underside of a herring gull, spitting sand

out of my mouth — and worrying if my bowtie was still on straight.

I must have been five years old, dressed by my mother in a V-neck pullover, smart shirt, bow tie and towelling trunks. If you discount the trunks, I looked like a child waiter. I can think of more appropriate beachwear. I mean it would have made sense if I were perhaps attending a wedding, or maybe a pool party, but a little formal for making sandcastles and paddling in the sea. It was as if my

mother was anticipating all eventualities: trunks for the beach, yes, but also ready for a full civic reception with a local dignitary.

Towelling really isn't ideal material for swimming trunks. In fact, if you had to pick the least effective material for swimming trunks, I would say that towelling is right up there. I would choose corduroy, or Harris Tweed, or loft lagging, or maybe even Bacofoil™ before I got to towelling.

For the uninitiated, a quick google provides the definition of towelling: 'A fabric with loops that can absorb large amounts of water, making it the perfect fabric for a towel.' Yes, that's the key word — towel. It's basically swimming in a towel that has been fashioned into trousers.

I think this is what may have put me off the sea from an early age, as my memories of trying to swim in them resulted in me becoming instantly waterlogged, followed by a valiant battle to stay afloat like a stricken freighter, holed below the waterline. Maybe my mother was building the towel part of the swimming experience into the garment itself. Self-drying trunks. Swim in a towel, dry off in the sun. Hey presto, you're sorted.

~~~~~~

Swimming in a towel is like potholing in high heels, dancing the paso doble in Crocs™, climbing Everest in espadrilles. It had quite a profound effect on me, so much so that throughout my adult life I have become a stickler for the correct bit of kit for the appropriate activity.

I recently found an old interview I gave to a Sunday newspaper. It was in the form of a questionnaire, you know the kind of thing, and what's notable is that my answers have a similar refrain:

'What would you tell your twelve-year-old self?'

'Wear the right footwear.'

'What's the secret of happiness?'

'Appropriate footwear.'

'Any tips for life skills?'

'Correct footwear at all times . . .'

With hindsight, I think the dog was a puppy and just a bit of a long-limbed, gangly, uncoordinated bundle of legs and fur. I remember a bit of a kerfuffle as the dog was admonished and words were had, but no harm done. I was embarrassed to have fallen over in a public place, but I ended up feeling a bit sorry for the dopey hound, which was only doing what young dogs do. He looked like a child who's just had a telling off.

In fact, it's something I think about to this day when our dogs are around small children. It doesn't take much to knock one over and it could be a little scary. But my own early tussle with that puppy didn't put me off and, shortly after the incident on the beach, we got our first dog, a West Highland terrier called Tinker. She was my first pet and went everywhere with us.

I think that being around dogs teaches you all manner of lessons. You have to look after them. You're responsible for them. You have to get outside and walk the goofball tongue-lollers. They are with you all the time. They're part of the family and get treated as such. My mother loved the family photo at Christmas. In our family photo albums there are many such assembled throngs.

'And now one with Tinker. Where's Tinker? Get the dog in the photo!'

The dog started to feature in them and can be seen in various states of bemusement, usually with two red or green eyes caught by the camera's flash. I've never met a dog that liked having its photo taken. There must be something about the tone of our voices when we're arranging a photo.

'Ok, stay. No . . . she's moved. Stay! OVER HERE . . . She's not looking . . . Get a bit of ham . . . Woohoo! Tinker! OVER HERE . . .'

Dogs instantly look nervous at the sight of a camera and refuse to comply. I realise they might think there's something unpleasant about to happen. Tiger, our old rescue hound, hated his photo being taken, so I resorted to using a long lens, from distance, like I was a paparazzo stalking him.

I recently found several photos of me holding Tinker up and one or two where the dog is lolling on its back. These photos usually have a hand discreetly placed over the genital area. As my mother would say, 'No one needs to see that.'

Chapter 2

Radioactive Sea Lice

'Look at these glow-in-the-dark woodlice. Never seen these before . . . You could put 'em in a jar and use 'em as Nature's disco . . .' I said, as we strolled on the beach near the Sellafield nuclear plant, up on the north-west coast of England.

We were on a camping holiday in Workington with my parents. They had brought their caravan. We were in a tent nearby.

Ok, it's not the most glamorous of locations, although the campsite proudly claimed to be 'right on the doorstep of the magnificent Lake District'. Which is sort of true, though the word 'doorstep' is doing a lot of heavy lifting here. But then 'handy for the Magnox Spent Fuel Rod

Reprocessing Plant' doesn't quite have the same idyllic appeal . . .

Sellafield, which for seventy years was the site of nuclear fuel rod processing, used to be called Windscale. The plant, which was plagued by accidents, including a very serious fire in 1957, was renamed Sellafield in 1981 as a 'fresh start' to hopefully regain public trust in the place. The fire and subsequent fallout measured level 5 on the 1 to 7 scale of serious nuclear incidents, but was played down by the British Government at the time for fear of damaging UK and US relations. The plant finally closed in July 2022, but not without concerns about the safe storage of the toxic sludge that still resides within.

It's fair to say that 'toxic sludge' and 'camping holiday' are not often mentioned in the same sentence.

I'd say, as campsites go, it might not have been my first choice, but if you ignore the apocalyptic skyline of smoking towers, it's quite picturesque and near the coast — and I imagine a lot easier to haul a caravan to than over the vertiginous passes of the Lake District. And at least it was on its 'doorstep'.

Caravan holidays were part of my youth and have always appealed to me. I've always loved the idea of just turning up, unhitching the caravan, getting on a brew — and there's your home.

I loved testing the rear indicator and brake lights for my dad. Were they correctly connected to the car's electrics? Left indicator? Check. Right indicator? Check. Such are the pre-flight checks of caravanning. The winding up of the tow bar, the hitching it on, the attaching of the extra wide wing-mirrors . . . These are the rituals of my childhood holidays.

I was reminded of this when, in Australia recently, I met some 'grey nomads'. This is the name given to retired folk who spend their later years criss-crossing this vast country, usually in a caravan or a *Mad Max*-esque four-wheel-drive camper. Many of them shared their accumulated tips and road knowledge with me. Like the need to attach a large screen to the back of the car, to stop the stones from pinging up from the car's rear tyres and cracking the caravan's windows.

Although they were often caravanning on dirt roads, endless unmetalled highways that stretch out before you for mile after mile of red nothingness . . . The A420 to Shepton Mallet it is not.

I have a warm fondness for these trips. Even though caravans are somewhat looked down on by visitors to motoring shows, they hold a huge nostalgic pull for me. Their innate comic flimsiness is their drawback — and yet also their greatest asset. In a storm, the sound of rain thrumming on the roof, and the thin walls weaving and bending in the wind, just enhances the sense of cosiness.

The smell of cooking on the gas stove, with the door open onto a grassy field. The sun on the awning and the smell of warm canvas. The aroma of cut grass and freshly fallen rain. Sausages on the grill . . . This is the caravanning sensory palate of my youth.

This particular trip to Workington with my parents and girlfriend (who would become my wife), turned out to be a huge success. We cooked in the van — well ok, my wife-to-be did the cooking, while I hopped about with onions and logistical support. She made a fantastic feast on this small camping stove, a legacy of her time working in a hotel in Aberdeen. My mum, who set great store by some-one's ability to cook, was suitably impressed.

One night we went for a romantic evening walk along the beach. Workington sits on a picturesque section of coastline that stretches from St Bees up to the Solway AONB. And its lovely beach is a world away from spent fuel-rod processing — an expanse of sand, with a few large boulders dotted around at the high tide mark. It was a mild and moonlit night, and as we strolled amongst the rocks, we spotted these little creatures scuttling over the seaweed-covered boulders.

Initially, I thought they looked like woodlice, but if so these were no ordinary woodlice. They were huge, bordering on giants of their kind. They scuttled in an unnervingly rapid and purposeful way — but even more than that, they emitted an eerie glow, pulsating with a bluish hue that made them seem bioluminescent in the moonlight.

Ok, I am convinced they were radioactive.

Radioactive giant woodlice!

Giant radiation-mutated rock lice!

Huge glowing slaters!

I mean, it's not beyond the realm of possibility, is it?

With hindsight, I should have probably described them to the Natural History Museum in case they were unknown to science. They looked as blue and mechanical as those electric fly killers in chip shops. In fact, I reckon I saw a fly land on one and it was immediately electrocuted. Ok, I may have dreamt that.

To this day, they are the strangest critters I've ever seen on a British beach. In terms of a film based around a nuclear incident, they're not really up there with the excitement of a British Godzilla. *Kong vs. The Woodlouse* doesn't quite conjure up the same epic battle, although in *Spiderman* Peter Parker is bitten by a radioactive spider, so surely Woodlouseman has potential?

> Woodlouseman, Woodlouseman,
> Does whatever a woodlouse can,
> Can he swing from a bridge?
> No he can't, he's under the fridge.

But their proximity to a nuclear reactor . . . not coincidental, surely?

After it was decommissioned as a fuel-rod processing facility, Sellafield became a storage depot. Buildings on its site are now being constructed to house tonnes of radioactive detritus to allow it to cool over thousands of years.

~~~~~~

The only safe way to render it harmless is to leave it alone over aeons of time.

My guess, though, is that when that day comes, the woodlice will still be there.

Chapter 3

Rocky the Boat Dog

When I lived on a houseboat in the late 1980s, my then-girlfriend, Kris, came to stay — and brought her dog, Rocky.

So I went from a bloke living on his own to three in a boat. Rocky was a Patterdale terrier, rust coloured and wire-haired, with a black stripe down his back. Patterdales are described as 'busy, clever, all-terrain, all-weather dogs, who are adept at digging and climbing and love to chase small objects.' I'd say Rocky was textbook Patterdale.

As the name suggests, they originate from the village of Patterdale in the Lake District. They were crossbred in the late nineteenth century from blue-black Border terriers and black and tan fell terriers as a useful all-purpose working dog. They were intended to be tough, brave and quick to train.

Rocky exemplified these qualities and long outlived the Patterdale's average lifespan of twelve years. He was a feisty and fiercely loyal dog, who had a character like no other I've encountered, and he became our ship's mascot. He loved his grub and slept with us in the bow in a little space where the bed fitted, and he would often sit up on deck in the fine weather, the canine captain of his ship.

We discouraged him from getting in the water, the tidal Thames being a less than ideal place for swimming, either for dogs or humans, but what we did have was a public park opposite the mooring and this park became his playground. We would exercise him there and take him for walks along the riverside, which opened out to larger parks and playing fields. He had plenty of attention, and other dogs to meet and run around with; he was, as they say, living his best life.

As for me, I had been living on the boat for two years already and it suited me fine at the time. It was an old US coastal patrol boat that had been refurbished with a small shower and khazi in the wheelhouse, a galley kitchen, a little living quarters comprising a small foam sofa and a 14″ TV perched on two beer crates, and a tapered sleeping area in the bows. It was a little cramped, but it was an inexpensive way to live in London. Mooring fees were about £15 a week, and my only other outgoings were for a phoneline and Calor gas for the cooker. There was a pot-bellied stove in the living area, which in winter I would stack with smokeless fuel like Coalite or compressed briquettes. When it was ablaze, it was toasty.

But if you didn't keep an eye on the stove, i.e. you nodded off and let it go out, in the morning the metal-hulled boat was as cold as a tomb. So as a backup, I'd got in one of those Calor-gas heaters on castors — which I soon realised was a terrible idea on a tidal river. Whenever a boat's wash flowed into the mooring, or there was a current, or the smallest of waves, it would trundle around like a drunk robot as the boat pitched about.

We didn't know it, but this would be the last year on Houseboat *Cormorant*. We were about to change our lives and buy a flat, move to dry land, and not be at the mercy of weather and tides. But that year, the whole summer stretched out before us . . . and Rocky was in his element.

Rock was obsessed with tennis balls. He was relentless in his pursuit of them and would grub them out of the most implausible of places. We could be round at someone's house and he'd be scratching and whining at the cupboard under the sink. On first inspection there would be nothing, but he wouldn't give up, scratching, yelping, whining . . . 'There's something there!'

Eventually, you would have to crawl in with a torch and, sure enough, wedged into the U-bend of the sink waste would be an old mangy tennis ball, often from the tenure of the previous owners. 'I never knew there was a tennis ball there,' was a common parting comment from many places we visited.

Rocky's love of a ball went beyond obsession, but in truth it made our lives easier in a way. Exercising him was a breeze: just throw the ball and he would run and fetch it until you got bored or it got dark, or there was a solar eclipse, or western civilization broke down irreparably.

Nothing would stop him.

As the days lengthened and the warmer evenings started to set in, we would have no need to fasten every hatch on the boat and huddle round the gas fire. We would leave the rear hatch open to let the cool air in. Rocky quickly realised that this meant he could take himself off to the park on his own.

He figured out how to scramble up the wooden steps from the wheelhouse, sidle along the boat's narrow gangway, hop onto the mooring, skitter up the wooden steps, squeeze under the gate and, hey presto, the park was his. He would find dogs to play with, then trot back for his lunch and a bowl of water, then off he would go again.

That summer, he was a latchkey dog.

And when he realised he could take his ball, well, that might just be the best thing that has ever happened to a dog. I would watch as he went up to someone stretched out sunning themselves and drop his tennis ball at their feet, then hop about manically, wagging his tail.

They would throw the ball and he'd bring it back.

On and on it went until they got bored, or left, then he would just take the ball to someone else . . . And so on, until he wanted his tea. It was the best summer of his life.

We had many adventures with Rocky over the years. Sometimes he'd come with me in my Sherpa van to gigs, curl up at the side of the stage and snooze through the show. On occasion he'd amble on and stretch out at my feet, to the crowd's great amusement. He came away on camping trips, he climbed fells, scampered through parks and forests, and ran along beaches chasing ball after ball. He lived a long and happy life to the rare old age of 20, a great innings for any dog.

But I don't think anything quite matched that summer by the river. Those were his halcyon days. Rocky's Brideshead.

Chapter 4

The Great Sandwich Heist

Shortly after we left the houseboat, we moved into a one-bedroom flat in Hammersmith in London, not far from the river. It had no proper kitchen or heating. Even the houseboat had those basics, so moving to dry land initially felt like a step down. We were grateful for the extra space though, and a bit of garden, even if it was a tangled mass of brambles and weeds.

Living on a tidal river comes with its own problems, particularly in the boats' sleeping quarters. The Thames has quite big tides, especially in spring, and sometimes the boat's keel wouldn't quite slot into its berth, having been moved around by the current. Occasionally, it would settle at low tide on a crazy angle, which meant your legs would be up the side of the hull and your body nearly upside down.

Living on this boat as a single man, I'd been prepared to overlook the odd privation or eccentricity, but when Kris arrived I knew things had to change. During an argument about conditions on board being unsanitary and too damp, I put up a spirited defence, including the devastating counter-argument that life on the boat was 'not too bad'. At which point Kris pointed to a large mushroom growing out of the wall in the kitchen.

So when we started to look for a flat, really I was just happy to be on dry land. I'd ask estate agents about local shops and utilities and ground rent and phone points and all that, but the real question was, 'Does the flat tip over when the tide goes out? No? Great. We'll take it.'

The flat had a flimsy outside wooden door that led down a side passage to the proper 'council' front door, painted a fetching shade of dark brown and with reinforced glass. It had a largish front room with a bay window, a fireplace with a boarded-up front, a small hallway with a lino-tiled floor, leading into the sole bedroom at the rear, and finally the tiny kitchen, a small jog right to the front door. I remember when a crazed fan broke into George Harrison's mansion and his wife heard tinkling glass in

~~~~~~~~~~~~~~~~~~~~~~~~~~~~~~~~~~~~~~

some distant part of the house. I used to say to Kris, 'Don't worry, if that ever happens I can reach every point of entry to the flat lying in bed with a pool cue.'

Not long after we had moved in, the kitchen was still a bit rudimentary. We had a gas cooker, a fridge and a sink with a drainer — and that was it. Kris had got into college to study theatre costume design, so I was at home alone with the dog, Rocky, and our grey Siamese Rex, Elsie.

I was taking my time to make a proper sandwich. Grilled brie on toasted ciabatta, garnished with lightly fried green and yellow peppers. Writing this now, I am impressed with my younger self and the level of commitment to the ingredients and the prep. The peppers were lightly sautéed, the brie was just melting, the ciabatta had been toasted . . .

I hopped from foot to foot clapping my hands, the pre-snack dance of eager anticipation. Rocky and Elsie watched intently, but this was a human-only snack.

Just then, the doorbell went, requiring me to open the inner door, go up the side passage and open the outer door. As I went, I heard Rocky's paws trip along the lino tiles in the hallway, then he launched himself at the door, closing it behind me.

When I got back from the door with the delivery, the full nature of the incident became clear. As the back door was locked and bolted, I was now shut out of my own house.

The cat, Elsie, was on top of the kitchen counter. I watched, helpless, through the kitchen window. She lazily padded over to the sandwich and inspected it.

Rocky sat expectantly, looking up at me. Was that a wry smile on his face or a look of guilt that he was trying to hide?

Elsie nibbled a bit of one half of the sandwich, then, as if batting a mouse, she knocked the other half onto the floor, which Rocky devoured in short order.

It then occurred to me that this was a heist. This was planned.

Elsie: 'Ok, when he goes to the door, you shut the door, I'll do the rest.'

Rocky: 'What's the cut?'

Elsie: 'Fifty-fifty.'

Rocky: 'I've got to shut the door.'

Elsie: 'Yeah, well, you can't get up on the kitchen counter so . . . This is a team effort.'

I think Rocky realised, too late, that the cat might just eat the whole thing herself. So there was a degree of trust there, which, despite losing my lunch, I found quite touching.

Thick as thieves, those two.

Chapter 5

Blackbirds

When I hear from friends that they've moved into a new place, my first question is not about the transport links or the schools or where the shops are, or can you get a falafel wrap within walking distance? It's always, 'What are the neighbours like?'

In order for us all to get along we need to cultivate good terms with our nearest dwellers, especially in a city. This is not always easy as people can be unpredictable and cussed and generally odd, but life is full of surprises and multifarious possibilities and pitfalls, and who knows when we might need to rely on our next-door compadres? Who knows when the next global pandemic might show up and we find ourselves stuck indoors, thankful for the home-made cinnamon whirls from them-over-the-wall? Who knew?

During lockdown I was doing some shopping for a neighbour who I had always thought was a quiet, introverted type. I never saw him with a goose, but I imagine that if I did he'd never say boo to it. One afternoon I went round to drop off the shopping, rang the doorbell and retreated the required two metres.

He took a while answering, then only opened the door a crack, though enough for me to see that he was dressed as a 1980s sitcom fortune-teller. He had a patterned red bandana wrapped around his head, he wore a bright yellow ruched shirt with a brown velvet jacket, and a large gold hoop dangled from his left ear.

'You alright, Stuart?' I said.

Stuart shifted awkwardly on the platform shoes I'd just noticed.

'I'm just in the middle of something.'

We have never spoken about this in the years since and the moment to do so has long gone.

*

After a year of living in our flat, a couple about our age moved in next door to us. It took a while to get to know them, but I always take this as a challenge. A friendly chat here, a polite inquiry there, a hand with the shopping and after a while they warmed up a bit.

Our invitations to dinner had always been politely declined, but, as in all things, I persevered. I am generally an optimist about life and about people, and, in my experience, when you make an effort people can surprise you. I suppose my interest in people is part of my general curiosity about the world and all it contains.

In my final year at senior school, we were encouraged to take part in a brand-new careers advisory scheme in the form of a lengthy questionnaire. The form teacher could barely contain his excitement at this cutting-edge technology as he explained how it worked. 'It's computerised!' he said, in tones of reverential awe. What it amounted to was just ticking a few boxes about likes, dislikes, preferences, first pet, which one out of ABBA you fancied (ok I may have made that one up, but you get the picture). This somehow offered an insight into your personality and was then posted off to a company with a 'computer' (ah, what innocent times).

After some algorithmic sorcery this daffy boondoggle somehow miraculously divined the ideal career for me. In hindsight it reminded me a little of the 1974 film *The Parallax View* in which a shadowy government agency sent out questionnaires to unsuspecting citizens and under the guise of this seemingly innocent form-filling were able to deduce who'd make the best assassins. Mine suggested my ideal career was either museum curator or member of the diplomatic service . . . and, now I think about it, either of these could have been a perfect cover for international espionage. There's an element of truth in both these paths in the way my life's turned out. I like collecting, the natural world, travel and generally trying to get on with folk. And when it comes down to it, what is my comedy — a mix of simultaneously mocking and celebrating Britishness to audiences around the world — if not a form of diplomacy?

*

At this point in the early 1990s we had a cat, BooBoo, a large velvety black rascal, a real handsome devil who was a play-away kind of feline. He got his food from various sources and multiple locations, he was 'known in all the boroughs', and when he hung out with us it felt like we were the chosen family for a while.

But when we hadn't seen him for six months, we assumed he'd just found a new home or, worse, that he'd been killed on the road. That was until one fine day I was parking the car and saw him jump out of the hedge from our neighbour's garden and saunter up for an ear stroke as if nothing had happened. So he became ours again and lolled around lording it over Rocky the dog, who tolerated his playful whacks to the head with good-natured forbearance.

One night, our neighbours invited us over for dinner, which was a significant development, so we thought we'd better be on our best behaviour, but from the moment we arrived, the evening started to go wrong.

I'd brought a bottle of wine, but as I proffered it, it was rejected with a rather curt, 'We don't drink.'

I have to say, as a British tradition, the bringing of a gift is pretty standard practice. So if a guest unwittingly brings you a bottle of wine, even if you don't drink, you might politely accept it, so as not to make your guests feel uncomfortable?

Or mention it in the invite:

'Please come round about 7pm. By the way, we don't drink alcohol, so no need for wine, although we don't mind you bringing some for yourself.'

. . . is what *I* would have said. And that's what you would have said, right? Or a variant thereof:

'If you're *sohhhhh* desperate for wine, bring some if you must . . . We promise not to stare at you throughout the evening, making you feel guilty for every sip.'

I mean, these days you also have to ask the question, 'Do you have any dietary requirements?' Fair enough. Except once in America I was asked this question by the PA of a well-known actor. I jokingly wrote back that my wife and I only ate a very rare kind of Tuscan pea.

'That's fine,' came the reply. 'We can accommodate that, just let me know the kind of pea . . .'

At this point, I started to think perhaps I was the one being pranked.

Anyway, the wine rebuff immediately caused an atmosphere. You can tell I'm still annoyed about it, even though it happened thirty years ago.

The fellow was Italian and was also the cook that night. I had genuinely been looking forward to this evening, the chance to connect with our neighbours and to bask in the warmth of community. A nice rounded glass of vino rosso and some-cooked Italian food, perhaps a delicious ragu or carbonara, maybe some veal Milanese, Osso Buco . . .

'We're vegetarian . . . So we're having vegetable pasta.'

Absolutely fine. No problem. I am happy with that. Lovely. 'Is that a dietary choice or . . .'

'We think it is immoral to eat animals.'

I was vegetarian for about two years, which was prompted by a trip to India for International Animal Rescue (IAR). This animal charity was attempting to stop the cruel practice of so called 'dancing' bears. The truth is, of course, that these bears are not dancing at all, merely scrabbling in pain trying to remove the rope that has been put through their sensitive nose. This cruel exploitation has been around for nearly 400 years and the bears are traditionally used by the Kalandar people as a means of income. It began as entertainment for a Maharajah's harem while he was away at battle. Ok, perhaps understandable back then, but surely we live in more enlightened times?

What I liked about this charity was the practical acknowledgement of bear-dancing as a source of income. It's all fine for us to wring our hands and say isn't it awful and please stop, but these dancing-bear owners were from the lowest caste in Indian society and thus on the breadline. How were they going to support their family when the bears and thus their income were taken off them?

IAR worked with local government to provide a grant for the bear-dance people to mitigate the loss of the bear and to assist them to start their own business.

My time there was characterised by chaotic cities, surreal traffic sights, cows ambling across the road, a man pushing a handcart of bright red peppers, some beautiful sunsets and the realisation that the tastiest street food was all vegetarian — thin, crispy breads, rice and dhal, and chana masala — a meat-free delight.

The Stoic philosopher Epicurus celebrated all that gave him pleasure. He saw it as one of the primary purposes of life — to achieve happiness — and I imagine he was always last to leave the Stoic Christmas Party. Growing up in Britain in the 1970s was to expect a life just short of pleasure, so in the spirit of Epicurus, I sometimes strive for contentment through pleasure, but when I can't get that a bowl of home-cooked Bolognese will do the trick.

In the spirit of Epicurus, I unscrewed the cap of the bottle of red I'd brought and went to find my own glass from their kitchen. I detected a certain frostiness in the air, which may or may not have been there before we arrived; a sense of a *moment* about to happen. There was palpable tension in the room, like a Van der Graaff Generator about to crackle into life; a sense of something unsaid between us; a lip-biting pause before the confrontation.

As an observer of human nature and interaction, these things fascinate me, although purely on an objective level, as the moment itself was awkward.

I am shocked, however, to read some statistics that say most people don't have an inner voice. How do they process the world?

My whole day is taken up with a constant jabber of competing conversations in my head, which offer arguments, counter-arguments and even a calm mediating voice that seeks resolution. Years of performing in front of strangers has attuned my sensibilities to the 'room' as we call it in comedy. 'Reading the room' is a key skill for a comic, i.e. deducing, sometimes in a few seconds, how the gig might pan out, starting with a litmus-test gag to see in which direction the show might go.

Right now, in the frosty ambience of this dining room, me downing a wine, silence from the kitchen, just the sounds of plates and cutlery clinking angrily, I was reading the room and if the room were a novel, the review would say, 'a bit of a slog, which ends unpleasantly'.

After a while, our host began a story.

'We found a baby blackbird that had fallen out of the nest.'

The way of telling seemed to have a rehearsed quality about it.

He had his head down, as if to say, 'Just get through this.'

'The mother was nowhere to be seen, so we took it in. It was quite poorly, so we carefully placed it in a little box with some cotton wool. We fed it with a pipette and gradually it got stronger.'

Kris made some approving remark, but I sensed something darker.

This was not going to end well.

'Eventually it opened its eyes, it had a few feathers and we could hear the mother calling for it. So today after we had nursed it back to health, we took it out on to the patio and we opened the box.'

We leaned in.

'It hopped out . . .'

I closed my eyes, the pay-off dawning on me.

'Then a big black cat jumped down *and bit its head off*.'

We knew immediately that this was our cat, BooBoo.

'Oh no, that's awful . . .' said Kris.

'What, right off? Its whole head? Off?' I said unhelpfully. 'Any idea where it came from?'

'It came from your garden.'

We both shrugged. There was a long, long pause.

'Terrible business,' I said finally, like I was talking about the Suez Crisis or crop failure in the Middle Ages.

We ate in Arctic silence.

I finished the bottle of wine in unseemly haste.

'Lovely evening,' said Kris brightly.

'Must do it again sometime,' I said as we left.

It wasn't and we didn't.

Animals, eh? Who'd have 'em!

*

There is a happy coda to this story, which much later made up for BooBoo's antics and hopefully led to us being a blackbird-neutral family.

One day a neighbour brought round a tiny blackbird chick that he'd found on the pavement. It was in a bad way and the fact that it was very young made it worse. It was clear we'd have to nurse it back to strength.

I wouldn't normally recommend hand-rearing an orphaned bird as it's tricky and the best care it will get is obviously from its parents. And if the chick is flightless, but full feathered, mum and dad are probably nearby, so it's best not to get involved at all. But in this case, with a tiny, unfeathered fuzzball with both eyes clamped shut and no sign of the nest or the parents, we humans were its only hope. We named him Pluto.

He was doing well and we made him a makeshift portable nursery out of a cardboard box. He needed constant care, so when I was performing at the Hay Festival, Pluto had to come, too, and hang out backstage, although sadly he missed Benedict Cumberbatch — he was too busy stuffing himself with mealworms we'd brought along.

When he was old enough, we let him go in the garden, but he continued to return most days, hopping around looking for a snack. Blackbirds don't tend to travel far from the nest and Pluto got used to the high life. Why forage around all day, when there's always a free meal at the Baileys'?

Chapter 6

The Cat Suit

The art of a good relationship that endures over time relies on many factors. Trust and openness, of course, but I also think a little spark of discord now and again that can elicit a certain *je ne sais quoi*. A fly in the ointment . . . a jolt of sharp piquancy in the ragu of life . . . some fermented century egg on the toast soldier that keeps things interesting. If you agree on everything, if you like the same things, if you never argue — where's the fun in that?

I always defer to my wife. I trust her judgement on most things. She has an unerring sense of what's right and I am happy to agree with her. This leads to a harmonious relationship and thus a harmonious life.

But once she talked me into wearing a smart suit so that we might impress a woman from whom we hoped to get a cat. This was a few years ago, early on in our long relationship. We were not married at this point. And yet, it was one of those priceless episodes, where I could legitimately say, 'You will never hear the end of this.' I can call this one up as a banker. Whatever I've done, or not done, at least I have this.

'Well, that may be true, but you made me wear a suit for a cat.'

Not just any ol' cat, mind. A Devon Rex. If you're not familiar, these are those weird hairless-looking ones with huge bat-like ears and wrinkled, pink skin like an old flesh cardie. They look alien, otherworldly, like cats kept by wizards or malign Bond villains. When Casper the Devon Rex lived with us in our office, we would sometimes get an RSPCA call where someone would report having seen a 'weird cat with no fur, clearly malnourished'. This cat was anything but – in fact it was pampered and well-kept – and I remember at least one occasion when the RSPCA came to the door, only for the officer to turn right round, muttering, 'A Rex, of course.'

When Kris got off the phone to the Devon Rex duchess-type woman she looked at me with my unkempt locks and my regular t-shirt, jeans and baseball boots combo.

'You'll have to smarten yourself up, because she said she won't let these cats go to just anyone.'

So I was instructed to wear a suit and tie, dressed to impress what we thought was Lady Lah-Di-Dah Hi Falutin', who spoke in a cut-glass accent and lived as she said, on 'the estate'.

On the drive up, I made my objections known, which consisted of me repeating the phrase 'I'm wearing a suit for a cat.' Over and over. The plan was that I was to keep away from the house until the cat was procured lest I blow the whole deal with my poorly ironed trousers. My instructions were: walk Rocky the dog for precisely half an hour, then come to the house, or sorry, 'the estate'.

In our minds, this estate to which she alluded was a huge country pile, a Brideshead-esque palatial gaff with fountains, ha-has, follies and extensive grounds. It would probably have an orangerie, a walled south-facing garden, a maze and a selection of erotic topiary, tapirs, reindeer, buffalo and a giraffe called Madame Bovary.

I parked near to where we'd been given an address and stumped up the road with Rocky, complaining to him the whole way. 'I mean, wear a suit for a cat . . .' Rocky listened to my diatribe and offered nothing more than a supportive bark.

'Yes, exactly!' I agreed. Then I realised he was barking at an alpaca, whose supercilious fizzog had just appeared over a hedge. Wait, perhaps she really *does* live on a posh estate, alpacas and everything!

But no.

When I eventually found the address, it turned out to be a small pebble-dashed house on a local council estate, up the road from the nearby large country house.

I rang the doorbell, which played 'London Bridge Is Falling Down'. When the door opened, I was met with two things: a visual and sensual overload.

On first impression, this was a sight to behold. A woman stood before me of an age that was hard to determine, perhaps in her 60s, or possibly 94, or maybe 37, with blonde hair grown out, a large jumper, huge glasses and a lot of make-up.

But it wasn't so much this sight that took me aback, rather the brutal, full-frontal physical assault of the brain-melting stench of rancid cat urine. I remember thinking, this must be where all cat whizz goes to die. It was like being hit in the face by a frying pan made of solid ammonia.

I recall that no birds were singing within about 500 yards of the house, nor was there any living thing in the immediate vicinity. Trees had died, there was no vegetation. It was a nuclear fallout zone of moggie micturition. The house would have had a thermal imprint visible from Saturn.

Every atom of my being was repulsed. I looked down at my suit and tie and thought, 'A hazmat suit might have been better deployed.'

So I was ushered in, although I remember physically recoiling as I ventured further into this hellhole. In a little sitting area there was Kris, settled in a stinking chair with a wild look on her face. Next to her was our neighbour Patsy, who had accompanied us on this crackpot adventure. Both her and Kris were struggling to put some Marigolds on in an atmosphere of stifled hysteria.

We sat in silence as a parade of minging cats were brought out from god knows where.

The gloves got me. Why yes, of course, let's not bring any germs into this Dantean circle of hell. God forbid there might be a hygiene issue in this foul midden.

The place looked a tip, as well. Cat fur covered every surface. The room looked half-built. As if noticing my gaze, Lady Cat Pee said, 'Yes, I'm having some work done.'

I felt like saying, look, before you get any work done you need to leave right now, just take the cats and get the hell out, skidaddle, and go through one of those jet-washing showers that you sometimes see in films when people have been exposed to radiation. Rinse yourself in that a few times, then have about eight baths, then check into a B&B in Alaska. Finally, as far as work on the house goes, I recommend you encase it in concrete then crane it onto a barge and drop it into the Mariana Trench.

She brought in another cat that was putrid beyond belief. 'She's very good natured.' I felt my eyes start to water and motioned to Kris that we had to get out of there. But the last straw was when she began lecturing us about proper cat care. Because, as she said, one of her cats had been bought by Jackie Onassis . . . !

Suffice to say, we did not leave with a cat. Only an assurance that we would 'think about it'. In the car on the way home, I drove in just a t-shirt and underpants having removed the suit, shirt and tie, and stuffed them into a bin bag. I consigned them to the boot of the car under a rug. Rocky curled up in the far corner with a look that seemed to say 'Well, that's cat people for ya. What can I tell you?'

An image started to form in my mind . . . I said, 'Can you imagine Jackie Onassis on that stinking sofa, wearing marigolds and our lady saying, 'Well, I don't allow these cats to go to just ANYONE!'

After much needed venting, we all agreed it had been character building.

And did it do any lasting damage to my relationship with Kris?

Reader, I married her.

Part Two

HOME

When people ask me, 'How come you've got so many animals?' I say, 'We started with a guinea pig and things just snowballed.'

Which is sort of true.

Our first rescues were a rabbit that no one wanted and a guinea pig that was similarly surplus to requirements. This odd couple of furry cast-offs got on very well and lived quite happily in an enclosure in the garden.

Once you venture down this path, a word of warning: be prepared to get inundated. In no time the word will be out: 'Animal soft touch — go go go!' In short order we found ourselves home to a veritable ark of forlorn guinea pigs, oddball cats, stray dogs and homeless parrots.

A bloke turned up at the door with a peacock once.

'I heard you look after animals,' he said shiftily.

'Where d'you get that?' I asked.

'I . . . er . . . found it.'

'Where?'

'Er . . . just up by the pub.'

I went inside to phone the RSPCA, or Find My Peacock, I can't recall which. Anyway, he was gone when I re-emerged.

Over the years, Kris and I have taken on more animals, and found room for them in our house and garden. And before you know it, chickens were in our shower, a chameleon was in the bath and ducks were under the table. It was a little chaotic at times, but we loved it.

We've opened our house to a gaggle of waifs and strays, and given them a home. Some of them have been given up on and we give them as much love as we can, and we get so much from them in return. Sharing your breakfast with four noisy parrots who love toast . . . means you start the day with a smile.

Chapter 7

Becks the Chameleon

When Victoria 'Posh Spice' Adams married David Beckham, it was tabloid heaven. The glamorous young couple would adorn the pages of papers and magazines, an incarnation of success and genuine youthful romance. They became the power couple that embodied the spirit of the 1990s.

It was around this time that we ended up looking after a pair of chameleons, and I guess their exotic glamour was the reason we named them Posh and Becks. I'd like to think that our choice of names also reflects the nature of fame and an ability to change, to adapt in the glare of the public scrutiny. Ok, maybe I've overthought this. But there is a kernel of truth here. To be in the public eye requires you to be a little chameleon-esque; to adapt as you get older and not necessarily wiser, under the scrutiny of merciless tabloid attention.

Before we moved them to an outdoor heated enclosure, we temporarily housed our chameleons in the bathroom. It wasn't ideal, but it was warm, as it had a heated mirror on the wall and our use of the bath meant that it was always fairly humid in there. Posh and Becks were about eight inches long and beautifully marked, with a curved, pronounced casque on their heads.

After a brief time when our chameleon couple were together, however, we very quickly realised that they had to be kept apart. In the wild, chameleons are solitary creatures, only coming together to mate, so if you put a breeding pair together, the male is not able to control himself. In a wild setting there would be a liaison, a brief encounter, then they would go their separate ways . . . They'd have the whole of Madagascar to roam around in. But confined to a bathroom in West London Posh was stuck with him and Becks' attentions lingered a bit too long for her liking. So we removed Posh to another enclosure. This allowed Becks to hang out on his own, exploring the branches and foliage we'd placed around the bathroom.

They are amazing creatures and quite stunningly beautiful. A myriad of greens and yellows and browns make up their markings. They have curious, almost pincer-like feet, that open and close like miniature tongs. As Becks made his way across the length of the branch we'd installed for him he would test the next step a few times, his tong-like feet making exploratory little air-grabs, delicate prods, before he placed his full grip. It gave the impression of a novice dancer, gingerly extending his limbs into uncharted territory. I can speak here from experience.

Becks was great value. We would sometimes (deliberately?) forget to tell visitors that there was a chameleon in the bathroom, which would sometimes result in a muffled shriek. Mostly people assumed he was a plastic model, until his great mouth opened and a long tongue would unfurl impressively.

It was always fascinating to watch him feed. A locust was his favourite snack, so we'd procure one and place it on a branch nearby. On spotting it, he would slink down silently to within striking range. His eyes would swivel forwards with great intent, his mouth opening slowly, like in *Alien* . . . and his huge tongue would suddenly shoot out, more than twice the length of his body, sticking to the grasshopper - and then slingshot back into his hungry gob.

The chameleon's tongue is a thing of wonder. A recent report in the *Nature Physics* journal has revealed that the sticky mucus on the end of their tongues is 400 times more viscous than human saliva.

Bon appetit!

I filmed the whole thing using the slo-mo feature on my phone and was amazed by the result. The sloweddown footage revealed another remarkable feature of these curious creatures. The chameleon's tongue, which I'd previously thought had such grabbing power due to its sticky coating, actually had a hollow cavity in it. So rather than just grab the prey with an adhesive pad on the tongue, the tongue itself would wrap around the prey, subsuming it in a fleshy tube, before being swiftly retracted.

And as for their famed ability to change colour, the truth of it was a revelation to me. Adult chameleons are beautifully marked, but this is a *permanent* colouring and doesn't change. But the young, new-born chameleon, of which we had a few when they bred well, can truly, for a short period, blend in exactly with their background.

Scientists used to think that chameleons changed colour by controlling the levels of pigment in their skin. Recent research, though, reveals an even more intriguing truth, as is usually the case. Their skin cells contain nano-crystals that reflect light — and in a relaxed state these crystals are densely bunched together, reflecting short wavelengths of light, such as the colour blue. Chameleons

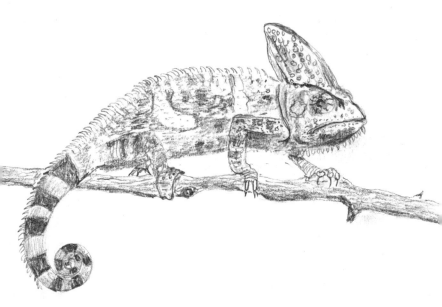

have yellow pigment in their skin, which, combined with the blue, produces their green colour. But when they get excited or agitated the nanoscopic crystals move apart and this reflects light at a longer wavelength, such as red and yellow, giving the impression of a change of colour.

When Becks was young he would sometimes get annoyed about something in his space — a fly or a moth — and he would inflate, puffing himself up to twice his size while turning a virulent blue-black colour and hissing alarmingly.

UNIDENTIFIED THREAT! ACTIVATE NANO-CRYSTALS!

. . . is how I imagine a chameleon's inner monologue sounds.

I would watch in fascination at the multiple colour-matching of our tiny new-born chameleons as they negoti-ated the foliage in their vivarium. The front half would be a pale green, but the section behind their body would turn the exact shade of the branch on which they were draped . . . An amazing ability that rendered them pretty much invisible — a perfect survival camouflage for when they're at their most vulnerable.

Our son Dax would come home from school and spend a while just staring into the tank at these colour-shifting marvels. At a point when they got slightly older, we moved them to a larger tank. We'd kept the old tank in case of any new arrivals and then we realised that Dax would still spend ages just gazing at the tank. We didn't have the heart to tell him they'd been moved, as it kept him focused and, as an extra win, meant he wasn't that bothered about TV, video games or other screen-based distractions.

I like to think it was creative parenting.

Chapter 8

The Rabbit and the Fox

In what looked like a scene from the *Teletubbies*, we once had two giant rabbits, one grey and one pure white.

They lived in our garden, and came out to nibble the grass and generally lollop about. They were enormous, implausibly big, and lent a surreal air to a London back garden. They were a breed of rabbit called the Flemish Giant, which originates in the north of Holland and Belgium, and was specifically bred for food. Well, if you're going to have rabbit, you might as well have one that's a meal deal.

We encountered the breed once in a pet shop and many years later it turned out that we were offered a couple to look after.

We built a hutch for them, which we then had to double

in size. It was more of a chalet by the end, a two-storey bunny duplex that they loved. Daytime would see them lolling around in there, when the weather was warm, sprawled out in a doze, their bunny eyes tightly closed, noses twitching as they dreamed.

The larger was the pure white one and it was as big as a medium-size dog or a human toddler, while its father was officially the Biggest Rabbit in Britain.

They were usually quite docile. We'd let them out and they would hop about on the grass, where they seemed happy. They were out every day, eating constantly, sleeping and fallumphing around the garden.

We have foxes that sometimes come into the garden, though, and obviously that was a worry. Most of the time either we were in or the dogs were around, so foxes were not generally an issue, but on one occasion, a scrawny juvenile fox got over the wall and began to stalk the white rabbit.

I feel like we all know from nature programmes that the adult lions have learned to avoid the hippos, while the teenage males, the immature adolescents, always try their luck and learn the hard way.

I doubt whether this fox had seen that doc, but even if he had I bet he'd never seen a rabbit that size. The rabbit was probably the same length as the fox's body, minus the tail, but heftier of midriff.

Anyway, the fox was creeping up on the rabbit, in broad daylight, and the rabbit suddenly whipped round to face the fox. The fox was momentarily startled, and stopped in its tracks, but then the rabbit flipped round again. They have enormously powerful hind legs and even small rabbits can be hard to hold when they start scrabbling, but this thing's legs were like industrial pistons.

You may or not have seen a B-movie schlocky horror film about giant killer rabbits. It's called *Night of the Lepus* (Lepus being the genus name). Which was chosen presumably because it sounds scarier than *Night of the Rabbit*. Although, as you are probably now thinking, hang on Bill, Lepus is actually the term given to all those of the Leporidae group that *aren't* regular rabbits, such as hares and jackrabbits. I bet a lot of people watched that film and thought, 'The taxonomic classification is all wrong! This is ridiculous!'

Apparently, giant Flemish rabbits like ours were used

in the making of the film, shot in semi-darkness and in slo-mo, and, I imagine, next to scaled down hutches to make them look even bigger.

This white giant could have easily screen-tested for that film. It had size and agility, but, more importantly, it had attitude. This rabbit was, as they say, a badass.

I imagine the fox was thinking, 'This rabbit is an easy mark . . . He hasn't seen me . . . Ok, always approach from the rear . . . It's oblivious to my threat . . . What a loser! Ha!'

The fox pounced, but before he got his teeth in, the rabbit had launched itself backwards and kicked back powerfully with its two hind legs. It was like a spring-loaded trap and whacked the hapless fox with tremendous force, full in the face.

It was the fox's turn to leap backwards and slink away, sorely chastened. Its ears flattened on its head, its tail lowered, it bolted across the garden like a lightning streak of rusty brown. It leapt onto the garden wall in a single bound and was gone.

And he never came back, I'm sure. I would have loved to be a fly on the wall later that night as he sat round in some foxes' hideout behind the bins in a Tesco carpark.

'So tell me again, you were attacked by a . . . rabbit?'

'Yeah!'

'Traditionally . . . foxes' prey?'

'Yeah, but I'm telling you this thing was massive . . . Took me right out . . . I went flying across the garden . . .'

'Wait, you telling me a rabbit did this?'

'Yeah, a massive white rabbit'.

'You sure, Gavin? You been licking those hallucinogenic toads again?'

'No, I swear!! This rabbit . . . It was a beast, like it's been working out, doing jiu-jitsu or something . . .'

'What, like sort of the Jason Statham of rabbits?'

'Yeah!'

'Gavin's lost it.'

And all the assembled foxes make chicken noises.

Chapter 9

Dolly the Tortoise

We inherited a rescue tortoise once. Godfrey, we called him, after the benign and slow-moving character in *Dad's Army* played so beautifully by Arnold Ridley. That was until a trip to the vet where we found out it was actually a *her*. So he was renamed Dolly, after Godfrey's sister. ('My sister Dolly has made some upside-down cake.')

Now it can be difficult to know how tortoises are doing. They're not very demonstrative and will just soldier on in discomfort, so you have to keep an eye on them. But tortoises can make excellent pets and, provided you get one from a reputable breeder with all the necessary paperwork, there's no reason why you shouldn't have one.

Dolly turned up one day . . . and in no time at all became part of the household. She would amble about the garden and, never having owned a tortoise before, I'd never realised how much they eat. She would be at the end of the garden, half hidden in the soil. I'd put a plate of veggies out and she would trundle down and begin munching.

Slowly, deliberately, she'd demolish a plate of veg.

She was, I wouldn't say *affectionate*, but certainly sociable, ambling towards us in the mornings as a matter of habit. It's amazing how attached you get to them. There's something about their strangeness, their ancient, prehistoric deliberations, that is hugely endearing. There's something of the delight you get watching Brontosauruses slowly munching leaves in Jurassic Park, albeit on a smaller scale, with a tortoise.

And although you would think it might be hard to fall for a creature that has a permanent air of disdain and world-weariness, somehow even this draws you in. Not for tortoises the endless mewing of a cat, the barking and wagging of a dog, the chirruping of a bird . . . or even the mild interest of a Giant African Land Snail. Just a withering look when you see them in the morning. 'Oh, you again. Well, have you got my food or what?'

And to watch them pee is quite a sight. I mean, if you've

got nothing else on. Placing them in a shallow tray of water is essential from time to time and a large amount of clear and white-coloured material appears. These 'urates' are entirely normal and the waste product of protein metabolism. It can be alarming at first, but the sign of a healthy creature. And just to give you a heads-up, if they've been eating a lot of dandelions, their pee might come out pink. Just so you know.

One of our dogs at the time, Ruby the Lakeland terrier, took a shine to her. Or rather, she claimed her as her own. She would stand over her and growl if our other dog, Bracken, went anywhere near.

It seemed an odd thing to do, but it became clear: Ruby had marked her out as her mate — or at least something more than mere friendship. I don't know if theirs was a reciprocal relationship — and certainly Dolly showed no affection back, rather the air of long-suffering acceptance that I guess all tortoises have — but this fixation took on a more physical form when Ruby's own possessiveness came to the fore. She would sometimes, well, there's no polite way of saying this, she would hump Dolly's shell. Friends with benefits?

When this curious show of affection began, Dolly would retreat into her shell at first, as you might expect. But as this became a regular thing, she seemed less concerned and would often carry on eating while this strange act of inter-species heavy petting was going on. If nothing else, her shell was always buffed to a healthy shine.

Sometimes people would be round and, of course, it always happened on those occasions. We'd be sitting at the kitchen table and would casually glance out to the garden, and there would be Dolly, impassive as ever, chewing on some lettuce while Ruby barrelled away merrily at her shell. It's amazing how quickly you get used to the quirks of animals, and you forget how bizarre this would look to neighbours and friends.

When we took Dolly on she was already quite long in the tooth, but she lived until a ripe age. Towards the end she wasn't moving well and a trip to the vet indicated arthritis. They suggested that we amputate the leg and offered to replace it a with a wheel, which apparently is not uncommon. But we never got to see this. Dolly became very ill and it was deemed kinder to say goodbye.

I think we spared her the indignity. Although, with hindsight, this may have discouraged Ruby from her daily ministrations. If I close my eyes now I can picture her trying to mount Dolly, on one wheel, gazing into the middle distance with infinite patience as she whirls round and round and round.

The circle of life. Or at least *a* circle of life.

Chapter 10

The Hissing Cockroaches
— or an Unusual Gift

I had just returned from a walking trip in Eastern Indonesia, specifically the Moluccas, and was preparing my script for the programme I was making about Alfred Russel Wallace (there's more about Wallace in chapter 20).

I'd been inspired by a birding book we'd taken on the trip, *The Birds of Wallacea*, an excellent guide to the avifauna of that part of the world. But what had really piqued my interest was the origin of the name 'Wallacea'. Here was a man whose name didn't really register with most people in the UK, a man who was pretty much unknown, and yet in Indonesia his life's work was recognised with an area the size of Germany. My simple question was: what's happened here? Why have this man's achievements, dis-coveries and lasting impact on a country slipped through our cultural consciousness?

I found out that one of the best minds on Wallace, a meticulous compiler of his letters and an expert on the man, was George Beccaloni, then Head of Coleoptera (that's beetles) at the Natural History Museum in London.

After a few swapped emails, Kris and I invited George and his partner Jan for dinner to discuss a potential TV pro-ject about the great man. If George was Head of Beetles, his partner Jan's speciality was arachnids. Beetles and spiders were their shared love and obsession. I didn't know it at the time, but this meeting would lead to many happy hours identifying weevils and katydids in the steaming jungles of Borneo, while Jan fascinated our son Dax by illuminating tarantulas and scorpions with her UV light in the velvety black tropical night.

That first night, at our house in London, George and Jan had brought us a gift. It was a pair of Madagascan hissing cockroaches.

'Most people bring a bottle of wine,' I said.

I'm going to make an assumption here, which is that

the vast majority of you will have never kept Madagascan hissing cockroaches, but they're actually quite sweet. They're less of the shiny-backed scuttlers lurking in dodgy motels and more like giant, furry woodlice about the size of a box of Swan Vestas.

Ok, I realise that even this might still conjure up the stuff of nightmares, but at least you'll be pleased to know that they do actually hiss, quite loudly in fact, like someone not too subtly trying to get your attention.

A proper sitcom stage whisper: 'Pssssst!!'

We transferred them to a glass tank that sat in my sunken garden office, which we nicknamed the Bunker, and I would sometimes forget they were there until I'd hear an occasional 'Pssssst!', causing me to involuntarily whip round saying, 'What? Oh yeah, it's you.'

One day I checked the tank and they had bred. There were suddenly six more, which is apparently typical for this species. Good that they felt so at home. Less so as now I was hearing higher pitched and multiple 'Pssssssts!' as if all the kids were now trying to get my attention.

I'm a patient man, but after a short while, let's say about ten minutes, it became so annoying that I decided to move them to the counter above the washing machine in the utility room. It was warm in there and they could hiss all day to their hearts' content.

Our son was fascinated by the cockroaches and, like all seven-year-olds, he loved to learn amazing facts. For children that age, impressing your friends with knowledge is still a potent currency, which can make you seem cool.

*

A few months later, I was working in New York performing my stand-up show in a theatre off-Broadway, down in the Lower West Side, and the family came out to visit. It was winter in Manhattan, so after a morning looking round the stores, getting pizza and enjoying a spot of ice skating, it was time for a trip to Central Park Zoo.

It's actually a great little zoo, and the seal feeding and the polar bears swimming underwater were big hits . . . But I then noticed there was an 'animal encounter' at 2pm. Sign us up!

Perhaps it was due to the enduring success of the *Madagascar* animated films, the first of which features an implausible escape from Central Park Zoo – but this animal encounter featured exclusively Madagascan critters.

First up was a tenrec, a small, spiny mammal indigenous to that island. It looks for all the world like a pygmy albino hedgehog, but they are only distantly related. Cue plenty of oohs and aahs around the room from all the kids and their parents.

Next up, who's taking top billing? Why, of course, it's our old friends and my office buddies, the Madagascan hissing cockroaches!

My son could barely contain his excitement.

After they were shown around the room, to a considerable ramping up of interest, they hissed obligingly.

A little girl put up her hand.

'How many babies do they have, Miss?

Momentarily stumped, by this, the keeper said, 'Well, to be honest, I don't actually know . . .'

'SIX!!' bellowed a voice next to me, my son now unable to withhold his precious hoard of knowledge. He had his hand up. 'THEY HAVE SIX BABIES!'

'Well, that's very helpful of you, young man. Thank you for that information, but can I ask, how do you know that?'

'BECAUSE MY DAD'S GOT SOME IN HIS BUNKER!'

At this point, the entire throng of kids lost all interest in the keepers, and the hissing cockroaches for that matter, and wheeled around en masse to gawp at these strange Brits and a bloke who keeps hissing cockroaches in a . . . bunker?

What is he, some kind of End-Of-Days prepper? Holed up underground with tins of beans and cockroaches waiting for the Apocalypse?

My son beamed with delight.

I looked sheepishly on. 'Er yes . . . They were . . . a gift.'

'A gift? Who gives cockroaches as a gift?'

'Woah, that is so cool!'

We slowly backed out of there, my son almost bowing with delight as his peers all wondered 'Who *was* that guy?'

Back home in London, I was preparing Dax's backpack for school one day and I noticed the lid of the cockroach tank was slightly ajar.

I slid it back into position. It was sitting right next to the laundry basket, with the fresh laundry folded inside. I was a bit worried that one might have got out and, sure enough, it was sitting quite comfortably on the underside of the handle on top of Dax's backpack. If he'd just used the straps, it could have quite easily made it into school.

I imagine that, had I not seen it, we would have got a call saying the school had been closed down and pest control had been brought in, along with a TV crew from BBC *London Tonight*. So it was a fortuitous find.

I dug around in the pile of clean laundry and put on a clean pair of jeans, but as I was buttoning them up, I felt something moving near my ankle . . .

'Pssssst!'

Sure enough, a large hissing cockroach dropped out of my left trouser leg.

I imagine this might be something from people's worst nightmares, like a scene from a horror film brought to life, but I just rolled me eyes, scooped it up and put it back in the tank.

Just another day chez Bailey.

Chapter 11

Teddy in Chelsea

One of the most extraordinary dogs we ever had was a street hound, a semi-feral Bali dingo called Teddy. They are related to the Australian dingo and similar looking in that they have the same foxy face and curving tail, but are overall smaller and slighter in build.

Teddy was a light honey colour and had beautiful eyes with long lashes. He was a handsome dog.

He came as a package with his pure-white sister, Bulé — who gets her name from the Balinese 'bule', a slightly derogatory term for a white person, basically anyone who isn't Indonesian — and Banjar, who was a half-Bali dingo crossed with a Labrador.

Teddy wasn't as beefy as Banjar and was more slender than Bulé, but he had a powerful charisma that commanded the respect of the others. He was a leader, most definitely 'top dog' in our house. The other two deferred to him; he was there to keep order. When I was away, Teddy would become more alert and jittery, as he assumed the job of protector of the household, but when I got back he relaxed, and was happy to go off duty and snooze.

Banjar, Bulé and Teddy . . . What a gang. Teddy, the leader, Banjar, the muscle, Bulé, the lieutenant.

Once, and only once, I took them all to Richmond Park. After trotting around quite happily, they caught sight of a huge herd of fallow deer and they were off, with Teddy leading the charge.

Bulé came back quite quickly. When we first took her out to our local park, she got a bit lost and hid in some bushes until it got dark. She was delighted to be back and I think never wanted to be lost ever again.

Banjar took a bit longer, but he still came as he was secretly a bit of a good boy and knew he ought to.

But Teddy . . . Well, he was a law unto himself. He chased those deer right over the hill, past the bluebell wood – and disappeared.

You might have seen a YouTube clip of a dogwalker

whose dog starts chasing a herd of deer in that very same park. The dog's name is Fenton and the clip is just this poor chap shouting 'Fenton! Fenton! Jesus Christ . . . Fenton! Fentonnnnn!' over and over, getting more frantic by the minute. The clip went viral and garnered a lot of views and hilarity. But I watched it and I cringed with the pain of having had the very same experience.

Knowing as I do a little about dogs that have a roaming instinct, I can tell you this: they tend to stick to one direction and keep going.

So I went back to the car and drove around the perimeter of the park to where I imagined he might be . . . and there, sure enough, making his way down the hill in his jaunty loping style, was Ted.

I drove up to him, opened the door and he hopped in without a word. Just as cool as you like, like, 'Oh thanks. Thought I might see you here. Just a lift back to the house, please.'

*

Teddy was out once with a dog walker and she called me in a panic to say that he'd gone, he'd run off, and she couldn't see him anywhere. They were on the south side of the Thames and a good mile or so from our house.

I was fixing some blinds to the front windows and had the phone to my ear as I took the call. But literally as she said the words, 'I'm worried he's gone missing,' Teddy trotted up the front path.

So while Teddy liked his little adventures, he always came back. That is, until one Saturday afternoon when the catch of the inner door had not closed properly. Teddy saw his chance, he was off. But for the first time, he was gone overnight. And the next day and the next . . .

After three nights, we were getting worried. We put up signs, we contacted all the usual dog centres, vets, police . . . even Battersea Dogs Home. As my mum might have said, we were having kittens.

And then, on the Wednesday morning, we got a call from someone who was ringing the number on Teddy's microchip. It was Battersea Dogs Home, where he had been since Saturday afternoon.

Someone had seen him trotting along the Chelsea Embankment, thought he looked lost and somehow got him into a vehicle and took him to Battersea. He'd been holed up there, so at least he hadn't been alone in London, on the streets. But feral street dog that he was, he wouldn't trust anyone enough to allow them to approach with a microchip scanner, which is why no one had made the connection when we called earlier in the week.

Eventually one of the kennel staff had gained his trust enough to get near him with the scanner and hey presto. I am forever grateful for their persistence.

Kris and I drove there immediately in a state of tearful relief. Teddy was delighted to see us. He wagged his tail so hard he could hardly walk, his whole body convulsed in a frenzy of delight. He looked a little skinny, but other than that no worse for wear.

We referred to it as his Chelsea 'holiday'.

Chapter 12

The Chicken that Went Bad

For reasons that continue to escape me, we once found ourselves in possession of three large Malay Chickens . . .

This poultry cohort consisted of a large Malay Game Fowl rooster and two hens. He was a magnificent specimen, about three-foot high and with a glorious array of red, metallic green and yellow feathers, an implausibly long neck, beady piercing yellow eyes and a fearsome looking beak, all topped off with a crimson coxcomb.

His large skull and projected eyebrows gave him a sinister, permanently suspicious expression. Malay cockerels are seriously intimidating creatures and have a high level of confidence. Indeed, at first glance they look more like dandy velociraptors than chickens.

It won't surprise you to know that these preposterous birds are officially the World's Tallest Chickens.

When he arrived, we were told that Malay Game Fowl had been brought to Britain in the 1830s specifically for cock-fighting, but the Victorians were so enamoured of their extraordinary size and splendid plumage, they preferred them as merely ornamental chickens. Apparently, we were told, over successive generations 'the fight's been bred out of 'em.'

Well, again, this should have rung a large alarm bell. Because if there's one thing I've learned about the many animals we've looked after over the years, we seem to get the exceptions, the outliers, the one 'they never managed to tame' or the one about which they might say 'He's never done that before . . .'

The Wrong 'Un.

The Chicken That Broke Bad.

The Godzilla of Roosters.

He was definitely an alpha male, a cocky show-off, who strutted around guarding his two 'ladies'. His two hens, while smaller and less scary looking, were equally beautiful in their own way. One was a pure white, the other black — and when the sunlight caught the black hen's plumage it shimmered in stunning, iridescent greens and purples. For his attitude and his flamboyant appearance, we named him Kid Creole, and the hens, Coco and Annie.

For many years, all was well. They ambled and pecked around the garden and the dogs kept a respectful distance. This fearsome outsize cockerel seemed to be a benign presence. Those long balmy days of the first Chicken Summer meant we often had the back door open. They would often wander absently into the house and on one occasion I found all three of them standing in the shower looking mildly stunned.

And then the trouble began.

Kid Creole just took against me.

I think he was being protective of his hens and seeing me became a trigger. Or maybe he just didn't like me? I'll never really know.

One bright morning in July I was crossing the garden and heard a sound behind me, which later turned out to be KC running at full tilt. He pulled up on this occasion, but the next time he ran at me he followed through. At the last minute he would launch himself, both feet forwards, ninja-style.

Of course, as we now know, this was only the start for him, first turning against me, then against the world. It was the moment he 'broke bad'. Somehow he'd got it into his chicken head that I was a threat to his hens and was challenging him, and he needed to assert his authority. But he was sly . . . Kid Creole only attacked me when there was no one around. No witnesses, my word against his — crafty!

And, of course, this had the net result of everyone thinking I was making it all up.

'He's charged me again!' I would say.

'Are you sure?'

'Yes, he just launched himself at my leg!'

'But the nice breeder said that the fight had been bred out of them?'

'NOT THIS ONE!'

'You must have wound him up. Did you wind him up?'

*

Looking back on that time, which I now know as the Chicken Years, I realise how I'd had to adapt my behaviour.

When there's a gradual ramping up of chicken-based violence, at first you don't realise it's happening. Everything appears normal, but then a simple walk across the garden means checking both ways to see if he is hiding and eventually turns into me running while holding two dustbin lids over my legs for protection.

That's no way to live. I was a figure of fun in my own house.

We were having some building work done at the time and, of course, my chicken duel provided great amusement for the Irish builders — 'Oh Bill, that chicken chasing you again? Heh heh heh' — followed by a few clucking noises, 'Who's the chicken?' etc., etc.

UNTIL . . .

I'd been away on tour for a few months and, when I got back, something had changed.

I found one of the builders hovering inside the back door. He was peering out, his hand poised on the handle, nervously scanning the garden.

'What are you doing?' I inquired.

'He's not there, is he?'

'Who?'

'The fecking chicken! That bastard nailed me good and proper on the back of the leg . . . Drew blood, he did. That chicken's no good . . . He's gone bad.'

My vindication was complete. 'You see? He's a hooligan!'

For years, I'd felt like the Boy Who Cried Wolf, But With a Chicken.

By now, Kid Creole was at war with the world. He attacked anyone and everyone. He was like Cato from the *Pink Panther* films. He would just launch himself out of the bushes, without warning.

Not now, Cato!

He knocked people over. He pecked and scratched like a wildcat. He was officially our Worst Pet Ever. Drop-kicks to the buttocks? It's just not what you want in a family pet, is it? I was a prisoner in my own house.

We kept the hens, who provided us with eggs for a good while after. But you won't be surprised to hear that KC had to go.

It was me or the chicken.

Part Three

WORK

Working in comedy came almost as an accident. It wasn't something offered in careers advice at school. It feels to me now, looking back, like a complete adventure. A carload of comics barrelling up the M1 to who knows where, to entertain a comedy club audience, or a room at the back of a pub, or a student union, or an enterprising arts centre who were running a comedy night for local enthusiasts. In London, the comedy scene was growing all the time and the proximity of comedy clubs meant that, with a bit of planning, you could potentially perform a few sets every night. Some nights we would fit in five twenty-minute sets, pinballing around town, ending up at the late show at the Comedy Store, after which I remember lugging my guitar along Oxford Street at 3 am and getting the night bus home.

I'd arrived in London to study English and Drama, so my initial intention was to pursue an academic career, while entertaining the romantic notion of being an actor, or maybe building a career in music. All perhaps precarious, and uncertain paths about which I had very little idea where to even start. But in comedy, I found a little of all of these options, and more than that, I found great freedom, a self-styled life path I never knew existed. A haphazard, make-it-up-as-you-go-along, punk style do-it-yourself ethic that felt, not just exciting, but my natural home. Just as I had made daft tape recordings in my youth, making up ridiculous nonsense, doing silly voices, now I had an audience. I could try out different characters, play instruments, rock out, act out whole scenes, like an alternative Nativity where Mary and Joseph's donkey somehow finds some cocaine, which means they get to Bethlehem a lot quicker, so they find that the inn is not yet fully booked and don't need to go in the stable. And at the same time, crucially, and wonderfully, make people laugh — an intoxicating feeling that stays with me to this day. Who knew that comedy could offer all this? Not me, certainly, and at the time I thought that it couldn't last; it was merely a temporary state of things, an exciting episode in my life, after which I'd have to think about a career elsewhere.

But, surprisingly, miraculously, comedy has led to all manner of unexpected opportunities, working with orchestras, acting in films and TV dramas and sitcoms, appearing on panel shows and dance contests, presenting a whole range of documentaries on anything and everything from wildlife, to history, the arts, both factual and comedic. As someone who has always had a keen wanderlust and a love of nature and the outdoors, it's been a source of great joy that comedy has also taken me all over the world, and along the way offered up all manner of animal encounters. I've watched kangaroos snoozing at dawn on the tarmac of remote outback roads in Australia, cuddled a wombat at an animal sanctuary in Tasmania, had Sulawesi macaques high-five me while filming in Indonesia and cradled the head of a magnificent jaguar, tranquilised for a documentary in Brazil, held the paw of a sun bear in India, narrowly avoided stepping on king coral snakes in the jungles of Colombia and sung to a whale on the Barrier Reef.

All this, along with equally marvellous encounters in these British Isles, watching sea eagles soar over the Isle of Mull and flocks of red knot swirl and morph in huge numbers over the wetlands of East Anglia.

~~~~~~

When I started doing comedy, I thought it might be a wave that I would surf as long as possible, a brief, glorious adventure.

Forty years on, I'm still surfing that wave.

Chapter 13

To the Bat Cave

I was once invited to perform on the little island of Boracay, in the Philippines. It came about when a local entrepreneur, working in a hotel on the island, persuaded the local hotel owners that comedy would be a good way to attract a few holidaying types and might boost the night's bar takings into the bargain. We had met him in Hong Kong, and he'd agreed a deal that would bring me and Kris, along with my fellow comedian, John Moloney, and his wife, Anna, to Boracay to perform a night of comedy.

At that time, there was a regular comedy gig across the South China Sea on Hong Kong Island, in the district of Wanchai. An enterprising local promoter had set up a stand-up night in an Indian restaurant, where patrons bought an all-inclusive ticket. You could enjoy an Indian buffet on the terrace in the warmth of a tropical night, nibbling on samosas while taking in the view across the bay to Kowloon. Then, fully sated, slip indoors to the air-conditioned section where a small stage was set up and comedians would perform. Perfecto!

It was a good arrangement and a gig that, joining several comic friends, was always a fun trip. In my early days of gigging in the 1990s you just went where the work was . . . which usually involved driving up and down the M1 at some point. Comics would often meet by chance in service stations, regular haunts that suited our nocturnal lifestyle. Many a night was spent in a drab motorway cafeteria sharing a reheated plate of chips and stories of gigs, mainly the bad ones. It was what we got into showbiz for. I think this might have been the time I described these places as 'cathedrals of despair'.

But, however fun those gigs at the Aston University student union might have been, even the lure of a 3am balti couldn't compete with an exotic jaunt and the romance of gigs in far-off lands.

Boracay is a little speck of land just off the north coast of Panay Island and south of the Calamian Islands, lapped by the Sulu Sea. It was historically home to about a hundred of the indigenous Ati people who, before the Spanish colonisation of the Philippines, cultivated rice and raised goats. It's in the Western Visayas region in the province of Aklan and about 200 miles south of the capital, Manila. It's about 10 kilometres long, shaped a bit like a dog bone, long and thin in the middle with rounded ends, and only about one kilometre wide at its narrowest point. It has some spectacular white sand beaches, turquoise seas and a warm tropical climate, making it one of the world's most popular tourist island destinations.

The German travel writer Jens Peters, in his 1978 book about the Philippines, described it as 'paradise on Earth', which prompted an influx of intrepid backpackers. Today, those modest numbers have exploded to the current tourist board's target of 2.4 million visitors in 2024. But thirty years ago, this was an odd place for a comedy gig. In fact, I would go so far as to say that it might have been the island's first ever.

The publicity was, I think the word is, rudimentary. One of my 10×8" standard black and white publicity photos had been faxed from my agent in the UK to the hotel, photocopied, and then these flimsy inked pages had been nailed to various palm trees along the beach. Rather than drum up excitement for a comedy gig, it had the effect of making me look like an outlaw or a missing person.

Either way, it had the desired effect and an audience was duly procured, a successful gig with a motley audience of Scandinavians and Americans. But what I really wanted to do was to explore the island.

I have to say, places like this don't normally hold any attraction for me as I quickly get bored sitting on a beach. There has to be another reason to go: a bit of history, a place to dive or snorkel, or especially a chance to encounter some animals.

When we were there, tourism was just being established. There were some hotels and a few guest houses, but there were also swathes of the island that were still untouched. The north, particularly, was a wild place and I asked around about the local wildlife. And that's how I found out about the bat cave.

I managed to find someone who would take me to see the bats and I set off in the evening, on the back of an ancient moped. The engine revved and the machine bumped its way over a rough path that wound increasingly further into dense vegetation. Large spiders' webs occasionally reared up to block our progress. I started to glimpse a rocky escarpment through the vegetation, which loomed ever higher as we pressed on through the dark green anonang trees, which I discovered had a local name of 'bird catcher tree' and had sticky fruit called 'glue berries'. And the rather lovely kulong-kulong coastal beach tree, with its curious pendulous flowers, known in English as the 'lantern tree'.

As we drew nearer, the sound of the bats became louder, until it was a constant screech. Fruit bats are the size of foxes, with pointy vulpine faces and large furry bodies – hence their nickname: flying foxes. On Boracay there are three different species: the common island flying fox, the large flying fox and the golden-crowned flying fox. This last species is endemic to the Philippines, a huge creature with a six-foot wingspan, beautifully golden in colour and, of all these bats, the one that perhaps most resembles an actual airborne fox.

They like to find a dark roosting place, sometimes in huge numbers. And so it was here on Boracay. They'd discovered a large cave on the north coast of the island, and we parked and set ourselves up near the entrance to watch the show.

The noise was deafening. Apparently, flapping while roosting is a common behaviour during this part of the bat's schedule, as is fighting and mating — hence the racket.

At night they would come out en masse to feed and return in the early morning — and what a sight it was, like something from *Jurassic Park* or perhaps your darkest nightmare: thousands of creatures screeching and flapping, leaving the cave in the fast-falling tropical night, where there is no gloaming, just a brief sunset, then blackout.

The entrance to the cave was slippery with guano and the smell was overpowering, ripe and fetid. It really is a smell like no other, making me gag as I nearly slipped head-first into the murk.

This was a spectacle that wasn't often seen by the sun-seekers in the south of the island — and I can see why. Bats get a bad rap and have inspired many a horror story. They seem other worldly and there is something of an evolutionary quirk about them, something half-formed, in

transition. Neither bird nor mammal. A grotesque. A flying thing. A gryphon. A dinosaur. A freak!

Since we were there almost thirty years ago, bat numbers have fallen into drastic decline. When I slithered and stumbled into that cave, there must have been thousands of creatures: a report from 1986 put the number at around 15,000. A recent survey found just 40 bats. This has a knock-on effect on the local habitat, as bats have a key role in the regeneration of trees as they disperse seeds all along their flight path.

According to local conservation groups on Boracay, bats need about a 650-foot buffer zone from human activity, which disturbs their roosting pattern. On this island, which was pretty basic back then, large swathes of the forest have since made way for resorts and golf courses, while helicopter tours over the island have forced the bats to seek out other sites . . .

On the face of it, Boracay could seem like a classic cautionary tale of a tropical island paradise gradually, then rapidly, ruined by mass tourism, which displaces local wildlife, degrades the reefs, the forest and beaches. And yet, from this depressingly familiar refrain comes a few notes of hope. In 2018, the island of Boracay was closed for six months to allow for an environmental clean-up, the installation of better sanitation and the replacement of diesel and petrol-engined vehicles with e-trikes and electric tuk-tuks. It seems to have been a success and bats, which had almost entirely abandoned the island, appear to be returning.

Perhaps the world's busiest tourist spots could all take note. Nature often just needs us to back off for a bit so that it can recover. I am always amazed that despite what seems like environmental oblivion, the natural world has this capacity to renew, to regrow, to regenerate.

Chapter 14

Dormice

In a tough competition with baby seals and hedgehogs, dormice might be the cutest creatures in Britain you've never seen: fuzzy little barrels of delight that spend almost two-thirds of their life asleep; snoozing furballs that I reckon most of you have yet to observe in the wild.

They might be the oldest mammals in Britain, too. The family Gliridae to which they belong has a fossil record that dates back to the early Eocene period. If you're a little rusty on your classification of antiquity, this was any time between around 56 and 33.9 million years ago. The term Eocene derives from the Greek 'eos', meaning 'dawn', so you could say these fuzzballs have been around since the dawn of time. And for most of those millions upon millions of years, they've been asleep.

They have dozed through a whole range of time periods, snoozed through the Renaissance, slumbered on blissfully unaware of the Industrial Revolution, world wars, plagues, even Metallica live at the Milton Keynes Bowl. This is presumably why they're relatively long-lived for a small rodent. Five years is a good innings when you only weigh 25 g and sleep in the bole of a tree for most of the year – especially when compared to the livelier vole, which on average lives for about nine months.

To be fair to the vole, it's not a protected species like the dormouse, plus voles are the staple diet of a variety of predators, from owls to kestrels, hawks, foxes, badgers, domestic cats, non-domestic cats, weasels, stoats and even gulls. It's a testament to the vole's resilience that, despite this volegeddon, there's a healthy 75 million population in the UK. But I digress.

The UK's resident dormouse species is the Hazel Dormouse and the name dormouse most likely comes from the Middle English 'dormous', with the 'dor' prefix probably deriving from the Old Norse slang 'dor' mean-ing 'benumbed'. So a typical Old Norse usage might be,

~~~~~~

'I have dronkene muche meade and I fele I have a dor-brain.' I imagine.

Of the many species of dormouse, the commonest in Western Europe is the one with the snappy taxonomic handle of *Glis glis* or the European edible dormouse, its name a relic of the time when they were considered a delicacy by the Romans. Just a side note here, if I were in charge of dormouse PR, I would maybe consider dropping the 'edible' from the name. Don't want to give people ideas.

The dormouse episode was part of the *Wild Thing* series I made for Channel 4 and we mostly filmed around Cheddar Gorge in Somerset. During the wildlife shoot I was also appearing in a different capacity as Sergeant Turner and his twin brother in the popular feature film *Hot Fuzz*, which was shooting in the nearby city of Wells. It was quite a commute. Getting fitted for a wig and police uniform, fun days filming with director Edgar Wright and Simon Pegg, then driving back to Cheddar to learn about the ancient practice of coppicing. It was peak West Country, one minute embroiled in the problems facing small town petty jealousies and grievances, the next learning about the gradual erosion of proper land management in rural Britain . . . This was very much the issue regarding the hazel dormouse, *Muscardinus avellanarius*.

If you're a bit out of practice with your woodland management skills, here's a brief history of coppicing. First practised in the Stone Age, it's an ancient technique that is an ingenious way to maximise the usage of one tree. The tree is cut down to the stump, which encourages new shoots to grow out, and then eventually the new growth of handy-sized poles is harvested and the process begins again. You may have found yourself in a forest where coppicing has been afoot and seen thinner, newer tree growth emerging from a central stump. Over time the word compressed to become the noun 'copse', meaning a stand of new trees.

Where this applies to dormice, specifically our own UK species, is that this practice was often done with hazel trees, which the mice inhabit. In fact our dormouse is more of an arboreal creature, but when it gets ready for hibernation it prefers a cosy nest on the ground. And a coppiced tree, with its many new growths, provides the perfect cover and security for a tiny sleeping rodent.

Unfortunately for the dormouse the practice of coppicing has been in slow decline since the eighteenth century as our fuel and construction practices changed. There wasn't the same need for firewood, as we relied more on coal or coke, and buildings gradually began using newer materials. These days, coppicing is something of a niche interest and only practised in a few isolated places for specialist requirements, such as staples for thatching and wooden hurdles for managing sheep. Coppicing is the kind of esoterica a bearded comedian might highlight on a show about the need to preserve ancient crafts . . .

The dormouse problem we were trying to address in the programme highlighted another consequence of the changing face of our countryside and indeed of the planet. Dormice hibernate for six months of the year, but milder winters mean they wake up too soon — and have nothing to eat. So their numbers are declining. And dormice are a flagship species, a signifier of the wider health of all the species of the woodland. The removal of old hedges means taking away a wildlife corridor, not just havens for insects, but romantic pathways to new adventures for fuzzy rodents. A problem that exists not just for dormice, but perhaps for many people today . . . where do we meet a partner? With the absence of dormouse Tinder, this was our mission.

My lasting contribution to dormouse introductions was my small part in building a tree-level mesh tube, which connected areas of ancient woodland known to contain a population of dormice, that had been bisected by a quarry access road. Getting the hi-vis on and a hard hat, and being elevated in a cherry-picker on a warm summer's morning is the fun part of dormouse conservation. Wrangling the mesh into place, affixing it, then just standing back and letting Nature take its course was enormously rewarding. I named this project the Tunnel of Love.

Back in my other life, I was on the set of *Hot Fuzz* as Sergeant Turner's surlier twin brother, this time with a magnificent curly wig rather than the one needed for the straight-haired sibling — a double-wigger as we say in the trade.

As I came to the line that has become notorious — 'Nobody tells me nothin'' — I glowered at the camera with a sour, yet heartbreakingly wistful, expression. If you watch the film there is undeniably an impressive range of emotions playing over my face and you can be sure one of them was dormouse related. I was thinking about the Tunnel of Love and hoping for the first tentative steps the dormice might take to a brighter future.

Chapter 15

Mrs Speckles

Some of my fondest memories of pets are of when we kept chickens and, of the many that shared our home, a large brown speckled hen, Mrs Speckles, was my favourite. She became so familiar, she would cluck into the house and then, in a flurry, fly up and perch on my head.

As several people remarked, she probably thought she was sitting on a giant egg, the biggest egg ever. An egg this size would require a lot of sitting and she became quite attached to it.

But what would my head hatch out into?

It was a curious way to be greeted on returning from a tour. I would often get back late and sleep in the next morning. At that time, the chickens were free to roam into the house, as the back door was open in the warmer months to allow the dogs to saunter in and out.

And in truth it felt like a special welcome. The dogs would come and fuss over me for a bit, until they had enough. Teddy, the street dog from Bali (you met him in chapter 11), known as a Bali dingo, but much smaller and slighter than his Australian cousins, was always a bit aloof and would only accept a short spell of fussing, then he'd just wander off, do his own thing. Bulé, his sister, was the same — she would get bored and find something else to do.

Banjar, another street dog, who seemed to be the product of a dingo and a Labrador, was, despite his out-ward bravado, really just a big softie. He would accept any amount of fuss and cuddling. He was clearly embarrassed about accepting this in front of the other dogs, but if they were out on a walk, or out of sight, he would get on my lap, roll over and lie there, getting a belly rub for as long as you could be bothered.

The birds, Molly and Jakob (you'll meet them formally in chapters 21 and 22), would be initially pleased to see me, then irritated in equal measure. 'You're here now, but where were you? So they would require a bit of attention. Molly would feign disinterest for a while, before accepting a grape, or a wing stroke and a scritch. Jakob would just sit on my knee, accept a cuddle, lie on her back, daft as a brush.

But Mrs Speckles was different.

She would cluck around me, accepting the odd crumb, and then hop on the back of the chair, then onto my head, where she would settle down, quite happily. Even as I got up to make tea she'd be there, until I had to shake her off and she hopped down most reluctantly.

Chickens naturally like to perch higher up, so I realised there was an in-built evolutionary advantage to her behaviour. And she was also the top of the pecking order, so she liked to lord it over the other hens. But I like to think it was her way of showing affection. Over the years I've learned that hens will do this and some will even become lap chickens. They've been our boon companions almost as long as dogs.

The farmyard variety of chicken is descended from South East Asian jungle fowl, and was probably domesticated as long as 10,000 years ago. So who's to say one

of my distant forebears, during some enforced domestic incarceration due to a long-forgotten airborne lurgy, didn't sit with a chicken perched atop his already slightly balding head?

In the long days of lockdown, when we were confined to our home, watching the hens was endlessly entertaining. They would scratch a little hollow in the earth and all pile in, on top of each other, like a chicken sleepover party. Slowly they became drowsy and their heads would begin to droop, and then one would get spooked by a noise. With a great cluck they would all suddenly jerk upwards, only to then gradually nod off again.

People would talk of being 'cooped up' in their houses. And I thought, we are literally in a coop, with actual chickens, and all the better for it.

Chapter 16

Whale Shark

In late October I am often to be found touring a stand-up show in Australia, usually every two years, global pandemics permitting. It's become a regular stop on my schedule, a long-distance love affair that began nearly thirty years ago when I first performed at the Melbourne Comedy Festival. That first year didn't always go to plan. Audiences had no idea who I was, or what I did, and festivals tend to have a huge programme of events that are spread out over a myriad of venues in the city, large and small, so often your audience is made up not of fans, or even comedy aficionados, but more your casual browser.

I was in perhaps the smallest room at the festival, a corner of the Melbourne Town Hall called the Powder Room . . . a quaint moniker that conjured up more elegant times when 'ladies' might retire to apply a dusting of powder, adjust their corsets or simply have a bit of a gossip.

On opening night, I was nervous. The room was nearly full, which meant an audience of around 80 people. Who knew if the press were in? Or what people might make of my show? These early gigs were usually a good signifier of how the whole three-week run might go, so, you know, no pressure.

A middle-aged couple, who were sat directly in the front two seats, looked bemused for most of the opening ten minutes. Not hostile, just wearing a look of mild befuddlement, the sort of look you have when you're not quite sure if you're in the right place. Over the years of touring, I've sometimes checked into the wrong hotel, strode purposefully to my room, sat down on a chair and thought . . . Where am I again? The expression I caught on my own face in the mirror matched that of this couple.

After about ten minutes, the couple conferred quietly, then made to get up and shuffled along the front row to leave. In a small room like that, there was no concealing it. A walk-out in the first ten minutes and on my opening night . . . This was not good for my confidence or for business.

I couldn't let the incident pass without comment, so as they shuffled sideways with their coats, I mumbled, 'Was it something I said?'

The bloke smiled back at me with typical Australian openness. 'Oh no mate, yeah, nah, we thought you were the juggler.'

This prompted a gale of laughter and the rest of the gig went off about as well as I could have hoped.

I've always wondered what this couple were thinking during those first ten minutes. His wife may have leaned across to him and whispered, 'There's not much juggling, Darren.' He may have leaned over and whispered, 'Any second now, he's going to balance that guitar on his chin . . .' Then, when that didn't happen, she would have said, 'Still no juggling,' to which he would have countered, 'It's probably some kind of post-modern juggling, where they just juggle with ideas and concepts.' And then his wife would have come back with, 'Well I prefer the more tradi-tional juggling — you know, clubs and balls and fire . . .'

But I guess I'll never know.

I think about that little exchange every time I return to Australia and wonder whether, if that first trip had gone differently, I'd have been encouraged to return. The fact that I did has led to all manner of adventures in this vast country. Another was about to unfold as I pulled on a wet-suit on a boat in North Western Australia as we chugged out to the Ningaloo Reef, preparing to swim with a whale shark.

I've always dreamt about whale sharks, ever since I first heard about them thirty years ago. They are the planet's largest fish, huge, slow-moving titans that cruise the trop-ical oceans. They're no threat to humans as they are filter feeders, sucking in great volumes of water and extracting plankton, krill, fish eggs, and tiny fish and squid.

I'd only ever previously encountered a relative of theirs in the waters of Indonesia, the Tasselled Wobbe-gong — a bottom-feeding carpet shark. The head of this extraordinary creature exactly resembles a mass of coral growth, which makes it an effective ambush predator. It reminded me of those heavily bearded mythical Medieval forest dwellers, like the ancient Green Man motif, that has branches and leaves and vines sprouting from his face.

It settles on the sea bed to wait for unsuspecting fish to stray near its be-tasselled bonce, then, fooled by the camouflage, the fish disappear into a vast maw as it gobbles up anything in the vicinity. The mouth's snap-open-and-shut action reminded me of Oscar the Grouch from Sesame Street.

While diving in Australia, I floated directly over the top of a Tasselled Wobbegong, only to spot it at the last minute. Suddenly, I made out the body and the tail curled behind the head, which was all but invisible.

The whale shark's beautiful star-like patterning on its back is an evolutionary remnant, a reminder of the camouflage needed for its life on the sea bed. Now, however, these markings are a means of identifying different animals and have little useful function any more as a camouflage, given that these gentle giants can reach 60 feet in length. They're hard to miss . . .

The faint buzz of the spotter plane was the only movement in the clear blue sky as I got my snorkelling gear ready. Under the wetsuit I had elected to wear a legging and waterproof shirt combo, both of which sported the rather fetching design of the whale shark markings.

In retrospect, they gave the general appearance of a man who has forgone all dignity for practicality and style. On the face of it, I had boarded the boat in a pair of novelty pyjamas.

As I stood on the jetty waiting for the tender to convey me to the whale boat, a returning group of whale shark enthusiasts were alighting from their excursion. As they filed along the jetty, which was a good few feet away, they all had the chance to get a good look at my whale shark outfit. A round of applause broke out, perhaps the first and only time this has happened due to my sartorial elegance. This I took as a good omen. Sure enough, by the time I'd got my wetsuit and fins on, the plane had radioed to the boat that a smallish adolescent whale shark was heading our way. Time to get into the water.

Every one of my previous trips to Western Australia had been a flying visit as part of a stand-up tour. A couple of days in Perth, maybe a visit to Broome if I was lucky, but always at the wrong time of year to see whale sharks. Their viewing season is a few months of the year, usually from around mid March until August. By the time my Australian touring schedule rolls round in October, the sharks are long gone, languorously swimming off into the blue yonder and their own agenda.

So this tantalising mismatch in mine and the whale shark's schedules has only added to their appeal, only increased their mystique and stoked my desire to see them. It had only taken me about thirty years, but finally I was about to meet them face to face.

I feared that my expectations could not be met; that I'd built this thing up too much. I am in awe of these fish, which have incredible adaptations to their environment. They possess a unique ability to retract their eyes deep into their sockets for protection and even have the facility to change the light sensitivity of their eyeballs. They can adjust the amount of light that enters their eyes to the extent that they can see their way at a depth of 2000 metres, in blue light. And then adjust again to the far end of the spectrum to allow vision in the sunlit shallows.

It's one thing to see any kind of megafauna on TV or a YouTube clip, but another entirely to meet one. Whale sharks may not be a threat to humans in any way and yet, when you're in the water, it's impossible not to feel a frisson of fear when a giant shape approaches you — especially one so smoothly adept in its world, a global marathon swimmer, effortlessly gliding through the planet's oceans. And then there's me, paddling about in a mask and fins and a pair of pyjamas.

The protocol in Australia was quite strict: don't get too close and allow it to swim alongside. Due to my usual ungainliness, it took a while to orientate myself so I would be able to watch it and not get in its way. And here it came, suddenly, a huge flattened head nosing through the water, its back a pattern of hundreds of stars. As it drew near, I had to catch my breath. I momentarily forgot to kick with the fins, as I struggled to take in its size. Even when I did begin to kick, I had no chance of keeping up with it, even though it seemed hardly to be moving. The great tail fin swept from side to side almost in slo-mo, yet it propelled this fish with such effortless speed and grace that I was left for plankton.

I tried to speak, a garbled exclamation of wonder as seawater gurgled into my snorkel and I coughed and spluttered with delight. The shark had disappeared into the blue.

'You want to go again?'

Yes, Yes, YES!

Such is the speed of these creatures, you have only a short window to swim alongside one, after which you have to get out of the water and back onto the boat, which then deposits you ahead of the shark, allowing you another swim-by as it cruises past. This time, my camera at the ready, I positioned myself to take in every detail, from the eyes, positioned at the corners of the mouth, to the enormous tail fin and the stunning ridges that run along the body.

Kicking as hard as I could, I kept pace briefly, before it began to overhaul me and recede into the ray-dappled blue.

'Again!' I shouted, like a small child being swung upside down.

Two more passes and I had no energy left. I hung off the back of the boat, bobbing about in the water as the sun was setting, beaming from ear to ear.

As I hauled myself up onto the ship's transom, a call came through from the spotter plane. A massive great hammerhead shark was swimming near the surface just off the starboard bow . . . We scrambled over to see it, an enormous beast immediately identifiable by its very large upright dorsal fin, its bizarrely shaped head disappearing beneath the waves.

'We can drop you in with it if you'd like, Bill?'

Great hammerheads are not necessarily known as a problem for humans, but they are huge, as big as a great white and are aggressive hunters, and sometimes a little prickly if disturbed. So you need to keep your distance. And I had no kick left in my legs, so I said, 'Just happy with me whale shark, thanks.'

These ancient titans cruise the planet's oceans alone for the duration of their long lifespans, which can be as much as 130 years. To us this seems like a desperately lonely existence, but this is just our own projection. Not having the faculty for self-awareness, they're just swimming along, swishing their tails, living their lives, consumed only by the moment. I feel drawn to whale sharks, their strangeness and beauty, these mysterious, ancient souls roaming the seas. For not only are they almost always solitary, as the sole surviving member of the Rhincodon genus, they are in every sense the last of their kind.

Chapter 17

Outback Story

Once when I was touring in Australia, I had done my back quite badly, to the point where I couldn't drive. It's a long story, but it did end in some interesting encounters with wildlife.

The injury had come about as a result of a piano prop I'd had made for my Edinburgh Fringe Festival show. It was a beautiful piece of kit that looked exactly like a black polished grand piano, except that it was merely a wooden shell. I had this idea to have a grand piano on stage, but one where the lid could be elevated by a hydraulic motor. I'd used this in my previous show, where I had a keyboard stand in the shape of an X-wing fighter from Star Wars. Well, why not eh? Keyboards, particularly electronic ones, are not that aesthetically pleasing, and playing one looks a little ungainly and uncool.

If you've ever seen the electronic pioneers Kraftwerk live you'll know they all wear identical suits and stand behind identical keyboard terminals operating the electronic beats and sounds. One way to look at them is that they subvert the usual rock and roll clichés, while carrying off a cool on-stage aesthetic. Another view is that they look like four bank managers checking their emails.

Anyway, my plan was to have an electronic keyboard concealed within the shell of a grand piano. This would make it prettier and more impressive to look at, while also having the flexibility of all the different sounds afforded by the electronic instrument. Plus I had a plan to place stage lights and a smoke machine inside the body of the prop piano, meaning that as the lid was raised, smoke and light would emanate from within.

The smoke machine sat on the floor under the piano and a flexible plastic hose conveyed the smoke under the lid. When we tried it in rehearsal, I was graced by the presence of comedy legend Ronnie Corbett, who had come into the theatre early to avoid the crowds. As the smoke machine was turned on, our dog, the indomitable Lakeland terrier Rocky, who had hitherto been snoozing on the stage, suddenly leapt to his feet and launched himself at the device, barking furiously and trying to attack the nozzle. Ronnie was slightly perturbed. 'Is this part of the show?' he inquired.

Rehearsal over, the evening performance went well and Ronnie was impressed. I was delighted and honoured to receive the approval of one of the greats, and so I'd say the whole endeavour was a success. Rocky was kept in the dressing room with a ham bone so as not to disrupt the proceedings.

A week after the festival ended, the piano was delivered to my house in London in a van. Because it was made from wood, it weighed quite a bit, but it came apart in two sections, the lid and the body. Individually these were manageable, but joined together it was a struggle for two people to lift.

The van driver was a cheery Scot from Edinburgh, who had travelled down on his own, and I was dismayed to see there was only one of him, as his mate was off sick. So it was just the two of us and the lid was indeed attached to the body. Too late, I realised this as we heaved and hefted it from the van, and walked it towards my front gate. I was walking backwards and I had to reach behind me to open the catch. I instinctively turned to open it and I felt something go in my back . . . DOH!

It was probably the last thing I should have done, but later that day I got on a flight to Hong Kong. By the time I arrived, I could barely walk. I hobbled off the plane and at the hotel my wife filmed me scuttling sideways like a crab (this was in lieu of sympathy). As I found out later, I had ruptured a disc in my lower spine and my body had gone into spasm to protect it. By sheer good fortune, the Hong Kong Rugby Sevens tournament was on, so the place was packed with physios and back specialists, and I ended up in traction, hooked up to a Tens machine. Electronic pulses pinged around my body, and partially alleviated the pain and lack of movement. But this good work was undone as I then had to fly to New Zealand to perform a stand-up tour . . . on my way to a tour in Australia.

By the time I got to Auckland, New Zealand, the back pain was worse. I couldn't sleep with the pain. I couldn't lie down or sit. In fact, the only position that was a little less painful was that demanded by my job — standing up. Two hours of standing and pacing about in front of an audience turned out to be the least uncomfortable part of the day.

Even then, though, it was problematic. I remember on my first night, I went to play my guitar and dropped my plectrum. The pain of bending to get it was too intense, so the song turned into a finger-picked version (actually not a bad version, but still). So I found a doctor, who prescribed some anti-inflammatories and some powerful painkillers.

That night a strange and disturbing thing happened to me on stage. A one-off — a single occurrence that I made sure never happened again. After the show, I was in the dressing room and Kris said to me, 'Is there any reason you told the same joke twice?'

Apparently, I'd done exactly that: once in the first half and again in the second. I had no recollection of this. I think I got away with it — the audience may have thought it was some clever, meta callback routine . . . but in reality it was because my brain was so fogged by the painkillers.

I stopped taking them after that night and every subsequent gig right up to this day. If I'm in pain for whatever reason, I just grit my teeth and hope the adrenaline kicks in, or else channel the pain into a rant about something or other — sometimes it's useful! Anyway, I finished the tour in New Zealand and headed to Australia, still aching . . .

After my tour was over, Kris and I had planned a trip to the outback. We'd hired a car and we aimed to drive about 14 hours north of Melbourne, towards a sheep station somewhere between Hay and Cobar. The instructions were: 'When you get to Ivanhoe, turn right . . . Set your trip counter to zero and when it gets to 140 km, there's a white post in the ground on your left. Oh, and don't drive at night. Make sure you get there in daylight.'

The thought of a fourteen-hour drive on outback roads was not thrilling, but this was something we'd long planned: to see the real Australia, away from cities and people. Just the red dirt, the open road, the desert sky.

I was in so much pain and discomfort that Kris drove, not something she'd done much of prior to this. But all seemed well as we barrelled along rutted, red dirt roads into the bush.

At one point, however, the road seemed bumpier than before and the rutted road seemed to merge with the desert.

Stop for a minute, I said.

As the car rolled to a halt, we turned off the engine and got out.

There was no road. That is, we were not on a road. We had left the road some way back and were now in the middle of the desert.

Kris: 'I thought it was a bit bumpier.'

Me: 'But you didn't say anything?'

Kris: 'Thought it would improve.'

Me: 'How long has it been "a bit bumpier"?'

Kris: ''Bout half an hour.'

At some undisclosed point back down the trail, we had left the road and for half an hour headed out into the unknown. Scary, exciting even, you might think . . . and we had probably just violated one of the terms of the car rental agreement. Either way, here we were, marooned in the Australian outback, no idea where the road was, with half a bottle of water and some wine gums. We had a map, but maps are only useful if you know where you are. And we didn't.

So we laughed, obviously, and joked that we would be found as two skeletons, one with a bony skeletal hand pointing at the map, the other shaking its skeletal fist.

We took a moment to observe our surroundings.

I'd wrongly assumed the desert would be a bleak and empty place, devoid of life, yet the opposite is true. It is, in fact, quite stunningly beautiful and teeming with life. All around, a profusion of different desert flora bloomed, stubbornly clinging to life. The striking red of Sturt's Desert Pea, the bluish button grass, the ancient, gnarled mallee trees conjured a captivating landscape of shapes and colours.

And then, as our eyes swept the horizon, we spotted in the distance a column of dust whirling into the diamond-bright sunlight. A truck! Which meant . . . a road! Hurrah! We were saved . . . so we drank some water and ate a wine gum to celebrate.

Back on the road, giddy with delight, we now encountered another unexpected hazard. The track was littered with dozens of lizards, ancient-looking reptiles about a foot long, with large, gaping mouths. They were blue-tongued lizards, prehistoric creatures whose defence mechanism is to open their huge mouths and show this alarmingly blue tongue while hissing menacingly. This might work for a fox or maybe a dingo, but not for a Mitsubishi Magma doing 80 kmph.

We had to weave around not to hit them, these 'sleepy lizards' as the locals call them, which did indeed have the bleary-eyed demeanour of having been rudely awoken.

After a few more hours' driving, we made a pit stop in the little town of Ivanhoe. Hungry for a snack, we inquired at the local store whether they had any hot food?

'We have pies,' came the drawled response.

Pies it is then. The adventure of losing the road had put us a little behind schedule. So with the words 'don't arrive in the dark' ringing in our ears, we made the final turn-off and set the counter to zero. This was a country track, a dusty red dirt road that wound its way through the low-slung flora. It gets dark quickly in the desert, without much warning, so soon we were in the deep blackness of night in the Australian bush. And now we realised why this was a bad idea.

Various creatures were popping up out of the gloom and kangaroos hopped in front of the car. As we now know,

it's the second kangaroo you need to watch out for, as you're so busy looking at the first one hopping off into the darkness. A wombat had ambled into the road, bugs flew around the headlights . . . and then the most extraordinary animal skittered into our path: an echidna, another unique creature, endemic to these parts.

An indescribable, spiny hedgehog-thing, part anteater, part porcupine . . . a true evolutionary hybrid. It hung around, as we got out to photograph it, this amazing and utterly Australian oddity.

In the dark we nearly missed the white post, which in hindsight could have meant us carrying on all the way north to Cobar, maybe beyond. We arrived at the sheep station to be met by our hosts, who were a little concerned at our late arrival.

'You didn't come up here in the dark, did ya? Crazy poms!'

Chapter 18

Koi

I never thought I'd get attached to fish, but our koi carp are always pleased to see me. I mean, they're pleased to see anyone, but I like to think they've recognised me.

They all have characters and some are pushier than others. When they see you approaching, they scramble to say hello, jostling for your attention.

During my time on *Strictly Come Dancing*, dowsing my toes in the pond was a great relief after a hard day's training. I would haul myself from the car, stumble through the house and slump outside the back door next to the pond. With great effort I'd cast off my shoes and socks, and shuffle forward so my toes dipped into the cool water. Immediately the carp would come to say hello and give me toes a good suck. After being crammed into hard, unyielding ballroom shoes all day, and initially suffering with blistered ankles, my feet thanked me.

I won't lie, it's an odd sensation, having your fingers and toes gently gummed by our gloriously hued fish friends. It's not for everyone, but I choose to see it for what it is — a gesture of fondness from these surprisingly affectionate aquatic nibblers.

Part Four

INDONESIA – A LOVE STORY

I grew up in the West Country, in the town of Keynsham, famous in my youth as the home of football pools
forecaster Horace Batchelor, who advertised his betting
system on Radio Luxemburg. His constant spelling out of
the town Keynsham — 'That's K-E-Y-N-S-H-A-M' — was
immortalised in a song of the same name by Neil Innes's
Bonzo Dog Doodah Band in 1969. Years later, the Bonzos
invited me to perform the song 'Keynsham' with them at
the Shepherd's Bush Empire, in a wonderful moment of
circularity.

After I left school, I travelled a bit, set up a comedy
club in Bath and invited acts to perform there. In that
same year I was performing with a school friend, Toby, in
a double act called the Rubber Bishops and it was after a
gig with the Bishops in Edinburgh that I met Kris, who
then moved to London. After a brief spell co-habiting on
a houseboat on the Thames we moved to Hammersmith in
west London and have lived there ever since.

Travelling east to seek adventure began in my youth.

Even as a teenager, a late-night excursion to Leigh Delamere services felt like we were on the outer limits of our home turf, as if we'd ventured into the exotic by way of the M4 Eastbound.

All-night pinball!

Even further towards the Orient were the faraway towns of Marlborough, Didcot . . . even Reading seemed impossibly romantic.

And right at the end of the M4, like some fantastical kingdom of Oz, was the capital itself: tempting, danger-ous, unknown. A place of infinite possibility, enticing and exciting . . .

It was irresistible, a tractor beam that drew you to it with the promise of bright lights and adventure . . . The Underground!

Many years later, work as a comic took me overseas, and the pull of further east again drew me to a country that Kris and I fell in love with: Indonesia.

But we nearly never went there at all.

I was performing in Hong Kong and had a couple of weeks before my next bookings back home, so we decided to explore the area a bit and initially we were headed for Thailand, a place neither of us had ever been. But on our preferred day of departure, all the flights were booked, so instead, on a whim, we headed to Bali, another new place for us. Such is the way of travel: a random occurrence often proves to be serendipitous.

Initial impressions of Kuta were not what we were after. I'd been touring in the busy cosmopolitan cities of Australia and then Hong Kong, which is the most densely populated place on the planet, so we were craving something different, the outdoors, the natural world, the path less taken . . .

Indonesia is a nation of around 17,000 islands, spanning 2000 miles from Papua in the east to Sumatra in the west, and strung out along lines of volcanic activity giving it the nickname Ring of Fire.

On the recommendation of a tourist guide at the airport, who was actually from Ambon, we caught a domestic flight to Makassar, the regional capital of South Sulawesi, the central of the islands in the Indonesian archipelago. From there we headed further east, to Ambon, and here we met two couples who were travelling to the Banda Islands.

So we just tagged along, as we seemed to be the only six westerners in the city. After a night in a little guest house, we all bought tickets for the huge passenger ferries that ply these waters. After an eight-hour voyage, we arrived at the Banda Islands, marooned in one of the deepest parts of the ocean and centred around a palm tree-covered, gently smoking volcano, Gunung Api – 'Fire Mountain'.

The sight of those islands, rising almost like a mirage from the endless blue of the surrounding ocean, is one I'll never forget. A sight that would have greeted the early Arab traders, the Portuguese, the British, the Dutch as they sought out its rare spice, nutmeg. A view that greeted Victorian biologist Alfred Wallace on his journey of scientific discovery. A view that greeted the writer W. Somerset Maugham and left such an impression on him that he chose Banda as the location for his novel, *The Narrow Corner*.

A mirrored lagoon, ringed by tropical islands shadowed by a cloud-wreathed volcano from which emanates a wisp of smoke. A colonial Dutch fort perched on a hill, wooden dugout fishing boats gently puttering home at sunset, a gaggle of excited children, waving and jumping into the water, a sight which, I imagine, hadn't changed much since Wallace first arrived here in the 1850s.

Confronted with this view, this stunning gem of a place, we decided on a whim to get married . . . And thus began our connection with this country, which continues to today.

The people we've met, the adventures, the extraordinary wildlife, the animal encounters have all tugged a little on the heart over the years. This huge and fascinating country always reveals something new, and you find yourself drawn back, as the writer Jon Swain said of Asia, by the 'warmth of humanity'.

Chapter 19

Birdwatching in Seram

Seram is a large island in the Moluccan Archipelago in Eastern Indonesia, known locally as Nusa Ina, 'Mother Island'. It's the largest island in the Maluku province and contains a huge amount of bird species that can be seen nowhere else on Earth. At about 6,600 square miles in size, a bit bigger than Yorkshire, it's teeming with life. It's also the home island of our very own Molly, the Moluccan cockatoo (chapter 21 is all about Molly). This, in part, was the reason we were skimming over a glassy sea in a speedboat from the regional capital, Ambon. Our plan was to trek into the forest, be hoisted 120 feet up onto a viewing platform, then wake up to the dawn chorus in the forest canopy . . .

Our travel companions were a mix of friends we've made over our many adventures through Indonesia. On this occasion, our main point of contact and tour guide was the estimable Djuna, a Californian potholer, caver and photographer, and it was she who had set up these viewing platforms on Seram. This could not have been easy, getting local bird-trappers to turn into bird guides, but such is her calm, persuasive manner, that is exactly what she had done. Using her caving experience she'd figured out a safe way to hoist guests and birders up to the platform.

The first challenge was just getting there. From Jakarta we flew to Ambon, a bustling market city spilling over with sights and sounds and smells. The spice markets are a thing of wonder, a vivid palette of colour and taste from where so many exotic flavours made their way to the tables of Europe during the Dutch colonial days. It's also a transport hub where the huge passenger ferries, vast lumbering PELNI ships with names like the *Bukit Siguntang* and *Rinjani*, named after the mountains of Indonesia, connect all points east.

Up to around the fifteenth century, Seram was under the authority of the Sultan of Ternate, based on Halmahera

Island to the north. Christian missions run by the Portuguese started appearing in the sixteenth century, and in the seventeenth and eighteenth centuries the island came under the control of the Dutch, as part of their Vereenigde Oostindische Compagnie — the Dutch East India Company or the VOC for short. The population is a mix of Christian and Muslim. In one part of town you can hear the call to prayer, in another, Christmas carols being sung, but it hasn't always been a peaceful co-existence. In 1998, sectarian violence swept through Maluku and the neighbouring islands, causing many deaths and huge amounts of displacement. Since the Malino Accord in 2002, though, things have returned to normal and a peaceful state of affairs has prevailed.

Seram is not a long hop from the regional capital Ambon, so a speedboat was enough to get us there, followed by a trip by car around the island to our first waypoint, the village of Sawai and a homestay built on stilts looking out over a turquoise lagoon, ringed by a reef.

A white-bellied sea eagle was perched on a tree branch near the shore and I watched, transfixed, as he launched himself on a hunting raid. Swooping low over the waves, he plucked his quarry from the water and returned to his branch to enjoy his spoils. A majestic sight. Except he didn't appear to be that keen on whatever he'd caught. I got my binoculars out and zoomed in to see that his 'catch' was actually a white sports sock. I think eagles always tend to look angry with everyone and everything, but this one had good reason.

The next leg of our voyage into the interior was a boat ride upriver. Packed into two narrow wooden skiffs with outboard motors, we roared off at dawn, making a wide arc across the bay and into the mouth of the river estuary. More white-bellied sea eagles saw us off, along with a few great frigatebirds circling high overhead.

After about half an hour the river began to narrow and we could see the wildlife emerging from the jungle. An enormous estuarine crocodile sat motionless on the bank, eyeing us with unblinking contempt as we slowly cruised past. 'Never get out of the boat. Absolutely goddamn right, unless you were going all the way. Kurtz got off the boat, he split from the whole programme . . .' Sorry, just reciting lines from the film *Apocalypse Now*. That film is never far from my thoughts and I'll find any excuse to quote from it. Gliding upriver by boat into a jungle interior, it seemed appropriate . . .

We pressed on as the channel became ever narrower, and we had to navigate huge fallen trees and a mass of strangler fig branches and lianas overhead. Eventually the boats could go no further, so we hauled out onto the bank, loaded up our backpacks and started to hike. Deer skittered away from the water's edge, we heard the call of jungle fowl, sulphur-crested cockatoos, bright green and red flashes of eclectus parrots, while huge Blyth's hornbills flapped overhead: living dinosaurs, modern day pterodactyls. Forest kingfishers, green leaf birds, rollers, flowerpeckers, spiderhunters and various sunbirds fluttered and screeched and filled the jungle with their calls.

We were walking through primal rainforest, the tangled layers of old jungle growth. Enormous spiked succulents and huge bamboo trees lined our way as we stepped over ferns and moss-covered fallen trees. We marvelled at huge ants, katydids and beetles, and fast-flying birdwing butterflies that allowed us only a glimpse of their fragile beauty as they flitted in and out of the filtered sunlit glades.

Indonesia has the second highest biodiversity on the planet, after Brazil — and the highest number of mammal species of any country. Indonesia has nearly 30,000 plant species in total and over 200 types of bamboo alone. This enormous profusion of species is what drew the great Victorian naturalist Alfred Russel Wallace to Indonesia and ultimately what allowed him to crack the theory of evolution, independently of Charles Darwin.

After four hours of walking through the steaming jungle we arrived at our camp: a few simple huts by a clear, shallow river, fed by a beautiful waterfall. We gratefully shed our packs and clothes, and luxuriated in the cool water.

The plan was to be hoisted up that night, spend the night in a hammock high in the canopy and observe the splendour of the dawn chorus the next morning. But not to be too indelicate, I was, as Samuel Pepys might say in his diary, 'much troubled by a looseness'. The only 'facilities' on this 12-foot × 12-foot platform was a small portable toilet, artfully screened off from the main platform with a tarpaulin. My natural British embarrassment prevented me from putting myself or indeed my travelling companions through an unnecessary gastric ordeal. So I chose to spend the night in the little hut at ground level, sleeping *en plein air.*

The next morning I felt much better. I had slept surprisingly well on a solid wooden bench and despite some biting insects nibbling me during the night I was in much better fettle.

With the entire party ensconced 120 feet up a tree some distance away, I had that rare moment on a jungle trek — privacy. I thought, well this won't last long, I'll make the most of it.

Stripping off entirely, I waded into the shallow river and showered under the waterfall, letting the morning sun warm my skin. With bright green parrots flying overhead and not a soul around I felt like I was bathing in a kind of Eden, where I was the only human in this pristine paradise.

At this moment of rapture two Australian blokes suddenly appeared out of the jungle.

One of them stopped in his tracks: 'Jesus Christ, it's Bill Bailey!'

I have been recognised in some odd places, but this was about as remote as it gets. I had to stand waist deep in the water and make awkward conversation until I could get to my clothes . . .

They were yachtsmen, sailing their boat around the islands, and had made the trek because they'd been told about the waterfall.

'What the bloody hell are you doing here, Bill?'

After a while I gathered my clothes, said my goodbyes and headed over to the platform tree. Being hoisted up in a caving harness is uncomfortable, but would have been impossible with my . . . *condition* the day before.

Once aloft, the real purpose of this entire endeavour was revealed in all its glory. Hawks, eagles and other raptors soared above a myriad of lizards, insects and hornbills. And then, finally. The sight we had travelled halfway around the world to see. Not just one or two, but a flock of huge, pinkish-white Moluccan cockatoos, foraging and screeching and fossicking in a way that was so familiar to us from our own dear Molly and yet also strange, as this was wild behaviour. A glorious and moving moment, to see them in their beautiful home, it gave me a pang of sadness that Molly couldn't ever return — but it also made us more determined than ever to give her the best life we could.

The nibbling insects on my leg the night before turned out not to be from mosquitos but sand flies, which are arguably worse. The bites became ulcerated and refused to heal, and this went on for weeks. Eventually, I ended up at a tropical disease clinic and the doctor became very animated and, I have to say, delighted.

'Jesus Christ, it's Bill Bailey!

No, he didn't say that.

'Ah, yes, this is subcutaneous leishmaniasis! Haven't seen this for AGES!'

This is a nasty parasite carried in the sandfly bite, though happily for me it's quickly cured with a hatful of antibiotics. Mine was only the variant that causes infinite ulceration if left untreated. The other leishmaniasis is nastier, he admitted. With that one, the parasites migrate to your eyeball and can cause blindness.

So, every cloud . . .

Chapter 20

Tarsiers

I was making a documentary about Alfred Russel Wallace who, as I mention elsewhere in the book, independently of Darwin discovered the mechanism for evolution — natural selection.

Part of this programme involved demonstrating how animals can change and adapt in remote environments, and one such creature is the remarkable tarsier, a small, velvety-furred primate: agile, bony-fingered and wide-eyed.

These saucer-eyed curiosities inhabit the forests of maritime South East Asia. They might look like little gremlins, but they are quite ruthless stalkers of insect prey. They really are unlike anything I've ever seen before or since.

We were on the Indonesian island of Sulawesi, where parasitic, strangler fig trees had gradually engulfed ironwood trees and in the process created a perfect habitat for tarsiers. During the day, these Gollum-like primates would hole up among the many intertwining branches, perfect cover for squirrelly predators.

Tarsiers are a bit bigger than a gerbil and as night falls they emerge from their daytime hidey holes to hunt, pursuing insects through the tree canopy. They have elongated feet or *tarsus* bones, from which they get their name. This adaptation gives them specialised skills in vertical clinging and leaping, which are perfect for an arboreal predator.

In evolutionary terms, they are very much a work in progress. Their eyes are obviously adapted for maximum vision at night and, in fact, their sight is their greatest asset: the larger the eyes, the better the night vision and the more chance of catching prey at night. Amazingly, each of a tarsier's eyes is bigger than its brain. So maths is not its strong point, but it can spot a cricket at a hundred paces.

Our plan was to film a sequence of them hunting grasshoppers and to show their usefulness to Wallace as

a creature 'in transition' that was visibly adapting to its environment.

We spent the day in the humidity of the Sulawesi jungle and, as darkness fell, the sounds of the night insects began, rising to a symphony of cheeping and croaking.

An unlucky grasshopper was procured as bait and we waited. In the deep darkness of the forest, the tarsiers began to emerge from their arboreal hiding places. I stood with my back to the tree as a tarsier appeared, close to my shoulders. As I watched, it leapt a huge distance and, in an instant, had grabbed the grasshopper and begun to devour it with fearsome little teeth.

The whole incident took less than a couple of seconds, so for the programme we slowed it to 50 frames per second, to be able to better see the action. It was an amazing encounter, a unique and rare experience, as these creatures are gradually becoming more endangered and are limited to only a few places in this part of the world.

The sequence was animated in the final show, to illustrate how the tarsier's eyes are crucial to its survival and have adapted over time to be so much bigger. This little sequence was a delight to film and it was fascinating to be close to these creatures, with the added thrill that this was a scene that Wallace himself might have witnessed.

The creatures themselves wouldn't have changed much in the intervening 150 years, and so, like much of Nature, despite the slow, generational adaptation of natural selection, we are reminded, too, of its timelessness; this vast panoply of life that spans human lifetimes, centuries and millennia; that delights and beguiles us in the present, but also provides a living link to the past, to our past.

Chapter 21

Molly in the Hotel

At one time, it seems an age ago now, we only had one parrot.

I mentioned her briefly a couple of chapters ago: she was named Molly and was a Moluccan or salmon-crested cockatoo, which is endemic to the forested, Indonesian island of Seram.

I once had a conversation with fellow bird-lover Bill Oddie about endemics − that is, species that are extremely localised and only found in a specific area, such as Molly and her kin. 'They're so exclusive, they are their own worst enemy,' he said, or choicer words to that effect.

Endemics don't venture beyond their range, which can make them vulnerable to disease, genetic weaknesses due to inbreeding or, in the Moluccan cockatoo's case, to poaching. They have a specific adaptation that binds them to their habitat, which if all goes well, means they can thrive. But their lack of adaptability means that due to the shifting patterns of zoological threats in the world, they are often endangered.

They are really magnificent-looking creatures: one of the largest of the cockatoo family, with white plumage and yellow underwings, culminating in a livid salmon-pink crest atop their heads. Molly came to us via a pet shop, where she'd ended up after various owners couldn't cope with the challenge. She'd been raised in captivity in the UK and had only known this life. Unfortunately, it wouldn't have been feasible to release her, even if we had wanted to. Cockatoos are very intelligent, but they need to be taught survival skills and how to forage for food by their parents. Captive birds have missed out on this vital bit of development and sadly wouldn't survive. So we vowed to make Molly's life as good as it could be.

Parrots can generally be quite destructive and messy eaters, so if you haven't arranged their accommodation to allow for this, you're in for a shock. Molly got out once, and nibbled the number 8 off the phone handset. In those pre-mobile phone days we lost touch with all the people with an 8 in their number.

Cockatoos are clever creatures, renowned for their curiosity and sociability. They need constant stimuli. They like to be around you and to see what's going on. They are creatures of habit and need a good night's kip in a quiet spot. When Molly first arrived she acted up for three months, hurling her food around and generally causing chaos. Apparently over the course of her life so far, most people could only tolerate this for about three months, then she was moved on.

But when the three months were up, she'd figured out that this was where she was going to stay and her behaviour changed completely. She became sweet-natured, funny and playful. She liked to sing. She liked elegiac music, like Elgar; slow, romantic sounds. She would sway on her perch and burble away tunelessly like someone on the train singing with headphones on.

We also learned that Moluccan cockatoos have one of the loudest screeches of any bird, reaching up to 135dB, which is almost as loud as a jet engine at 140dB just 100 feet away. When she decides to have a bit of a 'moment' and start screaming, it does sound quite alarming. On a few occasions I was on the phone to an interviewer and they asked, 'Is everything ok?'

'Yes, yes, it's just the parrot.'

Once our two birds were in a large cage each, side by side. Molly and Jakob, the odd couple. Jakob, loud and brash and always affectionate, who loved loud pop music. Molly, quieter, more thoughtful, who preferred romantic cello music. On one of the first occasions we'd left them in these cages, we came back to find that Jakob had figured out how to open one of the little hatches, had got out and was perched triumphantly on top of the cage. Molly, on the other hand, had managed to open *all* the doors and all the hatches . . . which all lay hanging open. But she remained perched *inside* the cage, as if to make the point, 'I could leave any time I like, but I choose to stay.'

*

We used to take Molly with us everywhere in her travel case. A clear, Perspex travel holder designed for parrots. American made.

It was called a Wing-E-Bago™.

In the leaflet that came with it, it claimed to be bullet proof.

One weekend in Brighton, we left Molly in the Wing-E-Bago™ with the cover over it and nipped downstairs to get some breakfast. As we later discovered, the nice housekeeping lady had come by to check the towels. Molly, in her cod-posh voice, had called clearly, 'Hello!' which had caused the lady to run down the corridor shrieking.

Later that day, not wanting to cause more consternation among the hotel staff, we took Molly to the pictures. It was a tense psychological thriller, *What Lies Beneath* . . . appropriately for what was under the cover at our feet.

At certain moments, the soundtrack veered away from disturbing, Hitchcockian single cello notes to be replaced by slow, elegiac, romantic strings, which of course Molly found to her liking.

She began singing, in a childlike, 'la la la' type of way.

A couple of people looked round, so I covered for her.

I sang a few notes to style it out. 'La la la!'

I heard a bloke mutter under his breath to his girlfriend, 'That weird bloke's singing.'

Not the first or last time I've heard this.

Chapter 22

Jakobi

For many years now, Molly's great friend has been Jakobi, a Triton cockatoo and a long-term pet who has quite simply become one of the family. She was named onomatopoeically, after the sweet little chirrup she gives: 'Jakobi!' Her remarkable life began in the wilds of Papua, the Indonesian half of New Guinea. At some point she was caught in a snare, which is sadly the fate of many pretty and entertaining tropical birds, trapped for the pet trade and trafficked and sold throughout South East Asia.

A British helicopter pilot who was working in Papua for a local mining company spotted her tethered to a perch in a local market and, seeing her hobbling on one foot in a miserable state, took pity on her. Realising her injury meant she would sadly no longer survive in the wild, he whisked her away to a new life. She ended up flying back to England with him in the relative luxury of Garuda Airlines in a duffel bag on his lap. I don't know whether she sampled the in-flight meal of nasi goreng or watched a movie, but she was now living the high life. Sometime after arriving, her helicopter-pilot saviour got a job with the Sultan of Oman, so Jakobi's international adventures began again. She ended up being fussed over in the Sultan's palace gardens for seven pampered years.

By the time she came to live with us, she'd been with the pilot and his wife for 25 years, though by then they were sadly no longer able to look after her.

As we had already had Molly and the community of rehoming parrots is quite small, our names came up as potential new guardians of this feisty and sparky bird.

Life with her was initially tough. She was terribly out of sorts, and not being with her family meant she hollered and screeched for weeks on end. All the research reading we did about these birds talks about how cockatoos are intelligent and affectionate birds, but you have to persevere. And persevere we did!

I will say straight out that I'm generally not in favour

of caged birds, mainly because in our experience so many of them don't have a great life. There's too often a basic lack of understanding about the birds' needs. Kris especially read every bit of research she could get, from how to handle birds, to what stimuli they need, the correct diet, where they might sleep at night and so much else. As with our other parrot, Molly, a return to the wild was not an option. Jakobi had been captured as quite a young bird and habituated to humans for so long, so she wouldn't have had the necessary skills to survive in the wild.

When she first came to us, Jakobi's diet was not great. She liked potato waffles, tinned sweetcorn, and chips . . . it seemed she'd turned into a perpetual student.

The sight of this funny little bird, with her bright sulphur crest, her powder-blue eye shadow, wobbling on one foot as she balanced on her perch, hollowing out a chip was a sight to behold. This was obviously not a sustainable diet so we gradually weaned her off it. Now the real joy is seeing her relish the food her parents must have raised her on, and the occasional glimpse of her wild self. Triton cockatoos' diet consists mainly of fruit and seeds, but they will eat the occasional insect. If a moth flies past, she sometimes grabs it and gobbles it down, spluttering with delight, much to Molly's disgust. It was a great surprise one day when I presented her with a giant mealworm: she expertly nipped it and hollowed it out, exactly as she'd done with the chip. So for all that time, the wild bird's instincts had been exercised in her love of skinny fries.

*

As I write this, she is lying on her back on my lap, getting a cuddle.

Of all our birds, I'd say she's now the most affectionate, the easiest to deal with and the one who loves the attention. She's over fifty years old now, having had quite a life, and she most likely will be with us for many more years to come.

As all the parrot books say, you never really own a parrot, you are just their companion for a while.

Chapter 23

Tiger on the Loose

I am trying to coax one of our dogs, Tiger, off the bed so I can lie on it. He's a large, ungainly bag of bones, half greyhound, half Indonesian street dog. Tiger is a rescue case, so when we first got him I put up with this nonsense as I felt sorry for him. 'He's had a hard life,' I would say. 'He's making up for the years of sleeping rough on the streets.' Now, after many years of doggie comfort, healthy food, exercise and love, this sympathy act he pulls is wearing a bit thin.

I look directly at him, jerk my thumb in the direction of the bedroom door and say firmly, 'Out!' He cocks his head in mock incomprehension, looks around as if I might be speaking to someone else, but otherwise there's not a flicker of movement.

Time for the secret weapon. For some reason, he dislikes cameras and phones. I don't know why, it's one of those odd quirks you discover with rescue animals. Anyway, it's a sure-fire way of getting him to move. I pull out my phone and start snapping away. As soon as he hears the sound of photos being taken, his lanky frame starts to stir; he draws himself up with an air of exaggerated disdain, stretches and totters off in a huff.

I am constantly deleting dozens of out-of-focus photos of Tiger that commonly feature the back of his head, his tail or a backwards resentful glance. Why do we put ourselves through all this for these creatures? Is it their wagging tails? Their dopey, imploring faces? Their constant capacity for public embarrassment?

We are all well aware by now of how they've been our pals for thousands of years; how they offer us love, unconditionally; how they seem to be empathetic and read our moods, and so much more. You have to be out in all weathers walking the dog, so pet owners tend to be more physically fit and are generally more socially outgoing. All this has positive knock-on effects that can counteract loneliness and even boost your self-esteem, making you possibly more attractive and generally brilliant all round (ok, this might be debatable).

Many studies will tell you this, and that's all marvellous, but what they don't mention is that you'll have dog hair on your clothes and poo bags in the pocket of every coat you own. A dog treat will get mixed up with your loose change, which will raise eyebrows with other shoppers at the twenty-four-hour garage when it appears you're trying to pay for an ice cream with a dog biscuit.

'Saw that Bill Bailey up the garage, trying to buy a Magnum with a Bonio. He's losing it,' said 'a source'.

The thing I love about dogs is that you get so much back from them — if you put the hours in, they repay you threefold. Not so much the praying mantis we had for a while. Every night I'd talk to him, tell him about my day, maybe sing a selection of eighties hits to him. He just stared indifferently at me from within his glass tank.

For some reason or other, we had a few giant land snails once. They lived quite companionably in a glass tank on top of the washing machine. I used to think I had formed a bond with one of them, as he seemed to respond when I whistled for him and would slide towards me expectantly.

But really, who was I kidding? Turns out, snails don't have ears. They have, though, got an excellent sense of smell. I still like to think he recognised me, but it was probably just the lettuce in my hand.

Now, even though he loved his home comforts, Tiger's time as a free spirit, living on the streets, never quite left him.

He was a challenge from the start. He was an escaper, a bolter, a repeat offender, a wandering soul. Tiger had a distinctive brindle marking down his spindly back, hence his name. We reckoned he was part Bali dingo, part greyhound and maybe a hint of giraffe. When we first saw him in the dog pound in a village in rural Bali, we instantly fell for this curious looking oddball. This place, Bali Animal Rescue Centre, has been the source of several scruffy looking mutts who have captured our hearts over the years.

He had an aura about him, a silent, authoritative presence that let the other dogs know to back off; but he also had a mournful look in his eyes, a melancholy borne of a keen sense of injustice. Tiger had been a domestic pet at some point, but for reasons unknown he'd been sleeping on the street for about a year.

We were drawn to this gentle giant, who always stood apart from the general pack of rough-and-tumble dogs. Standing a head and a half taller than most, he would stare intently through a little crack in the compound door, trying to catch a glimpse of the horizon.

He was like a lifer, pacing out his time in the exercise yard, keeping his nose clean, staying out of trouble.

He reminded me of the character Chief in the film *One Flew Over the Cuckoo's Nest*: a quiet, brooding presence.

*

When he arrived to stay with us with his companion, a fluffball called Louie, his thin coat — with the texture of a worn shammy-leather — was ill-equipped for the chilly London winter. I was nervous about how our established gang of Bali dingos would react to their new pound pals as I drove them through the darkened streets to our home. Once through the door, Tiger sloped off to our bedroom, unnoticed, for a long snooze. Louie was delighted to meet the gang, with whom she got on immediately.

Tiger slipped out to the garden to relieve himself, and

as he padded back inside the dingos finally noticed him and squared up to this odd-shaped stranger.

Tiger was feeling the cold and puffed out his chops. He stood, unmoving before these nervous dingos. We didn't quite know how this might pan out. Would they accept him? Tiger just fixed them with his usual doleful gaze. They inched forward . . . a standoff. Then, poor Tiger's teeth started chattering. Our gang considered this strange-looking ogre, his teeth clacking like castanets . . . and decided he was ok. His status as 'probably harmless, but so weird let's not find out' was sealed, and thus he became part of the household.

He was a bag of nerves and had clearly been traumatised by loud bangs. A car backfiring or a skip-lorry bouncing over a speed bump in the street would make him jump.

This, we later discovered, was due to gunshots.

At a time when there was a rabies scare on Bali, local authorities were taking the drastic step of shooting suspected animals, but sadly this cull wasn't very targeted and any stray dog who was unlucky enough to land in their sights was dispatched.

*

So, Tiger had already been through a traumatic time in his life when he came to live with us, back home in London. For the first few months, he just kept his head down. He ate, slept, woofed at the other dogs to keep back and that was that. His tail hardly moved, as if the wag had gone out of it.

Eventually, after months of perseverance, I had a breakthrough. I was out in the garden one day, encouraging him to play. Up to that point, this had consisted of me hopping about excitedly with various toys while he stood there impassively, a look of disdain — or perhaps pity — on his face. But that day, he suddenly put his front two legs down on the ground in what's known as a 'play bow'.

I whooped and immediately crouched down with him. He turned into a giddy pup and charged off round the garden, wobbling alarmingly on his lanky legs.

Even though he put on a bit of weight and his demeanour softened over the years, he was always a bit of a beanpole eccentric. His long back sagged in the middle, like a cow, and his thin legs looked like they could barely hold him up. When he shook himself, his hind legs would almost give way with the effort.

Tiger had large brown eyes and often looked a bit glum, but gradually his sweet nature came through, to the point that old ladies in the park would come up to us just to see him and give him treats, which he accepted gratefully.

On many occasions walking the other dogs I'd be spotted and his elderly fan club would inquire, 'Ooh, is Tiger with you?'

A bit like another of our dogs, Teddy (see chapter 11), he'd never really got the memo about coming back after an adventure. While our other rescues would always return, at least for a treat, he'd wander off, loping into the bushes, and he had to be clipped on his lead and walked out, otherwise he'd be there all day.

He loved being out and about and was very good with other dogs, who tended to defer to him anyway. He had a quiet authority, an air of 'I'm the boss', and the other dogs went along with it.

But we couldn't trust him off the lead.

One time, the door was slightly ajar and he saw his chance and was off. We only realised too late, by which time he was long gone.

I went out in the car scouring the streets for this errant

hound. It was a Saturday morning and we searched all day, but to no avail. At about 9pm we got a call saying they'd read the number on the collar tag.

'We've got your dog,' they said.

'Oh thank goodness for that. Where are you?'

'Ealing.'

He had travelled *miles*, which would have involved crossing roads, parks and the busy North Circular road west of London, and he was now standing in a street near Ealing Broadway, exhausted and a bit sheepish.

He jumped into the car without any resistance and I definitely got a sense of embarrassment from him. He'd gone out for a little wander, got a bit lost, panicked and kept going. 'I've messed up here, haven't I?' his expression seemed to say.

But it was a warning — don't let him get out again! Except . . .

It was Christmas Day and for some reason, which I can't really remember, we'd decided to have a Hawaiian-themed Christmas. I know! Why? The reason was that old classic: it seemed like a good idea. We had Hawaiian table decorations in the form of a Santa wearing a Hawaiian shirt, we had Hawaiian food and floral decorations. It was as if Maui had come to Hammersmith.

So, Christmas morning, my friend the American comedian Rich Hall and his family were coming over. They arrived — they had got the Hawaiian memo and were dressed accordingly — and began unloading presents and children, and a large trifle in a heavy glass bowl. Doors were propped open to allow easier ingress and I could sense that Tiger was just waiting for his moment.

Once all the bags and presents had been loaded in, the final item was the trifle. Wrangling the bowl, I made my way up the garden path.

And there was Tiger, poised at the door.

He'd figured out there was a gap in the fence to our neighbours' front garden in the far corner of ours. I edged towards it, clutching the trifle.

If you'd like to imagine the scene being played out over a spaghetti western film soundtrack at this point, be my guest.

Then I noticed the front gate was slightly ajar.

Guitar twang!

He noticed that I had noticed . . .

He glanced at the gate.

Looked back at me.

Tense harmonica chord!

I took a tiny step forward, balancing the trifle, as my eyes narrowed . . .

He edged a step forward.

Trumpet flourish!

And he was *off*, sprinting towards the gate.

I moved to intercept.

Huge brass and guitar combo!

At this point, and with the benefit of hindsight, the main life lesson I learned from this incident, was 'Never run with a trifle.' No good will come of it.

No one needs a trifle that badly that you have to sprint with it. And if you *do* find yourself holding a trifle and are suddenly required to run, as I was, please just put the trifle down. Honestly, it's not worth it.

I had an audience by now. Kris had come out to check on me, Rich was standing in the garden; Rich's wife, Karen, and my son, Dax, both appeared at the door.

As Tiger lolloped down the path to the front gate, I moved to intercept him. With an impressive turn of speed from a standing start I lurched across the garden, still holding the trifle, chilled by the December morning against which my flimsy Hawaiian shirt offered no real protection.

Fixing a slightly raised paving slab around the front pond was one of those jobs I'd always said I would get round to doing. Not a priority. I mean, who's going to be running round the pond with a large dessert bowl?

My foot caught on the offending lip of the raised slab and I became briefly airborne. Holding the trifle out in front of me like a rugby ball, I sailed horizontally through the cool morning air and perhaps the word 'Nohhhhhhhh!' may have escaped my lips.

At any rate, it had the effect of me scoring a try, with a trifle — a *tryfle*? Or, to Rich, it may have looked like a perfect touchdown in American football, if the game had a seasonal variation using party food instead of a ball.

I hit the deck with a thump, the bowl shattered and a quantity of trifle ricocheted off the path and up my nose. I also got a face full of earth as I landed half in the flower-bed. The bowl had landed on my outstretched thumb, which would later require a trip to A&E. Other than that, apart from the loss of the trifle, no great harm done.

As I picked myself up, retrieving sponge cake and earth from my nose, those who had witnessed the whole thing realised I was not seriously injured and the laughter began — and didn't let up the entire day. It lulled briefly now and then, but then someone would start up again, leading to more giggling, more cackling and eventually snorting.

We spent the next few hours of Christmas Day combing the streets calling for Tiger, a merry band of us, all dressed in Hawaiian shirts and grass skirts, eventually luring him back by waving a packet of ham around on a street corner. On more than one occasion we were asked, 'Are you filming a sketch?'

After these breakouts, we vowed that Tiger couldn't be trusted and thereafter we'd keep a close eye on him and always keep him on the lead. I mean, we wouldn't let him loose again . . . would we?

Chapter 24

Tiger in the Lakes

After his double escape and his unwillingness to come back when called, you might not think that taking Tiger on a walking holiday in the Lake District was a great idea. But he'd calmed down a lot by then. He was a lovely, placid-natured dog and on the lead he was absolutely fine. Our other little rescue at the time, Louie, was not such a calm prospect. She was a very sweet little Kintamani mountain dog from the volcanic region of that name in the mountainous north of Bali.

The Kintamani are a distinctly different species to the more common Bali dingo and are characterised by a shaggier coat to protect against the cooler climes at altitude, a robust body and sure-footedness.

As we checked into our self-catering cabin, I held grave reservations about the whole endeavour. Louie was a sweet dog, no doubt, and she'd not had the best start in life. She'd been abandoned as a puppy in a plastic bag and dumped on a rubbish tip. She'd barely survived, and only then due to the love and care she'd received at the vets, and afterwards at the Bali Animal Rescue Centre (BARC).

She was a ball of energy and affection and barrelled and pinballed around the pound with endearing goofiness. She seemed to have lost a little of her ability to function, because when she whirled around too fast chasing her tail, she'd get dizzy and fall over. We learned that she'd also taken to licking the backs of hallucinogenic frogs, which made her froth at the mouth a bit, drool, then sleep for hours at a time. Ok, there are no hallucinogenic frogs in the Lakes, but I wasn't sure whether she'd be a reliable walking companion. After all, she might have, I dunno, a flashback to a bad frog trip? Who knew.

We set off to walk up Haystacks, the classic hill that lies at the end of Buttermere in the Lakes. At the base is Gatesgarth Farm, a place where the family has a long connection. Kris's father, Peter, camped on the farm as a boy, made friends with the farmer's son, walked the fells over many summers, and formed a deep and lasting love of the whole area. Maureen, the matriarch of the farm, still ran the roost and was, at the time of our walk, the chair of the Cockermouth Mountain Rescue.

We set off and all seemed fine. We parked at the slate mine on Honister Pass and made our way up to the Innominate Tarn, where celebrated Lakeland walker Alfred Wainwright had requested his ashes be scattered. This, he claimed, was his favourite spot in the Lakes and it's not hard to see why. It's a good pull up the fell, but the views are stunning, taking in the whole of Buttermere and out to sea.

There are sections, as in all the Lakeland walks, where there's a couple of slightly hairy crossings or steep paths, but this is what gives the Lakes its wildness. If you start putting in railings, steps and safety furniture, then something about the place would be lost. It's a wild place, not without risk, but that's why it's a satisfying and rewarding climb.

I was worried that Louie would somehow slip her collar and charge about in a tizzy as she had done in London on occasion; but she trotted along very obediently and Tiger just plodded on upwards, his long legs navigating the tussocks and the long grass.

After eating our packed lunch at the Tarn, it was time to make the descent. Coming down off Haystacks was harder than I remembered from the last time I'd done it, with sections that require sliding on your backside off huge chunks of rock. Louie seemed in her element — of course, she was a mountain dog! Sure-footed and with boundless energy, she skipped easily down these awkward rocks and galloped off down the green sward, only to barrel back up again, as if rounding us up.

Tiger, on the other hand, was not doing so well. In fact, I'd say he was toiling. Ok, I'd go further, he was in a state of absolute refusal. It seemed that he was completely paralysed with fear about going down the mountain. This was an unforeseen problem. I mean, if he's fine going up? But then it occurred to us, perhaps he's never *gone* down a hill before. He dug in his bony feet and refused to walk another inch, so we were stuck up a fell, in the late afternoon, with two dogs, one a space cadet, the other a lummox with vertigo. Amazingly, the space cadet was brilliant and my fears for her had dissipated, but Tiger was going to be a big problem.

It was too far to retrace our steps, so we'd have to push on, but if he refused to walk . . . then what? As a last resort, I picked him up and slung him behind my head like a joint of meat. He lay there quivering, as I tried to negotiate the steep descent with this large, unwieldy, paranoid goofball.

I quickly realised that this was a terrible idea.

I was going to lose my balance, topple forward and we'd both end up ragdolling down the mountain in a heap.

I put him down and by now he'd had enough. He took off back the way we'd come, up the hill. We made a quick decision: Kris would try to follow him, and Dax and I and Louie were going to get help. Somehow, we'd have to get Kris and the dog off the mountain before it got dark.

We'd actually fitted Tiger with a light, a flashing night beacon, never thinking we might actually need it. So Dax and I and the space cadet dog quick-marched down the mountain and headed to Gatesgarth Farm, where I spoke to Maureen, who alerted the Cockermouth Mountain Rescue.

By the time the word got out that it was me and my dog . . . Well the whole gang wanted to come out for the fun.

'It's Bill Bailey's dog! Lost on the fell! I'm in!'

The entire rescue team came haring up the road in Land Rovers, picked us up and propelled us back up Haystacks, for the second time that day.

I brought my binoculars, to see if I could spot Tiger.

And amazingly there he was! Picking his way, carefully but steadily down the fell, with single-minded purpose. 'Just get me off this mountain. Whose idea was this?' etc.

We started climbing to try to head him off. As we got closer, I tried calling, but he was ignoring me. He was in the long tussock grass, so I waded off the path to intercept him. As he came close I lunged at him, but he was wild-eyed and a bit freaked, so he snapped at my hand. I lost my balance, and the binoculars swung wildly on the neck strap and clonked me on the side of my head.

Seeing stars, and now worried the dog was in a terrible state, we turned and clambered after him. Shortly after this, Kris appeared and we continued the pursuit.

But no errant hound is a match for the intrepid folk of Cockermouth Mountain Rescue. These amazing people, all volunteers, are the real masters of this terrain. They are there every day, rain or shine, hauling to safety sheep or people that have just become paralysed on a ledge and can't move — 'cragfast', as they say. They live to rescue ill-prepared people who've got lost, or run out of water, or have put their foot in a rabbit hole, or suffered some major health emergency, or perhaps just wandered off into these majestic but unforgiving wilds. I have a huge amount of respect for them and all that they do. Having got to know a few of them now, I know that not every rescue mission ends with a success, as the Lakes claims a few lives every year. So grabbing a dopey hound who doesn't like heights was a mission they all wanted to be in on.

Tiger was apprehended late that afternoon by several members of the Mountain Rescue. He'd been grabbed and wrestled under control, and a bandage wrapped around his nose to stop him from trying to bite anyone or hurt himself.

When we caught up with them, he looked in a sorry state. Photos were taken with him, us and the whole crew. That night, I bought them all drinks in the Bridge Inn at the other end of Buttermere. And later that year, I performed a show in Carlisle where the proceeds went to the Mountain Rescue. It made the papers, of course.

My old pal, Sean Lock, was performing a warm-up show in Workington of all places and in his dressing room was a copy of *Lakeland* magazine, which had the Tiger rescue photo on the front cover. He texted, 'Why am I looking at a photo of you and a dog with a bandage on its nose?'

But the *Lakeland Times* surely got the prize for extrapolating the most sensation out of this incident with a headline that read, 'CELEBRITY MAULED BY TIGER'.

Part Five

WALK ON THE WILD SIDE

I've been very fortunate that I have found something that I love doing and might make a few folk laugh along the way. One of the unexpected consequences of a life performing comedy is the way it has afforded me all manner of other opportunities. From performing with the BBC Concert Orchestra, to jamming with Deep Purple at the Albert Hall, and singing with Robin Williams, to presenting wildlife documentaries, it has given a breadth and variety to my life I never would have imagined. It's also taken me to some wild places around the world, from caring for a brood of baby adders in our garden in Devon to a momentous encounter with an enormous minke whale. It's a long way from being barrelled over by a dog at the age of five!

Chapter 25

Adders

Rarely seen and elusive, Britain's only venomous snake is a lovely looking creature.

I've moved them from busy road verges and relocated them from my own garden, so I've had the good fortune to observe them close up. They really are the most beautiful of animals, particularly the males.

The females are larger and have a two-tone brown colour, with the distinctive diamond marking along the back, while the smaller males are a gorgeous dark blue-black hue, a Malmesbury mamba. I've only ever seen them together once and that was a breeding pair in our garden in Devon.

My first TV adder experience was as part of the Channel 4 show, *Wild Thing: I Love You*, and we were investigating the problem of adders on the grassy verges of motorways. This unlikely habitat attracts adders mainly due to the absence of people, and for the same reason that kestrels and other birds like to hunt by roads . . . Small mammals like voles are plentiful here, drawn by the vibrations of the traffic.

Voles, the all-purpose snack of the animal world, face a triple threat of cars, birds of prey and adders. But in this case, the adders were under threat, too. The section of road was the A6 north of Carlisle, which was notorious for accidents. The motorway went from a three-lane to a two and this was the main cause of it being a blackspot. As part of the solution, the road was to be widened to a three-lane carriageway, but of course this meant that the established grassy banks were to be levelled. And nestled in the grass of these verges were several adders who had made it their home.

As part of the development process, contractors are obliged to check for any disturbance to wildlife as a result of their works, which is a good thing. So I found myself standing on the steep green bank of the A6 as adders were caught and bagged up ready for relocation.

The adders are quite a small stocky snake and tend to be coiled tightly, so the method for catching them was quite simple. Using large leather gauntlets, the catcher would just envelope them in the gloves and then gently but firmly, while holding the head, transfer them to a secure soft snake bag.

One of the adders took umbrage, as you'd imagine, and launched a little nip on the gauntlet, leaving two quite clear drops of venom.

This was quite a big defence investment for the snake — it takes them a while to produce venom — so he must have been really annoyed.

Luckily no harm done and when a good haul had been rounded up, the next phase was the relocation . . .

This involved me sitting in the back of a car, wrangling six bags of snakes. I could see them moving in the fabric of the bag, so this was a slightly unnerving road trip to the Lake District, where they were to be released. The area earmarked was a section where trees had been cleared as part of a project of land regeneration and therefore it had many good hiding places for our incoming snakes. It's always a thrill to release a wild animal and to see them take to their new homes was very heartening.

A camera placed in the entrance to a hollow under a tree beamed back evidence that the snakes had made their way in . . . Success!

On a slightly different scale, I was also involved in an adder relocation one particularly hot summer. Our bungalow in Devon is set back from the high sea cliffs that rise up from Combe Martin. The South West Coast Path wends its way in front of the place and Exmoor takes up the rear. It's a remote place, but starkly beautiful on any day.

In fact, the day we first went to view it was a bitterly cold, rain-sodden day in winter. Even then, I loved it. Sometimes it gets cut off in the winter snows, and in the height of summer, under a clear blue sky, I lie on the grass and watch skylarks disappearing upwards in a delicate plume of song. Over the years, many people have stayed here, many Christmases and New Years have been seen in. The seasons change, people come and go, but there is a timeless quality to this place and its wildlife plays a big part in that.

To encourage the adders and other critters, and to create a shady little habitat for them, we always leave an old piece of corrugated iron in a less well-trod part of the garden. Sometimes we find coppery slow worms under there or a grass snake. Once, after a prolonged period of hot weather, to our great delight we discovered beneath it a pair of adders, coiled up together — and not long afterwards three baby adders were seen. Almost a foot long, lithe and skinny, with bags of attitude.

Unfortunately these were, unlike their more worldly parents, unafraid of anything and willing to take on the world, much like human teenagers. This prompted the attention of our feral Bali dogs, who, equally, had grown up around snakes and weren't the least bit fazed by a hissing and lunging bunch of snapping tiddlers.

It did present a problem, so what to do?

My wife said we'd have to shift them out of the garden, but how?

Not having professional snake-catchers' leather gauntlets and uncertain of the snake-proof qualities of an oven glove, we improvised, using a soft broom and an old cardboard box. Not as impressive looking, but effective enough as we swept the lunging hissers into the box and harmlessly conveyed them to a wild bit of Exmoor, whereupon they were released — the terrain is classic habitat for adders: moorland, lots of bracken cover, and plenty of lizards and voles to eat.

Baby adders are fully independent from the minute they are born, in case you think we were taking them away from their mum and dad. In fact, once out in the world, adder parents have nothing more to do with them . . . so we were just helping them to find their own way.

I often think of this episode. Those baby adders went off into the wild with a helping hand from us, and I felt strangely responsible for them and often wondered how they fared. Adders can live for over ten years, so there's a chance these plucky youngsters would have been our neighbours for a while. Would they catch a glimpse of us and feel a filial affection, or just,

'There's that weird-looking thing that swept us into a box — steer clear of it.'

I feel very lucky to have witnessed this. Our homemade relocation was a rare and wonderful experience — and made more so now that adders are considered endangered in the UK. This sad state of affairs has come about due to a variety of factors, often down to the loss of hibernation sites through either destruction or disturbance.

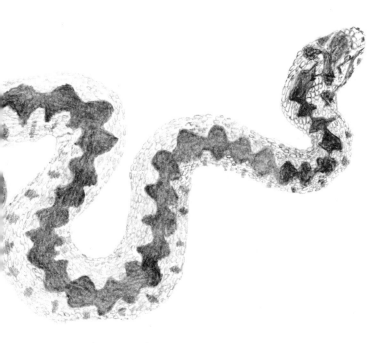

One thing we can all do to help is, if you have a garden, leave a patch of it to grow wild. This might be where an adder might pass through in a 'wildlife corridor' or even somewhere for it to hole up in the winter. It'll also benefit all manner of other wildlife, like bees and insects. Nature is resilient and often doesn't need much encouragement, but any helping hand we can give, we should, at every opportunity.

Chapter 26

Otters

I am standing next to a disused gravel pit, somewhere along Britain's north-east coast. The rain is that fine mizzling kind that soaks everything in its path. Hooded garments are no use, as this kind of rain appears to be able to travel *upwards*, inveigling its way into cuffs and collars, borne on a bitter east wind. Despite my waterproofs and many fleecy layers, the hours of standing about have left me cold to the bone, and I have a tearful and forlorn appearance, as occasionally a stray gust causes it to rain horizontally into my eyes. This is the reality of filming a wildlife programme. It's not all glamour. In fact, there's no glamour. None. It's an NGZ. A No-Glam-Zone.

To prove my point, in my cupped hands I hold some cold otter's droppings. This is what I got into showbiz for.

To explain about otters' behaviour and their diet, it's necessary to poke through their doings, or 'spraints', on camera, in the rain, with an upbeat demeanour. At this point in the shoot, this is the closest we had come to an otter.

Otters are notoriously difficult to spot due to their shy and reclusive nature, and they are still not that common. Otters have been up against it since the Industrial Revolution, when both land and Britain's waterways were co-opted for industry, driving the otters away from their habitats. The introduction of the American mink into the UK in the 1920s didn't help, either. The mink duly escaped and ran riot through Britain, occupying the niche previously held by the otter (and indeed another UK native, the humble water vole). An elusive, rarely seen, yet aggressive and wildly effective predator, the mink is now found in every part of Britain.

From the 1950s onwards, UK otter numbers plummeted further due to pesticides in the waterways. The problem was so severe that by the early 1980s otters were classed as an endangered species and their future in this country looked uncertain. But thanks to a combined and concerted effort by the Nature Conservancy Council, the Environment Agency and the Otter Trust, and a host of local conservation organisations, the numbers began to pick up.

There's a break in the filming while the cameras' lenses are all wiped dry, batteries are changed and new memory cards installed.

I clasp a cup of tea and shelter under an umbrella. In one hand, I still hold the cold otter's doings.

'Shall I put the otter's pellets down?'

'Not just yet, Bill. Could you hold on to them so we can match the shot?'

'Righto. No prob.'

I put the tea down and glance at the newspaper in the dry. An article about my old friend and fellow comic, Simon Pegg, catches my eye. I'm always keen to see how old pals are doing. I shift position on the folding chair, careful not to drop the otter's spraints.

'Simon Pegg to star alongside Tom Cruise in *Mission Impossible*.' A photo accompanies the article, in which the two of them appear smiling, tanned and impossibly glamorous.

I glance from the photo to the compacted otter turds in my hand.

Have I made the right choices in life?

Ok, so I was definitely in the NGZ™, but honestly, this is how I like it.

Filming a wildlife show involves being outside and this one is no exception. For *Wild Thing: I Love You* I had many fascinating encounters over the course of filming ten episodes. The point of the show was to identify a wild animal in some sort of strife and try to figure out a solution to their problem. I liked this approach, which made for a pleasing variety to the work. There needed to be some natural history — finding out about the animal in question and hearing the zoologist's view of what needed doing; and then there was the practical side of things — getting to grips with the issue at hand and trying to come up with a workable solution.

The episode on otters was a typical case in point. The show's researchers had learned that otters were being killed on the A1 near Newcastle. Otters don't normally run across roads, so there must have been some reason other than playing chicken. So why *did* the otter cross the road?

Because the culvert it normally used beneath the road had become blocked by years of accumulated vegetation! Ok, not the snappiest of punchlines, but one that nonetheless had fatal consequences for the otters.

The solution seemed to be straightforward: clear the culvert and happy days for our otter friends. Except this culvert hadn't been cleared in years and there were decades' worth of weeds and vegetation to move.

This is what I like about the power of television. It sometimes means that things just get done a bit quicker, cutting through what might have been months of paperwork and committees and consultation. It ended up with the local council wheeling a floating, weed-clearing device out of storage. It was a boat, but attached to its bow were large, extendable arms with rotating blades on the end: a giant Edward Scissorhands perched on the end of a dinghy.

I remember very clearly arriving to start filming, watching this weed-chomper being unloaded from a truck and then spending most of the day trying to get the thing started. Various attempts came to nought, but eventually, after much cajoling, WD40, knocking, oil checks and mechanical tweaks, the fearsome beast coughed and spluttered into life. With a brief burst of black smoke, it was up and running.

Once in the stream it was amazingly effective, carving through the knotted and clinging vegetation like a chain-saw through spaghetti, allowing the flow to resume. Job done . . . except, not quite. As subsequent CCTV footage showed, the otters were still not using the culvert. This was apparently because there were otter cubs and, in times of rain, the culvert would still, to a degree, fill up and the otter mums were not taking chances with the cubs. So part two of the solution went into action: the building of a bridge, a little trackway hung above the water level, for the otters to take their young families across the road.

When I finally spied an otter, I must admit that I was gripped with excitement. It's something that I don't think will ever leave me, that thrill of spotting a rarely seen animal or bird, particularly one that has come back from the brink and belongs here — a UK native, returned to its rightful place and giving the mink a run for its money.

I realised how significant this spot was when talking to one of our local guides. He said, in a thick Geordie accent,

'Ah've worked for the Northumberland Wildlife Trust for 25 yair and in all that time ah've neva seen an ottah.'

So I was doubly blessed.

'A lot of doggin' goes on around here, mind.'

Ah, that's not the kind of wildlife we're after, thank you.

that is truly horrible..

Chapter 27

Birdsong

Over the course of a week in summer, I walked the Ridge-way, Britain's oldest road. After I'd been walking outdoors for several days, I realised my senses were getting keener. I could feel changes in the weather, air pressure and temperature. It was uncanny, but also reassuring that we are able to revert to a less desensitised version of ourselves. Our animal senses are always there, it's just that they are not called on that often. I was seeing more, hearing more and, in particular, identifying birdsong: the distinctive intermittent drilling of a woodpecker, the insistent trilling of a yellowhammer, the raucous clamour of an alarmed pheasant, the surprisingly loud chattering of the wren, the mellifluous quivering of the blackbird . . .

According to some research, birdsong can help us to focus, improve cognition and reduce tiredness. It also masks background noise that can be distracting. It can initiate a state in us that corresponds to 'body relaxed, mind alert'. To me, it's no wonder we feel calm when we hear birdsong, because over thousands of years we've learned that, when birds are singing, we're safe. It's when they stop singing that we need to worry.

One of the features that makes birdsong so relaxing is that it is stochastic, a word derived from ancient Greek meaning 'pertaining to chance'. In this context, it means that although it's true individual birds have a certain song, it's not always predictable. The bird's song often changes slightly each time — a longer trill here, an embellishment there — plus the recurrence is also random. This has a positive effect on us, in a way that a repetitive beat from a radio, or a drill or anything non-organic might, well, drive us up the wall.

I remember waiting for a flight in Amsterdam's Schiphol Airport and being struck by a strange feeling of freshness, of lightness of spirit. It wasn't the excellent slender triangle of Gouda I'd just eaten with an olive chaser, or the glass of chilled Pinot Grigio, although that couldn't have hurt. There was something else, almost indefinable. Then I realised — it was birdsong. I spend a lot of time in airports and when I'm not trying to get onto the Wi-Fi, or just looking around for cheese, I spend my time watching people.

There's something quietly comforting about recognising familiar types among your fellow humans and at Schiphol it was no exception: the grey-faced travellers, dazed and pallid after just having got off a long-haul flight; the short-haul moochers, hovering about the coffee bars, texting and laughing; the grey-suited business people hurrying to or from a flight, talking formally into their Bluetooth earpieces; the families about to head out on holiday, all fired up and already dressed for the sunny destination in shorts and Hawaiian shirts, incongruous on this cold, drizzling January day in the Netherlands.

And throughout all this there was this familiar throng, the unmistakeable sound of twittering birds, a mix of starlings, robins, blackbirds. But where from? I mean, I have seen actual living birds in airports, the odd sparrow that's flown in by mistake or the occasional bemused pigeon, but

the sound was coming from lots of birds. My eyes roved around in the mass of wire gantries suspending the array of signs — and then I spotted them. There were speakers mounted in living trees planted around the concourse. And from these emanated this avian chorus I could hear.

This creative initiative seems to have had an impact on travellers. Last time I looked, Amsterdam Schiphol had over 11,000 five-star Google reviews extoling its virtues of 'freshness', its 'friendliness' and how 'relaxing' it was. Perhaps they didn't even notice the birdsong. Who knows? But its calming environment has not gone unnoticed in the airport world. A few years ago, Amsterdam was voted third best airport in the world at the World Airport Awards, to which my immediate response is, well done, well deserved and why wasn't I invited to host the World Airport Awards?

At the time of writing this, I'm at home with the back door to the garden ajar, the sounds of birds flooding through. It's a familiar chorus of our loudest and most enthusiastic singers: the soft fluting of a blackbird provides the backing vocals for the lead singer of a great tit, while the implausibly loud wren dukes it out with the nightclub MC shtick of a chaffinch.

Inspired by the composer Anton Bruckner, I'm recording the song of the wren. As you may know, Bruckner used the call of the great tit as an inspiration for the first movement of his 'romantic' First Symphony.

In this same spirit, I have recorded the wren's wild volley of chirps, whistles and metallic whirring and am in the process of sampling it, and playing it over drum and bass beats. I just need some other element, like Shakira singing a Colombian ode to wrens (or indeed all passerine birds) and I reckon it has Christmas Number One written all over it.

Or at the very least, the RSPB's 'on hold' music.

Chapter 28

Badgers

I'm standing on a proposed building site, in a mystery location near a place on the map called Brockton.

As you may know, 'Brock' is an old name for 'badger' and so the word's presence in a town name that is on an old Ordnance Survey map tells me that there have been badgers in these parts for a very long time.

Badgers, in case you're unfamiliar, are squat, short-legged creatures, about the size of a medium-size dog. Their bodies are greyish in colour, with distinctive black heads with white markings and a long, darker strip from head to tail. They have powerful claws, which are excellent for digging and grubbing up earthworms, which form most of their diet. They are the larger and more robust cousins of ferrets and polecats.

The programme I'm making is part of a documentary series for Channel 4 about animals, with a particular focus on the problem that faces a lot of new construction work: namely that there are now (rightly) safeguards in place to protect the nation's wildlife. The building company in question here have actually been the ones to flag up the fact that right where they're about to break ground on a new housing development there's clear evidence of badgers . . .

Badger dens, called 'setts', tend to be well-established, complex underground networks of interconnecting tunnels, which are often used by successive generations of animals. Badger housing is bequeathed to the new intake, with new badgers taking up residence and inheriting the family seat. In this way, badgers are very much like the aristocracy, but better at digging. Some of these larger setts can be hundreds of years old. Badgers tend to be quite territorial and inhabit the same setts year after year, so this compounds the problem. If the building goes ahead, they'll be made homeless.

As part of the programme, we had to establish which badgers were going to be affected by the construction work and this involved a neat trick. We put some food out for them and laced it with tiny, coloured plastic pellets. The pellets pass harmlessly through the badgers' digestive tracts and out the other end, leaving a clear marker where they have been.

The bait was peanut butter — apparently a bit of a fave. I mean, who doesn't like peanut butter? And it's not as if they can get it in the wild. So after a night of baiting, we waited for Nature to take its course.

And sure enough, after a day or so, we could see the brightly coloured pellets leading the way. Like Theseus in the Greek myth of the Minotaur, leaving a trail to get out of the labyrinth . . . Except with badgers and badgers' doings.

The brightly coloured line of pellets led through a field and into a wood, perched on a hill. As we investigated, more and more entrances became apparent, until we realised that we were standing on one enormous badger sett. These badgers would be ok, they were settled well away from the building site, but there was a second trail of plastic pellets leading back to where the diggers all stood in waiting . . .

Badgers have a long association with Britain in many ways. They crop up in literature, *The Wind in the Willows* being the classic children's tale, and they are a much-loved mascot of rural Britain. Since 1973 it's been illegal to kill a badger (other than as part of the recent culls intended to curb TB) or to disturb its sett. And fair enough, they're an important part of the ecology of British wildlife. Since the demise of the wolf and the lynx, they have endured as the UK's largest land-based predator. They keep other animals and predators, such as foxes, rats and mice, in balance. They are therefore known as a keystone species, crucial to the balance of UK wildlife.

And they have every right to be here. These ground-hugging, monochrome scufflers have been excavating Britain for half a million years and this iconic species is safeguarded by law. Since 1992, the Protection of Badgers Act has given them a wide-ranging protection.

The cruel practice of badger-baiting, where a badger is captured and set upon by a dog to 'test its mettle', has been around in Britain for hundreds of years. Badgers are docile animals in their natural environment, but when cornered they will fight with enormous strength, having a serious bite and powerful, sharp claws.

So popular a sport was this, that legislation against it began as far back as 1835 with the Cruelty to Animals Act, extended further in 1911 with the Protection of Animals Act. And yet, despite this long legal protection, badger baiting has persisted in a murky world of illegal fights, sometimes out in the woods, sometimes in houses with false walls put in, with a badger pit concealed behind. Large adult male badgers can be sold by gangs for up to £1,000.

This is why our badger TV shoot had an added layer of mystery. The location of the shoot, and thus the badger sett, was only revealed to a tiny number of us and did not appear on any call sheet or piece of paperwork. It lent an air of subterfuge to the whole endeavour.

No names, no pack drill. Keep it on the low down.

Actually it was a bit annoying, as I got lost on the way to the location. In frustration I made an illegal U-turn and got snapped by a traffic camera . . . So thanks, badger baiters – another reason to dislike you.

Anyway, it quickly became apparent that the solution to this badger problem was to relocate the badgers somewhere else . . . but where? The nearest sett was occupied by long-term residents who would not be enamoured of a bunch of newcomers. So a plan was made — to build a replica badger sett and see if our residents would be tempted to move in.

They'd need a water supply and some underground tunnels — but being creatures of habit, would they take to it? A friendly local farmer lent us some gear, we procured a digger and some volunteers . . . and we set about it. Plastic tubing was brought in to shore up the tunnels, and a design based on a typical sett was put in place. After a week of earth moving, digging and replanting, and a natural pond being dug in a nearby field, the stage was set. Night vision cameras were positioned in the tunnels and we sat in a darkened field, watching the monitor with trepidation.

After a long wait, YES! There was a tell-tale snout sniffling the air and slowly, cautiously, a line of badgers made their way into the tunnels.

Badgers sorted, the building work gets the go ahead — and everyone's a winner baby. It's not always like this, as you saw with my dating advice for dormice (see chapter 14), but hey, a win's a win!

Chapter 29

The Owl Incident

This is a tale of curiosity and it starts with a trip around China.

We were fascinated by a 60-minute documentary about Guangdong province in the eastern region of China, where all our e-waste ends up. It's where generations of obsolete computers and printers go to die, where the acrid smell of copper wire being stripped from cable drifts over a riverbank and a river turned black with printer ink oozes by in a slow current of Stygian murk. It was like some pre-industrial hellhole; a Dickensian nemesis for all our *stuff*; a bitter-tasting metaphor for our disposable society.

Out of sight and out of mind, this was where all our once-shiny phones and gadgets and screens found their final resting place, lying in a heap at the side of the road, being broken apart for a few dollars, a few yuan.

So, of course, once we'd seen that, we had to go! Let the party begin! And after a more traditional Chinese trip that had led us from the well-trodden tourist sights of Beijing to the terracotta warriors of Xi'an and on to the Great Wall, I was actually looking forward to this dark underside of the capitalist dream.

Flying into the regional hub of Shantou, we hired a guide to take us to the town of Guiyu in Guangdong province. The driver, our guide, talked constantly on one of his phones in low and intense Mandarin.

We arrived first at a phone recycling place and everyone there looked nervous. Perhaps there'd been too many TV companies around after the doco?

Well, we played up the harmless tourist vibe to be fair: me and my wife, our nine-year-old and our twenty-four-year-old Indonesian student friend, Mita. Perhaps that was the bafflement — why the hell are tourists coming here?

Either way it was grimly fascinating: piles of old faxes and ancient-looking answerphones, and that's with the worst of it no doubt being kept away from us by our 'guide',

who was actually a policeman. In fact *all* our contacts were
police, or at least on the payroll of the 'recyclers'.

After a bleak morning traipsing through a dull industrial backwater, we were getting peckish. Our guide,
relieved to get us off the streets, recommended a restaurant. Our son, who loves Chinese food, was delighted . . .

This place gave a hint at the sums of money being
made here: fancy new cars parked outside and a lavish, if
frayed and shabby, entrance. When we went in, we were
confronted with an unexpected sight. Not the prawns, the
lobsters, fish and other unfortunates you sometimes find
in the tanks of Chinese restaurants, but birds, including
cormorants, a giant salamander, stoats, weasels, civet cats,
all arranged in cages in the entrance.

It was never explicitly mentioned that these were part
of the bill of fare, but their arrangement right next to the
prawns etc., seemed to imply that anything was edible.
And there, pride of place in the entrance, was a cage housing a huge owl.

This was a large and impressive bird, and we soon figured out that it was a female Eurasian Eagle Owl. Not an
endangered species, it has an enormous range that spreads

from the mountains of Eastern Europe through to the outer reaches of Tianjin in the north of China.

Seeing a magnificent creature like this on display in a restaurant was shocking. We had to get it out of there. So, we asked if it was for sale.

Of course *everything* is for sale at the right price, especially in this town built on naked capitalism, so after much haggling we eventually got them down to 400 yuan (about forty pounds). As soon as the deal was struck, furious activity ensued. They must have been thinking 'let's just sell it before they change their minds.'

A gaggle of men, working quickly, opened the cage and two of them grabbed the owl, which was not happy. They fetched it out in a fury of talons and feathers, and proceeded to wrap some parcel tape around it. Trussed up like a package, it was loaded into a cardboard box and handed over. We got it into the taxi and instructed our driver to leave.

He was now on two different phones, a look of startled incredulity on his face. I don't speak Mandarin, but I've often imagined this is how that conversation might have gone:

'I thought they were just here to film the waste, but they seem to have bought an owl . . .'

It was one of those occasions where the day unfolded unexpectedly. From a strange and depressing view of the end of the line for outdated tech, our day had taken an even more surreal turn.

And as a conservationist, I was dogged by a nagging worry. Were we being too gung-ho here? I mean, perhaps they'd just sold us their family pet owl? The thing might be a softie and habituated to humans, and stand no chance in the wild. By letting it go, we might be condemning it to a worse fate. This bothered me, so I decided to get some expert advice. I just happened to have in my contacts the owl expert at London Zoo. It went to voicemail, so I left a message.

'Hi, it's Bill Bailey here. I'm in China and I've just bought an owl. Could you ring me back? Thanks.'

Not long after, he phoned back.

'What sort of owl, Bill?'

'Eurasian Eagle.'

'How does it look?'

'Really pissed off.'

'That's good!'

As I sat on the back seat of the taxi, the bird was glaring at me through a gap in the cardboard box, its yellow eyes ablaze with righteous indignation.

'Does it look well fed?'

'Hard to tell.'

'Could you give it a rat or something?'

'Not right now, I'm in a cab.'

I started to realise the limitations of my Mandarin phrase book.

Nothing in it that remotely resembled 'Can we stop to get a rat for the owl we've just bought?' Instead, I managed to say, 'Forest, can we go to a forest?' And that's exactly where we ended up.

We wound our way up a little country lane to a raised area of land with an adjacent strip of woodland. I'd already googled the main zoo in Shantou to see if that might be a better option, but when the website of the zoo finally loaded on my phone, its welcome page featured a photograph of a chimpanzee dressed as a train driver.

So maybe not there, then.

We managed to get the owl out of the cardboard box

and placed it gently on the ground, illuminated by the taxi's headlights.

It was absolutely *furious*.

Good!

We found a pair of paper scissors in the taxi's glovebox and carefully cut away the parcel tape. As the last strip fell away, the owl stepped to one side, taking in its surroundings. It shook its feathers, then glared at us with such vicious ferocity, I was at once convinced that this was a wild, caught bird. It shivered with feral energy.

I had worried that this might be a scam, that the owl was a homing owl and would fly straight back to the restaurant, only for some other do-gooders to fall for the old 'owl trick', but that glare convinced me. This was a truly wild animal. It had not been habituated. It had not been tamed.

It belonged in the wild, on the wing.

The owl hopped away and with one final backward glance of anger, it spread its huge wings and launched itself into the night. We all gave a huge spontaneous cheer, our arms aloft, shouting 'YESSSS!' into the gathering gloom.

That is one of my fondest memories. It was glorious, primal and we punched the air like loons.

The Chinese policeman was back on the phone.

'They've only let the bloody thing go!!'

'Come back to base, they're clearly not spies.'

Chapter 30

Encounter with Jaguars

Planning a trip to the wetlands of central Brazil to film a wildlife documentary about endangered jaguars posed a dilemma. Our son was very young at the time, but we were keen to take him. My wife and I have always loved travel, but when she became pregnant many of our friends issued dire warnings about how this would curtail our wanderlust. 'You'll have to get your travelling in now, you won't be doing that for a while when the baby arrives,' etc. But I think we both took this as a challenge, a gauntlet thrown down. We'll see about that!

By now he'd already been on the trails with us for a while; he was a good traveller. But as we investigated the trip in more detail, it turned out the filming was to take place during the wet season, when the mozzies are out in full force. This in itself is not a real problem, more an annoyance, but there was another level of risk nonetheless. Normally mosquitoes may carry malaria, which you can hopefully mitigate against with spray and the like, but at that time of year, the biting insects carry the far more deadly haemorrhagic malaria, which can be nasty. So he sat this one out at home.

Instead, I took my father, who at the time was sprightly and in good health and in his 70s. I mean, he's still sprightly and in fine fettle now, aged 91, but even more so then! And up for an adventure. I was at the time in my early forties, newly a dad.

Filming began near São Paulo, after which we would head into the interior. The Pantanal, the vast wetlands in the centre of Brazil, is an expanse the size of Belgium. I always feel for Belgium in these instances. Belgium is a proud, independent country, famed for its food, and especially for inventing the thin crispy chip known as 'French fries', which I imagine they're not happy about. I once suggested to a Belgian audience that they should all receive a royalty for every portion of French fries sold. And of course, I received a free bag of 'em — not that I was angling for them, mind you.

Belgium is the country of Jacques Brel and 'Le plat pays, qui est le mien', of Eddy Merckx, a place for which I have great fondness. I travelled round it with a theatre company once and marvelled at its organisation, its quality food and superb beer. And yet it has the misfortune to be used, traduced, as some kind of yardstick of global weights and measures. A Belgium is the size of two Liechtensteins and a Monaco . . . A swarm of bees 'the size of Belgium' . . . a vast iceberg 'the size of Belgium' heading for the shipping lanes. It's so much more than an international unit of peril.

The Pantanal is, as you might imagine, quite stunningly beautiful. Intertwining rivers leading to a myriad of interconnecting smaller waterways. Clouds of colourful exotic birds fly overhead, parrots, macaws and toucans, alongside a wealth of other strange and singular creatures, each with their own specialist skills: crab-eating foxes, giant anteaters, anacondas, black and spectacled caiman and, of course, piranhas . . .

Our guide, Rosalina, told us she loved to swim in these clear waters. But, she said with a blithe insouciance, you have to pick your times carefully. The piranha, she said, leave at the end of the season, so then it's time to get out the swimwear. One year, she said, she got cocky and went in too early. A straggler, a stray piranha left behind by his mates, was still hanging around.

She felt a sharp tug on her foot, no pain initially. She removed her sock to reveal a scar. Well, not so much a scar, more a chunk of her foot missing; a perfect scoop of flesh, neatly excised by the laggardly chomper, who presumably couldn't believe his luck and perhaps justified his decision to hang about for rich pickings . . .

*

We stayed in a lodge, about a ten-minute drive along dirt roads from the reception, a simple room on stilts that I shared with my dad. We ate at the lodge and, after the story of Rosalina's ankle, I ordered piranha soup out of sympathy. That'll show 'em. Who's the boss now? Who's soup? Yeah, you . . . (actually, quite palatable).

I didn't fancy a cooked fish in its entirety, the flesh is

quite soapy and full of dozens of little bendy bones. In fact, the great adventurer Redmond O'Hanlon described eating piranha as 'like sucking lard off a hairbrush', which I can attest through my own experience is an accurate description, which made me wonder if once, perhaps in a fit of madness or drug-fuelled experimentation, he actually *had* sucked lard off a hairbrush.

The jaguar is deemed to be endangered and, indeed, the title of the programme I was filming was *Last Chance to See*. But when talking to the locals a different picture emerged. Due to the fact that jaguars have been hunted and persecuted, it's true their numbers are dwindling. Such is the nature of these things, however, that their habitat was reduced to a narrow corridor of land that stretched from the Pantanal north all the way to the Brazilian border with Paraguay and Colombia, and if you happened to live in this corridor your impression of jaguar numbers might be a little skewed. As we found out when asking a local, hoping to get a response on camera along the lines of 'Ooh, no no . . . You don't see many of them anymore . . .' the responses were more like, 'Jaguars? Yeah there's loads of 'em! Place is crawling with 'em. Like pests, they are.'

We went on an exploratory drive into the bush. Our guide, Sandro, was keen for us to hear a jaguar luffing: a low, huffing noise that big cats make to let others know they're around. He had an ingenious bit of kit with which to do this, comprising a small cylindrical drum and a length of string. Kneeling down in the gathering dusk, Sandro wound the string around the drum and pulled the string sharply. Amazingly the instrument emitted a low, gruff sound, which accurately resembled that of a jaguar.

And there, in the warm and darkening gloom, came the distant sound of a responding luff. A jaguar had answered. Sandro looked at me with a big smile. Success. I was initially amazed. Wow, this thing actually works. And then another creeping sensation, like the shipping forecast when a storm is brewing: unease, building slowly, becoming fear. We were out in the wilds, with no means of protection, in the jaguar's natural habitat, deliberately challenging it . . . or, did I get this right, maybe . . . flirting?

At least we now knew there were jaguars around, as we barrelled back to the lodge.

The next morning we were to go on a jaguar hunt with the intention of trapping one with a tranquiliser dart and fitting it with a radio collar to track its movements. I'd forgotten my camera, so I popped back to our room. I walked in, made my way between the two beds, but as I turned I realised I was being watched intently by a large snake, which had reared up and had fixed me with a beady gaze.

It was an olive whip snake — not especially dangerous, but certainly venomous — and it was considering me as its tongue flicked speculatively in and out . . .

I backed out slowly, the snake watching me all the way. As the door closed, I could see through the window its aggressive posture relaxed and it continued to rummage around the room. As it disappeared into the corner, I skipped back into the room, opened the balcony door and legged it. I looked on from the window again as the snake, on its tour of the room, found the open door and slithered out. I mentioned this to my dad, who remarked casually, 'Yes, I thought I'd heard something in the rafters last night . . .'

Before they became a protected species, the traditional method of hunting jaguars was to use dogs. One of the most experienced of the old school of jaguar hunters, Francisco, was on our small expedition. He was a large and rangy man from a tougher time, more used to hunts that ended in a kill than a radio collar. He had some words of wisdom for our band of neophyte jaguar hunters:

'You are not a man if you kill a jaguar with a rifle . . .'

'Oh,' I said.

He paused, for dramatic effect.

'No . . .' he looked off into the distance. 'No, a real man will use . . .'

My dad and I leaned forwards, the thick jungle air close, and at this point I was thinking, his bare hands? A spoon? A *sock*?

'A PISTOL!' said Francisco, waving a pistol he'd just whipped out with a flourish.

I thought, yeah, but it's still a gun.

Although when I eventually saw the jaguar, I realised that I wouldn't feel in any way safer with this little pop gun.

The hounds were baying as the 4×4s rolled up and we were eager to get going. Gauchos on horseback galloped and quadbikes roared off at first light.

Off we went into the bush, dogs baying, horses bridling and Francisco tootling on a little hunting horn. I have to say, I am not a fan of hunting, but I found myself gripped by the primal feelings of a chase. Even though the end point was not in this case to kill the beast, only to tranquilise it, the same atavistic feelings were apparent in the throng: the urgency and thrill of the pursuit, the sense of a quarry!

We were bound together with a single purpose, but something more was at play here I think. We are descended from hunters and this is what our ancestors had to do, just to survive, so in that moment I felt a keen connection with the past. It reminded me that we are, in our primal state, just animals too. And if we'd skipped a few random mutations in our DNA it could be us being chased by highly evolved jaguars. Would they drive Jags? I think they would.

The radio crackled . . . A jaguar had been 'treed' by the dogs, meaning that it had taken refuge in the branches above us and the dogs were keeping it there. We hared across the bush, car bucking and rolling as the engine revved and whined. I could see my dad's head bouncing up and down, clanging off the inside of the car's roof a couple of times. I craned forward — 'Are you alright, Dad?' — but he was in his element, beaming and laughing. This is what animals add to our lives. They put us right there, in the moment, and we truly know what it means to be alive . . .

Suddenly we arrived, met by a gathered throng of gauchos, and there was the jaguar, coiled in a crook of the tree. Francisco sidled up to me and, in a dramatic aside, said, 'Don't look into its eyes.'

Of course, I immediately stared right into its eyes. They burned with fury and indignation and annoyance. This animal was not afraid. It was seething with anger, if anything. It seemed to lock eyes with me and, not for the first time, I felt that primal fear. This was an apex predator, perfectly adapted to this environment, a sleek, skilful and indomitable boss cat, capable of spatchcocking anything in these parts, unafraid of humans or anything else.

As the biologists, zoologists and various gauchos milled around, it seemed to be eyeing up its escape. 'Right, jump down, take him out, knock her over . . . Head for the big fella, take him out, the scared beardie guy won't be a problem, maybe just slash him for fun, then leg it . . .'

At this point, a gun was brought and a tranq dart carefully loaded. The gun was aimed and fired. A good strike, right in the shanks.

And now we waited.

After a few minutes, the jaguar began to slump. It was asleep in the crook of the tree, but still about a good five metres up. At this point something extraordinary happened. The shooter put down the tranq gun and with no hesitation, like a man for whom this was another day at the office, he started to climb the tree.

I could scarcely believe it. I mean, he was wearing wellies. But the urgency was due to the fact he had to get the jaguar down before he woke up and it appeared to be trickily snagged.

~~~~~~

While this ~~absolute nutter~~ incredibly brave gaucho climbed the tree, a net was stretched out below. This nimble cat-wrangler had now reached the jaguar and started to gently manoeuvre it so that it finally flopped down into the net.

Action stations! The jaguar was gently laid out while samples of its blood were taken and I was invited to take a closer look. I found myself holding the jaguar's head. An adult female, youngish, with a tooth missing and an infected gum. A discussion as to what to do broke out. To treat or not? But in the end, the experts decided to let Nature take its course.

What struck me was the sheer size of it, the weight of its head. I had previously imagined a jaguar to be no bigger than a small leopard, or a serval or a puma even, but this was *huge*, more like the size of a tiger. The local people call it *onça* — the beast that kills with one bite. Its head was enormous, beautiful, *regal* . . . I have never, before or since, beheld a wild animal as impressive.

All my senses were heightened by the chase and the softness of the fur, the sheer weight and mass of her head, the wild beauty, they are all imprinted, still fresh in my memory, along with the awareness, as it was happening, of the incredible good fortune I had to witness such a marvel.

The jaguar started to stir, coming round from the effect of the tranquiliser, so an injection was administered to help wake it up. We all backed away . . .

It stood groggily for a few minutes, regarding us with undisguised loathing (especially me, it felt like), before loping off into the bush.

Later, data from the radio collar said that she travelled 100 km north, in a dead straight line. I mean, I could have told you that's what she'd do. That's what *I* would have done.

Data analysis proves that jaguars are not daft . . .

Chapter 31

Jaguar Story 2 — Army Base

For the jungle section of the jaguar documentary we travelled to Manaus, in northern Brazil. It's a large bustling city and the capital of the Amazonas region. Here the Amazon is as wide as an inland sea and Manaus is a busy shipping port — yet it's extraordinary to think that we were a thousand miles from the coast. It really brought it home to me, the scale and size of this mighty river.

Manaus is a jumping-off point for forays into the interior of Brazil. There's a large army base here and we were invited to film there as they had a jaguar as a mascot. I mean, this does put a regimental goat in the shade somewhat. In fact, a jaguar could probably eat most other regimental animals. There can't be many other mascots that are apex predators? British Army mascots tend to be a horse or a pony, or maybe a wolfhound, and were typically brought in to raise morale. A jaguar is the mascot of all mascots. I was keen to meet her . . .

When we arrived at the base and were being driven to the jaguar enclosure, the first creature I saw was perhaps even more impressive. A truly massive anaconda was coiled around the top of a tree. This thing was monumentally large and the thickest part of its body was like a man's torso.

Apparently, this particular monster was the real-life star of the 1997 movie *Anaconda*. In animal films, there's always someone on hand to wrangle the beast, primp it to look good, cajole it with treats and rewards. Often in films where dogs are required to sit, beg, bark or look cute as part of a scene with an actor, you can see that their eyeline is off camera as the trainer gives the commands. I worked with a dancing dog once, a collie on the TV show *Skins*. In the show, my character's hobby was line dancing with a dog. I had a day to train with the dog, who was amazing, and quickly trusted me enough to dance backwards around me on its hind legs. This was many years before my success on

Strictly Come Dancing, but there were clearly early signs of how well I would take to rhythm and choreography.

I couldn't imagine anyone cajoling this anaconda to do anything. It was probably just a case of keeping it fed so it didn't eat any of the human co-stars. Like so much about the jungles of Brazil, there is wildlife here that defies description and is surprisingly bigger — and scarier — than you had first thought.

Anacondas are excellent swimmers, can hold their breath for up to an hour and are seen as a genuine threat along the banks of the river. As we got further upstream, stories emerged of anacondas taking dogs, livestock and even humans from the shallows. I was convinced that this terrifying reptile in the tree would make short work of anything up to the size of a cow or maybe even a hippo. For now it looked well fed and docile, but I noticed that the soldiers all gave it a wide berth.

Further into the compound, we came to the jaguar enclosure. This was not what I had expected. Instead of a smallish caged area, more of a zoo scenario, this was a ten-hectare fenced off wild area. When we approached the door, I noticed the soldiers had machine guns, one held a huge length of metal chain and they all looked jumpy.

As we passed through the heavy metal doors, I was reminded a little of *Jurassic Park*. I asked where the jaguar was. Our guide said, 'She's in here somewhere.' So the picture now started to become clear. Somewhere in this densely foliaged enclosure was a (semi-) wild sort-of pet jaguar, which no one seemed to know how to deal with or claimed to know where it was. I thought, how is it fed? Then a thought crossed my mind. Maybe *I'm* the food. Maybe it's being fed now . . . Hello? Grub's up!

The soldiers hoisted their automatic rifles and checked their safeties. The large, muscular bloke hefted the huge metal chain and glanced around nervously. Often the mascots for these jungle battalions are wild animals rescued or confiscated from hunters and in some cases they are raised as cubs, so while they're not exactly wild, they're not exactly tame either.

'Lulu?' the handler called gently.

I suddenly had a moment of clarity. At any moment now, a large, semi-wild big cat was going to jump out of the undergrowth. I needed a bit of a briefing as to what to do if and when that happened.

A rustling in the trees, a half snarl and snicker, and Lulu suddenly appeared. Leaping down from a high branch she landed soundlessly and, surveying the assembled throng with disdain, she padded towards me.

I noted that the soldiers had fanned out in formation and I was being presented as . . . as what, an offering, a starter?

I asked the handler, 'How should I behave? Should I run away or not run away?'

'Ok,' he said. 'Very important, Bill. Just stay calm, but important to remember this one thing.'

'What's that?'

'Always approach from the front.'

'Ok, good to know.'

This made excellent sense to me. Don't creep up on it. 'Don't go sneaking around behind a jaguar' seemed to be perfectly sensible advice. But a nagging thought wouldn't go away: isn't that for nervous, skittish animals like horses or gazelles or emus? Could that really be the right advice for the *onça*, the beast that kills with one bite?

As the jaguar padded towards me, I duly approached it from the front.

The handler suddenly erupted in a volley of words.

'Oh sorry, never! I meant never!'

'Whaaat?'

'Sorry my English! NEVER approach from the front!'

Too late, I was already doing just that, and as if to prove the point Lulu, the semi-feral killing machine, launched herself at me. In that tiny moment, I had the briefest of flashbacks to the red setter hurling itself onto me on a Devon beach. It happened so fast I'd hardly time to react, but some self-preservation instinct kicked in and I turned away from the incoming claws and massive teeth. The net result of this was that she grabbed me as I turned, and rolled me onto to the floor like a toy. The lunge was so quick, I barely had time to register it, but the chain-wielding guy sprang into action, got a leash around Lulu's neck and managed to at least yank her off me. After the initial shock of a big cat attack, I realised no damage done, her claws were retracted and she was playing. A playful tussle with a killer.

Of course you don't approach from the front. What was I thinking? My earlier instincts were correct. The jaguar is

at the top of the food chain, the king of the jungle, lord of its domain.

So what if you're behind it? You pose no threat. It knows that whatever is creeping up behind it is very, very foolish.

There's nothing out there that it can't deal with. One turn and swipe and it's goodnight Vienna.

But if you approach from the front, you are directly challenging it. You are taking it on as an equal, mano a mano. A stand-off. Or, in my case, a helpless bearded play-thing for it to just toss around like a ball of wool.

A heavily armed phalanx of worried-looking soldiers hustled me out of the compound in short order. On our way out, I noticed the anaconda had gone from the tree and was loose in its own compound.

I didn't wait to find out the correct way to approach it.

Which is probably 'don't'.

Don't approach an anaconda from any direction.

Chapter 32

Baboons: Majestic Rascals of the Cape

The flight from London to Cape Town takes about ten hours, flying due south along the whole length of the continent of Africa. Cape Town is on a similar line of longitude to the UK, so while ten hours of flying east or west would usually mean quite a bit of adjustment for jet lag, this long journey had the curious effect of me being able to slot into the time of the place without too much disorientation.

Just as well, as filming schedules tend to be full on. This was my first visit to Cape Town, a place I'd long hankered to see, famed for its beauty and fascinating wildlife. I was presenting a six-part series about baboons for ITV and, as is often the case, timings, filming permits and availability of contributors meant we started at 6am the next morning. Fully briefed, researched and ready to go, maybe a swig of coffee and a bite of toast if you're lucky — ah, such is the life of an itinerant presenter/comic/troubadour.

Cape Chacma baboons have been resident here for a long time, perhaps as much as 40,000 to 50,000 years. They are impressive beasts, one of the largest of all the monkeys. The big males can weigh up to about 45kg. Adults sport a huge set of teeth, with the comparative bite strength of a lion. So they're quite fearsome looking, about the size of an adult Rottweiler dog and not to be trifled with. They live in large family groups, or troops, and tend to be quite territorial. They're largely veggie and spend long hours feeding in the bush, often on proteas, the large, colourful native South African plant that grows plentifully on the Cape.

But here was the problem.

Us. Humans.

In fact, this programme, although it was centred around a relatively small area of the Cape, was really a microcosm of a global issue. As the human population grows, we all need somewhere to live. So we expand outwards from cities into areas that hitherto were uninhabited by humans — that is, to areas inhabited by *other* living things . . . And so the displacement and conflict happens.

This was exactly the problem for these baboons. For years they had lived happily on this stretch of land, with enough room for all the various families to get along fine. But now, as the bulldozers rolled in and ground was broken for housing developments, a host of problems had appeared.

Firstly, these baboons weren't going anywhere — I mean why should they? But a large, noisy bunch of whooping and chattering monkeys skittering over your lawn? Well, it's not ideal.

The Cape is a place teeming with wildlife. Never mind the baboons, there are cheetahs, leopards, wild dogs, hyenas, lions, rock hyrax, eland, zebra, rock python, grackles and even penguins.

The waters around the Cape produce a huge upwelling of food and cold water straight from Antarctica, so it attracts all manner of marine life. You'll perhaps have seen footage from this part of the world of people cage diving with great white sharks, which are attracted to the crowds of seals that come here to breed.

Large numbers of humpback and right whale come here to feed, too, to mate and to gambol in the cooler waters off the Cape. And the Cape National Park is a perfect vantage point from which to observe them. As a result, large numbers of tourists come in their droves, park their cars on the raised bluffs and take in Nature's great show.

And therein lies another of the baboon's problems. Despite the many warning signs up at the entrance to the park saying, 'Do not feed the baboons!', people can't resist — and for the baboons it's a bonanza. The kind of food that tourists have — sandwiches and fruit — contains sugar and carbohydrates, a high-value meal compared to what the baboons might forage in the wild, with a strong concentration of what the baboons need in order to thrive. The amount of nutrition gleaned from plants would take a long day to find compared to a few tasty snacks from these tourists. Baboons are highly intelligent, they learn fast and they've figured out that working the tourist lines not only provides rich pickings for the whole troop, but it saves time foraging the bush for plants. In short, it's changed the behaviour of the troop and led to rival troops showing up for a share of the bounty. Normal wild baboon behaviour would mean that competing troops would keep their distance and forage in their own 'range' . . . So this was causing a real problem. Like two buskers showing up to the same pitch at the same time, tempers will flare.

And while it might be cute to see a troop of baby baboons being shepherded across the road by a kindly female, perhaps an aunty, this itself can cause an incident. The alpha male of the troop is responsible for the safety of the younger members of the clan, and in the confusion of people and cars, noise and food, he will sometimes lose sight of them, feel threatened or be cut off from his family. In this situation, he might make a sudden movement, or barge a tourist out of the way, which can be alarming.

It is extraordinary to see the level of sophistication these baboons have. I watched a male baboon, showing great dexterity, loping along a line of parked cars, trying the door handle of each. Some of the older, more experienced males have even figured out that when they hear the 'blip' of a car alarm being activated, it's not worth trying the door!

These scallywags are smart and captivating, and brilliant characters. But they're also big and intimidating, and this leads them into ever more trouble.

A video clip emerged of a female German tourist who was holding a sandwich. A large male baboon leaps up to snatch the snack, but unfortunately knocks her over in the process. She shrieks in fear and it does look genuinely scary. This was shared widely online, of course, and the baboon in question, Fred, became *baboon non grata*.

Other problems started to appear. Because the baboons were eating tourist snacks and food out of bins and people's gardens, they were now suffering from bad teeth, from raised blood sugar and obesity.

Our story centred around Fred, who was a big male. My first day filming with the baboons led to an unexpected encounter. The adults tend to leave humans alone and not interact, preferring instead to burglarise their bags or cars for food. But younger animals, adolescents, can't contain their curiosity and, like human teens, will goad each other into ever-more adventurous dares.

I sat on the grass overlooking the sea and the baboons gradually edged closer. After a lot of chatter and nervous darting forward, one young baboon came right up to me and very gently laid a paw on my arm. As he did this, he looked right into my eyes, as if to say, 'Are you alright with this?' It was a sweet moment and, like so many animal encounters, one that I shall never forget.

These moments are especially poignant with primates, as we see a little of our own features, as if gazing into a fairground mirror. We are different, but somehow our

shared ancestry is briefly revealed. The expressive subtlety of this little ape's face, his eyebrows dancing up and down, the remarkable softness of his paw, the gentle gesture of friendship . . . Just a few million years of evolution separate us, our DNA almost the same, but there is this gulf between us, our two worlds so far apart, yet somehow we came together for a brief moment.

It only lasted a couple of seconds and then all his mates started shrieking about like teenagers out on the town, as if to say 'He touched it! He touched it! Can't believe he touched it!'

Baboons are protected animals, so even though, through no fault of their own, they've become a bit of a menace, it's illegal to kill them. But they'd become such a problem that various baboon-deterrence measures had been put in place. This consisted of a group of volunteers who would bang sticks and blow horns to encourage the monkeys to move on, and local residents, tired of having their bins routinely rummaged by monkey marauders, had figured out what they thought was a foolproof scheme. They had installed large, hinged clips that fitted over the wheelie bins and fastened in a catch.

But these primates are too smart for that. In the voice-over for the series, as we see the clipped and protected bins, I say, 'Local residents have fitted their bins with robust clips to stop the . . . ah.' At which point the footage shows a young baboon tipping a bin over, expertly levering off the clip and then getting into the bin, hurling stuff over his shoulder like a manic gremlin.

I interviewed some of the local residents, one of whom had a story to tell about an up-close-and-personal encounter with a large male baboon. He had heard a disturbance downstairs, pots and pans rattling, and, venturing into the kitchen, was confronted with the sight of a large male baboon who had opened the fridge and was standing on his hind legs, surveying the contents, for all the world like a peckish fourteen-year-old looking for a late-night snack.

The fellow recalls saying to the baboon, 'Take anything you want, mate.' Even though this must have been quite a scary sight, the homeowner was sympathetic to the baboon's plight. 'I mean, I like them,' he said, 'but they are rascals!'

Rascals is right, but it's probably one of the nicer things said about them. Large, aggressive male baboons terrorising tourists is not good for business and unfortunately proved too much for the Cape Tourist Board.

While we were filming, we heard to our dismay that the big male, Fred, had been euthanised — a sadly inevitable demise that was indicative of a failure to really deal with the problem. We humans move in and expect the wildlife to accommodate us. Fred had become a casualty of the conflict sparked by our encroachment on Nature, just one of many around the world.

Even though the news about Fred put a dampener on our experience, I still felt immensely lucky to have seen these beasts in their natural environment. The sadly ironic thing was that a photo of Fred had been used in the Cape tourism brochure as one of the attractions of the area.

From poster boy, to most wanted . . . From mascot to outlaw.

Chapter 33

The White-tailed Sea Eagle

An amazing sight soaring over the Highlands, it was like a glimpse into the past, a window on a wilder age.

The white-tailed eagle, sometimes called the sea eagle, was declared extinct in these isles early in the twentieth century due to persecution by humans, and was thought to be lost for ever. Thanks in part to a scheme in which eagle chicks were imported from Norway in the 1970s, the population is now doing well, with over 200 breeding pairs.

According to historical accounts, white-tailed eagles were once common throughout UK, the largest raptor in these islands, with sightings as far south as the Isle of Wight. But the persuasive idea began to spread that these magnificent birds were a threat to livestock, while another, more macabre, myth tells of an eagle snatching a new-born baby from a mother's arms. There's a pub in Oxford called the Eagle and Child and the sign depicts this exact occurrence. While never corroborated, it's a powerful and terrifying image, and no doubt helped to stoke the long, merciless campaign to trap and kill these magnificent birds.

Alongside issues such as the loss of habitat and socio-logical changes, with ever bigger farms and more efficient methods to kill birds, the sea eagle finally blinked out in the UK in 1918, when the last one was shot in Scotland.

I first saw one on the Isle of Mull off the west coast of Scotland while filming a birdwatching TV show. I arrived in Oban, a place which I've become fond of over the years, before taking the CalMac ferry over to the Isle of Mull. As we drove around the different locations, it occurred to me what a diverse mix of characters there were in these parts. People were here from all over the world. A Finnish couple were running the pub by the jetty and various regional accents from all around the UK greeted us wherever we went. It became clear to me that this place exerts an extraordinary effect on people. It draws them in and compels them to move there, to leave their former homes

and, in many cases, their former lives, and start anew here among the eagles and sea lochs.

And why not indeed. From my vantage point on a hillside, the low cloud suddenly parted to reveal the mainland of Scotland across the water, a panorama of snow-capped mountains and receding peaks of purplish hues. A fine vista and my first sighting of an eagle was equally dramatic. It was deer-stalking season, so the eagles were out on the scavenge. When a deer is shot, the hunters will gut it in the field, leaving all the innards or 'gralloch' out for the wildlife. We slowly cruised around the inner sea loch and could see the figure of a bird high overhead.

First impressions: a huge wingspan, up to eight feet across, perhaps the largest eagles alive, wings extended stiff as boards, with feathery 'fingers' raised at each tip. Gradually it circled lower, but close enough to make out clearly, in the binoculars, the majestic shape, the wings, the bright yellow beak and the white tail, and two sets of huge, fearsome talons. It almost doesn't quite look real, more like a cartoon version of an eagle, such is its size and dynamic intensity. It's an apex predator, which means that nothing will compete with it — except us.

As I continued to watch, I was struck by its out-stretched feathers at the wingtips, gloriously aesthetic, like a painting. Like so many wildlife encounters, it made me catch my breath. These birds were always part of the UK fauna and they have a right to be here. In fact, they should be here and still would be were it not for centuries of per-secution. It's not like they just had a good evolutionary run then died out; we finished them off!

When I see success stories like the re-introduction of sea eagles to our islands, it instils in me something more than just a sense of wonder at Nature in all its raw beauty. It actually gives me hope, rather like when I hear music that speaks to me in a certain way. I hear a phrase, a chord change, a lyric that chimes with me and my reaction is instant: aha! Someone else feels this; someone else has had these thoughts! And I feel connected.

Seeing these eagles back in their natural home gives me hope. If these creatures can be brought back from the brink, then there's a chance for all nature under threat. Wildlife these days is increasingly marginalised and pushed out as habitats disappear, as more and more of us need more space. These creatures remind us of an older, wilder time, when we were less demanding inhabitants of these isles.

I watched as a single cormorant skimmed across the sea loch as a lowering mass of black cloud pressed downwards. It felt ominous and as the sky darkened the colours leached from the landscape, rendering the view down to layers of monochrome. But, as I've learned over the years, the weather of the Western Isles is capricious and can change in a moment . . . and so it was now. Within minutes the cloud lifted, allowing brilliant sunshine to burst through above and below, a great flood of light blocked by some huge, floating monolith.

The low beams shimmered with a diamond sparkle off the loch, dazzling the eyes, while those rays facing skywards pierced the cloud like an illustration from an Old Testament Bible.

I was transfixed. This is why people come here and re-settle, out on the edge of humanity, on these isles in the cold, hard Atlantic. Yes, it might be a wrench to uproot and start again, to find your own niche, to get along and find something meaningful to do. I don't doubt it might be a challenge. But when you witness a moment of such elemental beauty, a spectacular lightshow greater than any made by human hand, where Nature in its indifferent majesty stops you in your tracks, it works its magic on you, you feel a pull, a yearning to be forever in a wild place like this.

Chapter 34

The Dwarf Minke Whale

About two days' sail north from Cairns, in Australia's Far North Queensland, you arrive at a spot at the limit of the inner Great Barrier Reef. The water is relatively shallow, and despite recent heat blooms and coral die-off, the coral bommies and reefs are teeming with marine life. On my morning dive, I was greeted with a dizzying variety of marine abundance. Bull rays cruised past, delicate Moorish idols browsed in pairs, the peripheral glimpse of a whitetip reef shark quickened the pulse, a profusion of tropical reef fish shimmered by, from parrotfish, angelfish, orbicular batfish, puffer fish, rabbit fish, all shapes and sizes, down to the tiniest dazzling gems of nudibranchs cohabiting among myriad coral types: fan, cabbage, brain and fire.

Which sounds like the title of a motivational podcast.

But as glorious as this aquatic spectacle was, the skipper of the boat, Ross, mentioned to me,'If you want to see something truly amazing, come in the winter.'

Of course, that is our mid summer in the UK, July to be precise . . . but circumstances prevailed and I did return. The glassy aquamarine waters of an Australian summer were replaced with choppy dark blue waves and cooler temperatures, but the marine life was even more extraordinary. Because for a short window of time, this part of the Great Barrier Reef plays host to a natural phenomenon, a bit of cetacean playfulness, that I wouldn't have believed possible had I not seen it with my own eyes.

The moniker 'dwarf' minke whale is a misnomer. Yes, they are a little smaller than regular minke whale, but not by much. They're still about 30 feet long, with slender, extended heads and sleek, gunmetal grey bodies built for speed. They have white body markings behind the pectoral fins that are individual to each creature and form part of the database of identification.

But how do you go about seeing a whale? I mean, ok they're not tiny . . . But still, the ocean's a big place and cruising around hoping a whale will show up seemed a little speculative.

Turns out, that's exactly what we did. These whales are inquisitive creatures, and they will actively seek out a boat and swim around it, spy-hopping and circling to get our attention.

I stood on the rear transom of the boat as a huge, glossy whale surfaced a few feet away, its head calm and still amid the choppy waves as it caught a glimpse of me. It is still a moment I treasure. Encounters with wild animals are often like this. Everyone I've ever met who's had a similar experience feels this way. An eagle flying low overhead, a deer pausing to gaze at you, a badger at dusk, a butterfly landing on your hand . . . It doesn't matter how big or small, these moments tend to leave a deep impression on us.

But why is this? I think it's because we are losing our connection with Nature and thus the animal kingdom. We used to be intimately part of it. In many areas of the world, including pre-industrial Britain, animals slept on the floor below or around our families; their body heat warmed us through the cold winter nights. Animals were quite simply more plentiful: deer, wolves, lynx, birds of prey, they were common sights, they were *neighbours*. Now, I fear that we see animals as an abstract, a distant, exotic, mysterious phenomenon, unconnected to our human world.

I was recently in Singapore, a modern cosmopolitan city. Interconnected malls, bustling streets and a densely built-up environment surrounds you. But this is still the tropics, a place of abundant wildlife, so gradually, here and there, I have glimpses of that other world. A kite soars in front of an office block, its reflection shimmering and flickering between a thousand mirrored glass panels. A huge cicada buzzes along the street . . . Wildlife is here, but you have to look for it, seek it out.

And this animal abundance is even harder to find in London, the city I call home — but it is there all the same. Occasionally, you might look up and see a peregrine falcon, the world's fastest creature, perched on a stone cornice high above the street hubbub as people busy themselves, oblivious to this aerobatic marvel.

The magnificent footage we see in wildlife documentaries amazes us and is breathtaking. We marvel at the colours, the drama, the skill and dedication of the camera crew, the animal stories, the daily struggle for existence. But I fear that, incredible as they are, these TV images may just blur together with so much other visual brilliance that we receive through our laptops, phones and streaming services. We see, but we don't *feel* the nearness of our animal cousins.

The sheer mass of this whale, its beautiful dynamism, the sound of its spouting, the spray hitting us, cannot be replicated.

Not much is known about where these dwarf minke whales actually go when they head south or even why they seem to like hanging out in this particular part of the reef.

But then, they might think the same of us. It seems, from observation going back a few years, that they're mainly younger whales, adolescents, who are perhaps sizing each other up. Flirting, like at the school disco? Whatever reason, there's only a brief window to see these gentle giants before they head off to the cold waters of Antarctica.

I am getting into my wetsuit with a mixture of excitement and trepidation. To be able to see these whales close up is a tantalising prospect, but I am also well aware of where we are. Whales are not the only large creatures inhabiting this part of the ocean. The skipper says breezily that it'll be fine, but that we have to get out of the water when it's getting dusky. 'Ok,' I say, perhaps a little too hopefully. 'For the visibility?'

'Yes, there is that, but also it's when the bitey things come out.'

Ah yes, the bitey things. Point taken. I'll be ready to come out waaay before that.

Entering the water, the bubbles clear, I note the visibility is excellent . . . about 60 feet. In this clarity, with no point of reference, it's easy to feel disorientated as you float not really aware of up or down. For a while, I see nothing, just endless blue, with the sunlight causing starbursts of refracted light that flicker like an underwater mirrorball. And then, from the distant blue, I start to make out a shape, the telltale gunmetal grey and white, and its body bucks and undulates as it propels itself forward.

The minke whale gets closer and just keeps getting bigger. Under the water their size is so much more apparent and, even though they are benign and mean me no harm, the sight of a huge creature under the water always gets the heart pounding.

It gets closer still and eventually makes a pass in front of me. I can see its large eye tracking me as it cruises past . . . I notice a few round pock marks along its flank. These are apparently bites from little 'cookie-cutters' — small sharks, only a few feet long, that have a round mouth and a set of tiny, razor-sharp teeth. They take neat round bites out of larger fish. And anything else, I imagine. One of the 'bitey' things.

As I look around, I can make out more and more whales, large shapes cruising in every direction. They take turns to glide past and one is so close that I can see the eye in great detail.

It rolls towards me as it passes. An extraordinary moment. Even though this huge creature is passing just in front of me, I feel no threat. No menace. Just a wonderful, benign presence . . . and something else. Curiosity? It's just checking me out. Observing. I wonder what on earth it thinks of *me*. 'What a strange little thing.' A spindly, black, ungainly thing in my wetsuit. Perhaps we look like detritus, or a piece of driftwood, or seaweed, but it clearly has us down as living things. In that moment all I can think is *how I wish I could communicate.* Just to ask it a few questions. What do you think of us? What's it like being a whale? Why are you here? And another million questions, but instead all I can do is watch in dumbstruck awe as this perfectly evolved giant silently slides past. And, of course, maybe all it feels is indifference. What are we to them, anyway?

In recent years, using hydrophonic microphones scientists have recorded the song of the dwarf minke whale. It consists of four notes, with the last one a lower pitch and held for a longer time: DA DA DA DAAAAH . . .

It sounds remarkably like the opening notes of Beethoven's Fifth Symphony.

And there, in that moment, I hear this faintly, pulsing through the water. I should be clearer: it is not so much heard, as *felt.* But why these notes? What message did it wish to convey? It just confirms that we need to keep discovering and that the world is still an unknown, enigmatic place that contains magical mysteries like this.

Through my scuba regulator, I hum back the answering phrase:

'DA DA DA DAAAAH!'

It answers.

Could this be the greatest moment of my life? Trading Beethoven phrases with a whale?

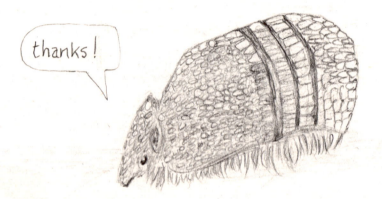